Dugald Butler

**John Wesley and George Whitefield in Scotland**

Or, the influence of the Oxford Methodists on Scottish religion

Dugald Butler

**John Wesley and George Whitefield in Scotland**
*Or, the influence of the Oxford Methodists on Scottish religion*

ISBN/EAN: 9783337243364

Printed in Europe, USA, Canada, Australia, Japan

Cover: Foto ©Lupo / pixelio.de

More available books at **www.hansebooks.com**

# John Wesley and George Whitefield in Scotland

or, The Influence of the Oxford
Methodists on Scottish Religion

BY THE

## REV. D. BUTLER, M.A.

ABERNETHY

WILLIAM BLACKWOOD AND SONS
EDINBURGH AND LONDON
MDCCCXCVIII

# PREFACE.

In the following pages an endeavour has been made to write a short history of the visits made to Scotland last century by two of the most outstanding men of the period—the Rev. John Wesley and the Rev. George Whitefield. Although the visits were but a very small fraction of their vast work, they are of great interest to the historical student, and to every one that takes an interest in a most remarkable revival of religion, the results of which are still felt in the life and work of the modern Church. Wesley and Whitefield influenced Scottish Religion most profoundly, and the movement of which they were the outstanding leaders became to a considerable extent a religious movement *within* the Scottish Church, moulding both life and work ever since. The outstanding feature of the great Methodist Revival is that its indirect influence was as important as its direct influence. The literature it created, the hymns it inspired, the work it called forth, the spiritual atmosphere it created by the organisation of a great religious communion, acted upon all the Churches, and left no Church afterwards the same. Spiritual force cannot be limited in its area of direct action, and the great Methodist Revival of Religion, while it is visibly embodied in the Scottish Churches that still bear Wesley's honoured name, cannot be measured in extent by them. The general movement has assimilated itself into the life and work of all sections of the Scottish Church, and has acted as an expansive force on religion and on religious work. Whitefield brought it by his preaching, which affected the Scottish towns as Savonarola's did Florence of old : Hervey expressed it in the religious literature which was widely read in Scotland : Charles Wesley has sung it into the Scottish devotional life by his hymns : John Wesley brought it by his literature, his hymns, his apostolic labours ; by the direct and indirect influence of organised Methodism, and the religious life it has inspired.

The literature connected with the general movement is vast, but the interest connected with the Scottish work is distinctive, and an endeavour has been made to give it a treatment which, while narrating the particular facts, yet connects it with the general movement. The letters and journals of Wesley and Whitefield are the original sources from which the information has been acquired, but other literature relating to the period has also been helpful. The letters and journals (especially Wesley's) are not only valuable as a record of the movement, but are also of historical value in casting light upon Scottish Church life in last century —an interest, too, which will increase with the years. It is to be observed that the movement was also indebted to Scotland, for a Scottish book —Scougal's 'Life of God in the Soul of Man'— had an epoch-making influence over Whitefield's religious development (pp. 5 to 11), and was well known to both Charles and John Wesley (p. 7 and pp. 67, 68).

D. BUTLER.

THE MANSE,
ABERNETHY, PERTHSHIRE,
*November* 18, 1898.

# CONTENTS.

# WESLEY AND WHITEFIELD
# IN SCOTLAND.

———◆———

WESLEY [says Mr Leslie Stephen] founded a body
which eighty years after his death could boast of twelve
million adherents : and its reaction upon other bodies
was perhaps as important as its direct influence.[1]

The Methodists themselves [says the late Mr Green]
were the least result of the Methodist revival. . . .
A yet nobler result was the steady attempt, which has
never ceased from that day to this, to remedy the guilt,
the ignorance, the physical suffering, the social degra-
dation of the profligate and the poor. It was not till
the Wesleyan impulse had done its work that this philanthropic impulse began.[2]

Although the career of the elder Pitt [says Mr Lecky]
and the splendid victories by land and sea that were
won during his Ministry form unquestionably the most
dazzling episodes in the reign of George II., they must
yield, I think, in real importance to that religious

---

[1] History of English Thought in the Eighteenth Century,
vol. ii. p. 409.

[2] A Short History of the English People, vol. iv. pp. 1618,
1619.

revolution which shortly before had been begun in England by the preaching of the Wesleys and of Whitefield. The creation of a large, powerful, and active sect, extending over both hemispheres, and numbering many millions of souls, was but one of its consequences. It also exercised a profound and lasting influence upon the spirit of the Established Church, upon the amount and distribution of the moral forces of the nation, and even upon the course of its political history.[1]

Such are the opinions of three modern historians regarding this remarkable and unique religious revival, and Mr Tyerman holds the bold statement to be strictly true—that "Methodism is the greatest fact in the history of the Church of Christ."[2] The present study deals with the historical facts regarding the introduction of Methodism into Scotland; with the influence it wielded, the opposition it had to contend with, and the spiritual force it brought within the Church itself. The area for inquiry is circumscribed, yet the movement within Scotland was real and pervasive, and what it lost in extent it gained in intensive power. Methodism was in Scotland, as in England, a purely religious movement, as spiritual as anything on this side of time can be; it had as its marching-order and inspiring force a great object, fraught with good to the Churches of the country—viz., religion "not as the bare saying over

[1] History of England in the Eighteenth Century, vol. ii. p. 521.
[2] The Life and Times of John Wesley, vol. i. p. 12.

so many prayers, morning and evening, in public or
in private; not anything superadded now and then
to a careless or worldly life; but a constant ruling
habit of the soul; a renewal of our minds in the
image of God; a recovery of the divine likeness;
a still increasing conformity of heart and life to the
pattern of our most holy Redeemer." [1]    These
words of John Wesley, written in 1734, embody
and express the aim of the great revival of last
century, and it cannot but be of interest to trace
its development in Scotland.

The Scottish movement chiefly centres around
the names of John Wesley and George Whitefield,
who both visited the country; and in order to
understand John Wesley's work, it will be necessary to begin with George Whitefield, as he was
the pioneer of Methodism in Scotland, and influenced the Church of Scotland most profoundly.

[1] Tyerman's Oxford Methodists, p. 19.

# THE REV. GEORGE WHITEFIELD.

GEORGE WHITEFIFLD was born in the Bell Inn, Gloucester, on 16th December 1714. When eighteen years of age he entered as servitor Pembroke College, Oxford, where he spent four years, from 1732 to 1736. Twelve years before, John Wesley had been admitted to Christ Church College, and during the interval had been elected Fellow of Lincoln College, had taken his degree, and been ordained deacon and priest. Charles Wesley had been six years at Christ Church, and had taken the Bachelor of Arts degree, and had become a college tutor.

William Morgan, one of the first of the Oxford Methodists, died a few weeks before Whitefield entered Pembroke College. For three years past Clayton had been at Brasenose. Ingham had already spent two years at Queen's. In 1726 Gambold had been admitted as servitor in Christ Church, and in 1733 was ordained by Bishop Potter. Hervey, born in the same year as Whitefield, had in 1731 become undergraduate in Lincoln College, where Wesley was tutor. Broughton was in Exeter College. Kinchin was a Fellow of Corpus

Christi. For twelve years Hutchins had been Fellow
of Lincoln, where also for some time past Whitelamb
and Westley Hall had been studying, to the content
of Wesley.[1]

At Oxford Whitefield was brought into contact
with the earnest company of students known as
the Methodists, and was profoundly helped and influenced by them. The "Holy Club" before long
perceived the earnestness of the Pembroke servitor,
and admitted him into their fellowship. It is interesting to record that a religious book, written by
a Scottish professor, was one extensively used by
all of them, and had no small influence in shaping
their religious development. It is a book now
much forgotten, but one that ought to be better
known—'The Life of God in the Soul of Man.' A
subjoined footnote gives a narrative of the life of
its author, Henry Scougal (1650-1678), and an analysis of his religious teaching.[2]  Those acquainted

[1] Tyerman's Life of George Whitefield, vol. i. p. 14.

[2] Henry Scougal was the son of Patrick Scougal, Bishop of
Aberdeen, and was born in 1650.  He was educated at King's
College, Aberdeen, and entered it when fifteen years of age.
He was a regent in the University for four years, and when
only eighteen years of age wrote the 'Private Reflexions and
Occasional Maxims'—a valuable book that will repay careful
perusal.  He settled as minister of Auchterless at the early
age of twenty, and afterwards became Professor of Divinity in
Aberdeen when twenty-five years of age.  This office he held
until his premature death in 1678.  Although his life did not
extend beyond twenty-eight years, he accomplished much
within it, and he will be gratefully remembered as the author
of several valuable sermons, but chiefly as giving to the world

with the early position of the Oxford Methodists
will recognise how deep and potent was the influence of Scougal's book over them. John Wesley

'The Life of God in the Soul of Man,' which influenced the
Wesleys and the early Oxford Methodists, and was to
Whitefield what the 'Theologia Germanica' was to Luther.

"Learning and piety," says Dr Grub, "never appeared in a
more attractive form than in his life and in his writings. In
an age of strife and controversy, when most persons in main-
taining what they believed to be the truth, seem to have lost
sight of charity, he discharged his duties faithfully and yet
with meekness and humility. Beloved by all while he lived,
his memory continues to be cherished by the Church which he
adorned. His writings have always been highly esteemed.
The work which is best known—'The Life of God in the Soul
of Man'—in its purity and beauty the faithful picture of his
own mind, which so many great writers have delighted to
praise, and which has been the source of so much good to
devout persons of very different opinions, was published during
the author's lifetime by Gilbert Burnet."—Grub's Ecclesiastical
History of Scotland, vol. iii. pp. 269, 270.

'The Life of God in the Soul of Man' begins by stating what
religion is not. It is not to be placed (1) in the understanding nor
to consist of orthodoxy—this leads to sectarianism ; nor (2) in
the outward man, external duties and model of performances ;
nor (3) in rapturous hearts and ecstatic devotion ; nor (4) in
wickedness and vice and the hallowing of corrupt affections.
True religion is a union of the soul with God, a real participation of the divine nature, the very image of God drawn upon
the soul or Christ formed within us. It is called a *life*—(1)
because of its permanency and stability ; (2) because of its
freedom and unconstrainedness. It is called a divine life
because God is its author, and it bears a resemblance to the
divine perfection. The root of the natural life is sense : the
root of the religious life is faith, and its chief branches are (1)
love to God, (2) charity to men, (3) purity, and (4) humility.
As religion is better understood by actions than by words, there
is the constant necessity of turning to the life of Christ for
inspiration, and His life exhibits—(1) diligence in doing God's

knew it: Charles Wesley knew it well, and gave
the use of it to George Whitefield, who is open
in giving strong testimony to the influence of the

will, patience and submission in suffering God's will, and constant devotion in so far as His whole life was a prayer and
communion with God; (2) charity to all men; (3) purity; (4)
humility; for He was so absorbed by a sense of the infinite
perfections of God that He appeared as nothing in His own
eyes. The four lessons are then applied to the soul of the
believer. (1) Divine love is excellent, for it is the right temper
of the soul, and fixes the affections on the divine perfection.
It advances, elevates, and makes the soul supremely happy.
To love God is to find sweetness in every dispensation, and
the duties of religion become delightful. The next branches
of religion are (2) universal charity and love; (3) purity, or a
contempt of sensual pleasures; (4) humility arising from a
calm and quiet contemplation of the divine purity and goodness. For the growth of the divine life in the soul Scougal
states the following directions: (1) We must shun all manner of
sin; (2) know what things are sinful; (3) resist temptations by
considering their consequent evils; (4) keep a constant guard
over ourselves; (5) often examine our actions; (6) restrain ourselves in many lawful things; (7) strive against the love of the
world; (8) do those outward actions commanded; (9) strive towards internal acts of devotion and charity. As helps or means
Scougal indicates the following: (1) Consideration is a great
instrument of religion, and "spiritless and paralytick thoughts"
are to be avoided. (2) We must consider the excellency of the
divine nature; (3) meditate on God's goodness and love; (4)
remember that all men are nearly related to God; (5) that they
carry His image upon them. (6) We must consider the dignity
of our nature: (7) meditate often on the joys of heaven; (8)
consider our failures; (9) contemplate God's perfection, which
creates humility. (10) We must often use prayer as an instrument of religion; (11) religion is advanced by the same means
with which it began; (12) the use of the holy sacrament is
peculiarly appointed to nourish and increase the spiritual life
when once it is begotten in the soul.

Such is a short analysis of Scougal's inspiring book (pp. 1-74).

Scotch minister.   Referring to an interview he had
with Charles Wesley, Whitefield says :—

I thankfully embraced the opportunity (and, blessed
be God ! it was one of the most profitable visits I ever
made in my life).   My soul at that time was athirst
for some spiritual friends to lift up my hands when
they hung down, and to strengthen my feeble knees.
He soon discovered it, and, like a wise winner of souls,
made all his discourses tend that way.   And when he
had put into my hand Professor Frank's treatise against
the 'Fear of Man' and a book entitled 'The Country
Parson's Advice to his Parishioners,' the last of which
was wonderfully blessed to my soul, I took my leave.

In a short time he let me have another book entitled
'The Life of God in the Soul of Man' (and, though I
had fasted, watched, and prayed, and received the
sacrament so long, yet I never knew what true religion
was till God sent me that excellent treatise by the
hands of my never-to-be-forgotten friend).

At my first reading it I wondered what the author
meant by saying "that some falsely placed religion in
going to church, doing hurt to no one, being constant
in the duties of the closet, and now and then reaching
out their hands to give alms to their poor neighbours."
" Alas !" thought I, "if this be not religion, what is ?"
God soon showed me ; for in reading a few lines further,
that " true religion was a union of the soul with God,
and Christ formed within us," a ray of divine light was
instantaneously darted in upon my soul, and from that
moment, but not till then, did I know that I must be
a new creature. . . . From time to time Mr Wesley
permitted me to come unto him, and instructed me as
I was able to bear it.   By degrees he introduced me
to the rest of his Christian brethren (the Methodists).

They built me up daily in the knowledge and fear of God, and taught me to endure hardness like a good soldier of Jesus Christ.[1]

Again he says at a later period of his life (1769)—

I must bear testimony to my old friend, Mr Charles Wesley. He put a book into my hands called 'The Life of God in the Soul of Man,' whereby God showed me that I must be born again or be damned. I know the place : it may perhaps be superstitious, but whenever I go to Oxford I cannot help running to the spot where Jesus Christ first revealed Himself to me, and gave me the new birth. I learned that a man may go to church, say his prayers, receive the sacrament, and yet not be a Christian. How did my heart rise and shudder like a poor man that is afraid to look into his ledger lest he should find himself a bankrupt. "Shall I burn this book? shall I throw it down? or shall I search it?" I did search it ; and, holding the book in my hand, thus addressed the God of heaven and earth : "Lord, if I am not a Christian, for Jesus Christ's sake show me what Christianity is, that I may not be damned at last." I read a little further, and discovered that they who know anything of religion know it is a vital union with the Son of God—Christ formed in the heart. O what a ray of divine life did then break in upon my soul ! I fell a-writing to all my brethren and to my sisters. I talked to the students as they came into my room. I laid aside all trifling conversation. I put all trifling books away, and was determined to study to be a saint, and then to be a scholar. From that moment God has been carry-

1 Tyerman's Life, vol. i. p. 17.

ing on His blessed work in my soul. I am now fifty-
five years of age, and shall leave you in a few days;
but I tell you, my brethren, I am more and more convinced that this is the truth of God, and that without
it you can never be saved by Jesus Christ.[1]

Such is Whitefield's testimony, and there can be
no doubt that Scougal's remarkable book was in-
strumental in creating an epoch-making influence in
his spiritual life. It led to the "awakening of the
soul," and thus a Scottish teacher discharged no
unimportant part in the shaping of the greatest pulpit orator of last century; and Scotland, while it
received much from Whitefield, also gave much to
Whitefield. His conversion was in 1735, and in
1736 he was admitted by Bishop Benson into holy
orders. 1737 was a year spent by him in preaching
throughout England when Wesley was in Georgia,
and Gloucester, Bristol, and London were stirred by
him in a way they had never been stirred before.[2]
He became a "Gospel-rover," and as Charles Wesley
originated Methodism, so George Whitefield originated itinerancy and began the evangelical revival.
"The doctrine of the new birth and justification by
faith in Jesus Christ (though I was not so clear in
it as afterwards) made its way like lightning into
the hearers' consciences,"[3] and in his great work

---

[1] Eighteen Sermons preached by Rev. George Whitefield,
revised by Dr Gifford, p. 359.
[2] John Wesley, by J. H. Overton, M.A., p. 86.
[3] Tyerman's Life, vol. i. p. 73.

Whitefield was as happy as a man could be outside of heaven. Scougal's influence had leavened his thought : "Some place religion in being of this or that communion ; more in morality ; most in a round of doctrine ; and few, very few, acknowledge it to be, what it really is, a thorough inward change of nature, a divine life, a participation of Jesus Christ, and union of the soul with God." [1]

His first visit to America was in 1738, and on his return to England in December he found all the churches, with few exceptions, closed against him. In January 1739 he was ordained a priest by Bishop Benson, [2] and commenced the outdoor preaching which was afterwards to be so pronouncedly associated with his name. He anticipated the Wesleys, as Dean Farrar said, " in having been the first to make the green grass his pulpit and the blue heavens his sounding-board." [3] On May 9, 1739, he received from the trustees of Georgia five hundred acres of land for his Orphan House, [4] and as far as Scotland is related in the movement it henceforth received periodical preaching-visits from Whitefield, and helped him very liberally by contributions to his philanthropic work. As we are here chiefly concerned with his influence in Scotland, it will now be necessary to state the facts regarding his early visits. The Rev. Ralph Erskine, one of the four

[1] Tyerman's Life, vol. i. p. 96.      [2] Ibid., p. 158.
[3] Wesley : The Man, his Teaching, and his Work, p. 183.
[4] Tyerman's Life, vol. i. p. 215.

brethren of the Associate Presbytery, wrote him
regarding a visit to Scotland.   His Diary states—

*May* 18, 1739.—Received an excellent letter from Mr
Ralph Erskine, a field-preacher of the Scots Church, a
noble soldier of the Lord Jesus Christ.[1]

Again :—

*July* 22, 1739.—Received a letter from Mr Ralph
Erskine, of Scotland.   Some may be offended at my
corresponding with him, but I dare not but confess
my Lord's disciples.[2]

The following is Whitefield's answer to Mr
Erskine's letter, referred to in the above extract :—

LONDON, *July* 23, 1739.

REVEREND AND DEAR SIR,—Yesterday with great
pleasure I received your kind letter.   I was afraid lest
I should have offended you.   If this should be the case
at any time, reprove me sharply, and I shall thank
you with my whole heart.   I bless God that my sermons are approved of by you.   I am but a novice in
the school of Christ, but my Master enlightens me
more and more every day to know the exceeding great
riches and freedom of His grace to all who believe in
Jesus Christ.   By this time I hope you have seen my
journal, and have given thanks for what great things
God has done for my soul.   An appendix will be
printed shortly.   The success of the Gospel increases
daily.   Opposition also increases daily ; but as opposition abounds, so does my inward consolation.   . . .
My tenderest affections await all the Associate Pres-

---

[1] Tyerman's Life, vol. i. p. 216.          [2] Ibid., p. 267.

bytery. I am opposed for owning you ; but to deny
our Lord's disciples, in my opinion, is denying Christ
Himself. Providence detains me here. Pray write by
next post to, rev. and dear sir, yours most affectionately
in the bowels of Christ,      GEORGE WHITEFIELD.[1]

Erskine in his reply expresses the hope that there
will be "a happy union in the Lord" between the
Oxford Methodists and the Associate Presbytery,
"not only in a private and personal, but even in a
more public and general way." With regard to
the Secession he adds :—

You say that so long as the Articles of the Church
of England are agreeable to Scripture, you resolve to
preach them up, without either bigotry or party zeal.
This is the case with us. We preach up and defend,
doctrinally and judicially, those Articles of the Church
of Scotland, agreeable to the Scriptures, which the
judicatories are letting go. Hence, I conclude, you are
just of our mind as to separation from an established
Church. We never declared a secession from the
Church of Scotland, but only a secession from the
judicatories in their course of defection from the primitive and covenanted constitution, to which we stood
bound by our ordination engagements.[2]

About this period Whitefield became somewhat
pronounced in the Calvinistic position. It is
known from his Journal[3] that he had been reading
the sermons of Ralph and Ebenezer Erskine, and
probably this is the source of the change, which

---

[1] See Life and Diary of Rev. Ralph Erskine.
[2] *Ut supra.*                    [3] June 9, 1739.

was also accelerated by the correspondence already
referred to. Whitefield visited America in 1739,
when the views to which he was previously inclined
were strengthened by his intercourse with Jonathan
Edwards. It is said "that he caught the tone and
imbibed the opinions of Edwards,"[1] but the
Erskines evidently laid the foundation upon which
the superstructure was afterwards built during the
American visit. Mr Tyerman, while "totally dis-
believing his Calvinian doctrine," adds :—

Whilst sorrowing that his embracing those doctrines
should have occasioned a temporary breach of the
friendship existing between him and Wesley, it is an
unquestionable fact that this opened to Whitefield a
wide field of usefulness, which, without it, neither he
nor Wesley could have occupied. Without this Whitefield could not have had the sympathy and co-opera-
tion of the Presbyterians and Independents of America.
It was this that prepared the way for his popularity
in Scotland. But for this he would have lacked the
important patronage of the Countess of Huntingdon.
This was one of the prime sources of the immense
influence he exercised over Hervey, Berridge, Romaine,
Venn, and many other contemporaneous clergymen of
the Church of England ; and it also, to an untold
extent, enabled him to move and quicken the Dissenting ministers and congregations of the land.[2] It
is also right to add [continues Mr Tyerman] that
Whitefield's Calvinism never interfered with his warm-
hearted declarations concerning the *universality* of redeeming love, and the willingness of Christ to save

---

[1] Life of Sir Richard Hill, p. 171.    [2] Life, vol. i. p. 275.

*all* who come to Him. Doubtless there was some degree of inconsistency in this; but it only shows that the man's heart was larger than his creed.[1]

Whitefield's Calvinistic evangelicalism was the source of his influence last century in Scotland, and it opened for him doors of access that were shut to Wesley.

Whitefield started on this second visit to America on August 1739, and did not return until March 1741. The following was written during his voyage, and was addressed to the Erskines and their followers :—

Though I know none of you in person, yet, from the time I heard of your faith and love towards our dear Lord Jesus, I have been acquainted with you in spirit, and have constantly mentioned you in my poor prayers. I find the good pleasure of the Lord prospers in your hands; and I pray God to increase you more and more. Scotland, like England, has been so much settled upon its lees for some time that I fear our late days may properly be called the midnight of the Church. I cannot but think a winnowing-time will come after this ingathering of souls. O that we may suffer only as Christians, and then the Spirit of Christ and of glory will rest upon us. In patience possess your souls. I will leave my cause to God. The eternal God will be your perpetual refuge. He who employs will protect. As your day is, so shall your strength be.[2]

From America he wrote the following to the Rev. Ralph Erskine, which shows that he had

---

[1] Life, vol. i. p. 305.   [2] Ibid., p. 311.

scruples regarding the Scottish Seceders, and regarded them as bordering on Cameronianism :—

I bless the Lord, from my soul, for raising you
and several other burning and shining lights to appear
for Him in this midnight of the Church. My heart
has been much warmed by reading some of your
sermons, especially that preached before the Associate
Presbytery. I long more and more to hear of the
rise and progress of your proceedings, and how far you
would willingly carry the reformation of the Church of
Scotland. My ignorance of the constitution of the
Scotch Church is the cause of my writing after this
manner. I should be obliged to you if you would
recommend to me some useful books, especially such as
open the holy sacrament. I like Boston's 'Fourfold
State of Man' exceedingly. Under God, it has been
of much service to my soul. I believe I agree with you
and him in the essential truths of Christianity. . . .
My only scruple at present is " whether you approve of
taking the sword in defence of your religious rights?"
One of our English bishops, when I was with him,
called you *Cameronians*. They, I think, took up arms,
which I think to be contrary to the spirit of Jesus
Christ and His apostles. Some few passages in your
sermon before the Presbytery I thought were a little
suspicious of favouring that principle. I pray God
your next may inform me that I am mistaken ; for
when zeal carries us to such a length, I think it ceases
to be zeal according to knowledge.[1]

From Savannah on January 16, 1740, he again
wrote to the Rev. Ralph Erskine :—

---

[1] Tyerman's Life, vol. i. pp. 333, 334.

You may depend on my not being prejudiced against you or your brethren by any evil report. . . . I assure you, dear sir, I am fully convinced of the doctrine of election, free justification, and final perseverance. . . . I think I have but one objection against your proceedings—your insisting on *Presbyterian Government,* exclusive of all other ways of worshipping God. Will not this necessarily lead you (whenever you get the upper hand) to oppose and persecute all that differ from you in their church government or outward way of worshipping God? Our dear brother and fellow-labourer, Mr Gilbert Tennent, thinks this will be the consequence, and said he would write to you about it. For my own part, though I profess myself a minister of the Church of England, I am of catholic spirit ; and if I see any man who loves the Lord Jesus in sincerity, I am not very solicitous to what outward communion he belongs.[1]

On February 16, 1741, he writes again to Mr Erskine :—

You and your brethren are dearer to me than ever. Your 'Sonnets and Sermons' have been blessed to me and many. The former are reprinted in America. I want all your own and your brother's works. Since I have been on board I have been much helped by reading the 'Marrow of Modern Divinity.' I have just perused 'Boston on the Covenant' ; and this morning have been solacing myself with your 'Paraphrase upon Solomon's Song.' Blessed be our Lord for helping you in that composition ! . . . I hope my love will find acceptance with your dear brother and

1 Tyerman's Life, vol. i. p. 352.

all the Associate Presbytery. My prayers always attend them. I should be glad to sit at their feet and be taught the way of God more perfectly.[1]

George Whitefield thus sympathised with the objects of the Scottish Secession, came to Scotland on the invitation of the Erskines, and at first proposed to preach under their auspices. John Wesley differed from him in this, and was most pronounced against such movements.

Although [he says] we call sinners to repentance in all places of God's dominion ; and although we frequently use extempore prayers and unite together in religious society ; yet we are not dissenters in the only sense which our law acknowledges. . . . We are not Seceders ; nor do we bear any resemblance to them. We set out upon quite opposite principles. The Seceders laid the very foundation of their work in judging and condemning others ; we laid the foundation of our work in judging and condemning ourselves. They begin everywhere with showing their hearers how fallen the Church and ministers are. We begin everywhere with showing our hearers how fallen they are themselves.[2]

Whitefield came to Scotland on the invitation of the Erskines, and with the resolve to ally himself in religious work with the Scottish Secession. The most pronounced and outstanding in this movement were Ebenezer Erskine of Stirling ; Ralph Erskine of Dunfermline ; William Wilson of Perth ;

---

[1] *Ut supra*, pp. 461, 462.
[2] Wesley's Works, vol. viii. p. 321.

Alexander Moncrieff of Abernethy ; James Fisher of Kinclaven. They seceded from the Church of Scotland on account of the doctrinal defections of the period and the prevalence of Arian and Socinian views within the Church ; they also maintained the rights of the people in the election of ministers, and protested against the patronage laws. In so far as the Secession was an earnest endeavour to restore the religious spirit of the country and maintain purity of doctrine, the Scottish movement corresponded much with the English evangelical movement, at the head of which were the Wesleys and Whitefield. George Whitefield, however, was more in harmony with the doctrinal position of the Scottish Seceders than John Wesley. Like Whitefield, they were evangelical Calvinists, and like him, they had inaugurated a new period of field-preaching, which had not been a novelty to the Scottish people during the time of the Covenants in the previous century, but had fallen into abeyance since the Revolution Settlement. The seventeenth century in Scotland was both characterised by a popular struggle for civil and religious liberty, and also by an earnest religious revival. The religious life of the country had been quickened by the preaching of the Covenanting ministers on the moors and hillsides, and when Whitefield adopted it, he was on the line of mighty association and quenchless memories. What was a novelty south of the Tweed was familiar to the people north of the Tweed, and helped Whitefield to become a great religious force in Scotland.

After his return to England in 1741, with his Calvinism strengthened by a long intercourse with Jonathan Edwards in America, Whitefield was urged to visit Scotland. Ralph Erskine renewed his warm invitation : April 10, 1741, he writes :—

We and our people have all a notion of you as being in the way of reformation. I am persuaded that your coming to us would be matter of great joy. How great is our need of such awakening gales of heaven as you speak of in the last visit you made to Georgia !

Come, if possible, dear Whitefield, come. There is no face on earth I would desire more earnestly to see. Yet I would desire it *only* in a way that, I think, would tend most to the advancing of our Lord's kingdom and the reformation work among *our* hands. Such is the situation of affairs among us, that unless you come with a design to meet and abide with us of "the Associate Presbytery," and if you make your public appearances in the places especially of their concern, I would *dread* the consequence of your coming, lest it should seem equally to countenance our persecutors. Your fame would occasion a flocking to you, to whatever side you turn ; and, if it should be in their pulpits, as no doubt some of them would urge, we know how it would be improved against us. I know not with whom you could safely join yourself, if not with us. . . . You are still dearer and dearer to me. By your last Journal I observed your growing zeal for the doctrine of grace. RALPH ERSKINE.[1]

---

[1] Life and Diary, p. 322.

Whitefield's answer is contained in the following letters to the Erskines :—

BRISTOL, *May* 16, 1741.

This morning I received a kind letter from your brother Ralph, who thinks it best for me wholly to join "the Associate Presbytery" if it should please God to send me into Scotland. This I cannot altogether agree to. I come only as an occasional preacher to preach the simple Gospel to all who are willing to hear me, of whatever denomination. It will be wrong in me to join in a reformation as to church government any further than I have light given me from above. If I am quite neuter as to that in my preaching, I cannot see how it can hinder or retard any design you may have on foot. My business seems to be to evangelise, to be a Presbyter at large.

When I shall be sent in your parts I know not. I write this that there may not be the least misunderstanding between us. I love and honour "the Associate Presbytery." With this I send them my due respects, and most humbly beg their prayers. But let them not be offended if in all things I cannot immediately fall in with them. Let them leave me to God. Whatever light He is pleased to give me, I hope I shall be faithful to it.

GEORGE WHITEFIELD.[1]

FIRST VISIT TO SCOTLAND, 1741.

Whitefield arrived in Scotland on July 30, 1741, and spent his first night with Ralph Erskine at

[1] Tyerman's Life, vol. i. pp. 505, 506.

Dunfermline, who the next day wrote thus to his brother Ebenezer :—

DUNFERMLINE, *July* 31, 1741.

Mr Whitefield came to me yesternight about ten. I had conversation with him alone this forenoon. I only mention this one thing about his ordination : he owned he then knew no other way, but said he would not have it that way again for a thousand worlds. As to his preaching, he declares he can refuse no call to preach Christ, whoever gives it ; were it a Jesuit priest or a Mahomedan he would embrace it for testifying against them. He preached in my meeting-house this afternoon. The Lord is evidently with him.[1]

On August 5, 1741, Whitefield met " the Associate Presbytery " at Dunfermline, and an account of the conference is given in a letter he wrote to a friend in New York :—

EDINBURGH, *August* 8, 1741.

MY DEAR BROTHER,—" The Associate Presbytery " are so confined that they will not so much as hear me preach unless I will join with them. Mr Ralph Erskine, indeed, did hear me and went with me into the pulpit of the Canongate Church. The people were ready to shout for joy ; but, I believe, it gave offence to his associates.

I met most of them, according to appointment, on Wednesday last. A set of grave venerable men ! They soon proposed to form themselves into a presbytery, and were proceeding to choose a moderator. I asked them for what purpose ? They answered to discourse, and set me right about the matter of church government, and the Solemn League and Covenant. I replied

---

[1] Life and Diary, p. 326.

they might save themselves that trouble, for I had no scruples about it; and that settling church government and preaching about the Solemn League and Covenant was not my plan. I then told them something about my experience, and how I was led out into my present way of acting. One in particular said he was deeply affected; and dear Mr Erskine desired they would have patience with me; for that, having been born and bred in England, and having never studied the point, I could not be supposed to be so perfectly acquainted with the nature of their covenants. One, much warmer than the rest, immediately replied, "that no indulgence was to be shown me; that England had revolted most with respect to church government; and that I, born and educated there, could not but be acquainted with the matter now in debate." I told him I had never yet made the Solemn League and Covenant the object of my study, being busy about matters, as I judged, of greater importance. Several replied that every pin of the tabernacle was precious. I said that in every building there were outside and inside workmen; that the latter at present was my province; that if they thought themselves called to the former, they might proceed in their own way and I should proceed in mine. I then asked them seriously what they would have me to do? The answer was, that I was not desired to subscribe immediately to the Solemn League and Covenant, but to preach only for them till I had further light. I asked, why only for them? Mr Ralph Erskine said, "They were the Lord's people." I then asked whether there were no other Lord's people but themselves? and, supposing all others were the devil's people, they certainly had more need to be preached to; and therefore I was more and more determined to go out into the highways and hedges; and that if the Pope

himself would lend me his pulpit, I would gladly pro-
claim the righteousness of Christ therein. Soon after
this the company broke up ; and one of these, otherwise venerable men, immediately went into the meeting-
house and preached upon these words, " Watchman,
what of the night ? Watchman, what of the night ?
The watchman said, The morning cometh, and also
the night : if ye will inquire, inquire ye : return,
come." I attended, but the good man so spent himself in the former part of his sermon, in talking
against prelacy, the Common Prayer Book, the sur-
plice, the rose in the hat, and such like externals, that
when he came to the latter part of his text, to invite
poor sinners to Jesus Christ, his breath was so gone
that he could scarce be heard. What a pity that the
last was not first, and the first last !

The consequence of all this was an open breach. I
retired ; I wept ; I prayed ; and after preaching in
the fields, sat down and dined with them, and then
took a final leave. At table a gentlewoman said she
had heard that I had told some people that " the
Associate Presbytery" were building a Babel. I said,
" Madam, it is quite true ; and I believe the Babel
will soon fall down about their ears." But enough
of this. Lord, what is man ? what the best of men ?
but men at the best ! I think I have now seen an
end of all perfection. Our brethren in America, blessed
be God ! have not so learned Christ. Be pleased to
inform them of this letter.—Ever yours in our common
Lord,                         GEORGE WHITEFIELD.[1]

The Associate Presbytery thus rejected and afterwards openly denounced Whitefield, and he declined to work under the narrow limits they were

---

[1] Tyerman's Life, vol. i. pp. 509, 510.

fixing for him. He found, however, a hearty welcome from many of the ministers and laity of the
Church of Scotland, and within the pulpits of the
Establishment and in open-air preaching a larger
and more open-minded audience than the Associate
Presbytery could have given him. While the
pulpits of the Church of England were since 1738
closed against him, Whitefield found many of the
pulpits in the Church of Scotland open to him; and
it is only historically just to acknowledge this
larger charity, and to rejoice in finding it during a
period when the Church of Scotland has been much
assailed. Whitefield's catholicity was recognised
by the Establishment and also by the Scottish press
of the period. "This gentleman," says the 'Scots
Magazine' (July 1741), "recommends the essentials
of religion and decries the distinguishing punctilios
of parties; mentions often the circumstance of his
own regeneration, and what success he has had in
his ministerial labours."

"The pulpit for Christ," says the late Dr John
Stoughton, "was virtually Whitefield's life-maxim,"[1]
and he had now a great opportunity for declaring
this in Scotland.

A literary work by Whitefield and Wesley had
also helped to prepare the way, for one of their
earliest joint works was 'An Abstract of the
Life and Death of the Reverend, Learned, and
Pious Mr Thomas Halyburton, M.A., Professor

---

[1] The Pen, the Palm, and the Pulpit, p. 108.

of Divinity in the University of St Andrews,'
with recommendatory epistle by George Whitefield (dated London, 5th February 173⅜) and
Preface by John Wesley (dated London, February
9, 173⅜).[1]

Both of them had been benefited by Scottish
streams of piety as they flowed through Leighton,
Scougal, Rutherford, and Halyburton, and they
were not slow to make the acknowledgment; it was
to open up these streams again within the Church
that their labours were henceforth to be chiefly
directed, and ultimately to be so pronouncedly
successful.

George Whitefield's Diary and Correspondence
tell their own artless tale regarding his work in
Scotland, and they give us the portrait of a most
interesting man. Whitefield awoke the slumbering
energies of the Church and gave an impulse to
philanthropic and missionary work. His first visit
lasted for thirteen weeks, and the record of it is a
heroic one. He writes :—

EDINBURGH, *August* 8, 1741.

On Sunday evening (last) I preached in a field near
the Orphan House to upwards of fifteen thousand
people ; and on Monday, Friday, and Saturday even-

---

[1] Thomas Halyburton was born on December 25, 1674, at
Duplin, in the parish of Aberdalgie, near Perth, where his
father was parish minister. He was educated at Perth and St
Andrews. He was appointed minister of Ceres, Fife, in 1700,
and was admitted Professor of Divinity at St Andrews in 1710.
He died shortly afterwards, and left an autobiography (pp. 176-

ings to near as many. On Tuesday I preached in the Canongate Church ; on Wednesday and Thursday at Dunfermline ; and on Friday morning at Queensferry. Everywhere the auditories were large and very attentive. Great power accompanied the Word. Many have been brought under conviction.

His preaching appealed to all classes, and a letter under date August 9, 1741, describes one of his Edinburgh audiences :—

Numbers of all ranks, all denominations, and all characters came to hear him, though his sermons abound with those truths which would be unwelcomed from the mouths of others. Three hours before noon he appoints for people under distress to converse with him.[1]

He received two invitations : one from the Rev. Mr Willison, minister of Dundee, to visit his parish ; in his reply he speaks of "the divisions of Scotland as affecting and will occasion great searchings of heart." Another from the Rev. Mr Ogilvie of Aberdeen, invited him to visit the northern city ; and in his reply he again expresses himself as grieved at the Scottish divisions and indicates their remedy :—

I find it best simply to preach the pure Gospel, and not to meddle at all with controversy. The present

298), which was conjointly published by Whitefield and John Wesley. (See Jackson's Library of Christian Biography, 12 vols. : vol. i. containing John Wesley's Preface, pp. 171-175.) He was known as the "Holy Halyburton," and his autobiography was extensively read.

[1] Gillies' Memoirs of Whitefield.

divisions are a sore judgment to Scotland. This is my comfort, Jesus is King. . . . O that the power of religion may revive! Nothing but that can break down the partition wall of bigotry.

To Lord Rae he writes :—

Why should we, who are pilgrims, mind earthly things? Why should we, who are soldiers, entangle ourselves with the things of this life? Heavenly-mindedness is the very life of a Christian. It is all in all.

To the Marquis of Lothian :—

I thank your lordship for your intended benefaction to the poor Georgia orphans.

His letters manifest a mind elevated above the secondary matters of religion, absorbed in the advancement of the kingdom of God and Christian beneficence. They also give the glimpse of a spiritually awakened people concerned about eternal things. In a letter dated "Edinburgh, August 15, 1741," he writes :—

Every morning I have a levée of wounded souls. At seven in the morning we have a lecture in the fields, attended not only by the common people, but persons of great rank. I have reason to think several of the latter sort are coming to Jesus. Little children are also much wrought upon. Congregations consist of many thousands. I preach twice daily, and expound in private houses at night, and am employed in speaking to souls under distress great part of the day.

At the end of August Whitefield preached in the
Scottish provinces, and after his return to Edinburgh
wrote thus to a friend :—

EDINBURGH, *September* 24, 1741.

On Sunday last I preached here four times, twice in
a church and twice in the fields ; in the evening I
collected £20 for the Royal Infirmary. On Monday
morning I visited the children in the three hospitals,
and preached in the evening in the Park. On Tuesday
and Wednesday I preached at Kinglassie, Aberdour,
and Inverkeithing. On Thursday I visited the prison,
and in the evening preached to the children of the
city, with a congregation of near twenty thousand, in
the Park.

At Glasgow he preached ten times in the High
Churchyard chiefly, and eight of his sermons were
printed at the request of his great Glasgow audiences.[1] His orphan-home at Georgia was now completed, and Scotland helped him in the beneficent
undertaking. During his first Scottish tour he
received by private benefactions and collections
£572, 16s. 5½d. ; from four Scottish towns he received the compliment of honorary burgess-tickets—
viz., Glasgow, Aberdeen, Stirling, and Paisley.[2]

The Earl of Leven and Melville, his Majesty's
Commissioner to the General Assembly of the Church

[1] See Appendix to ' Revivals of the Eighteenth Century,' with
Sermons by Whitefield.
[2] Tyerman's Life, vol. i. p. 523. The same honour was con-
ferred upon him by Irvine in 1742, and by Edinburgh in 1762,
*ut supra.*

of Scotland from 1741 to 1753, and his Countess,
Mary Erskine of Carnock, aunt of the Rev. Dr John
Erskine of the Greyfriars' Church, Edinburgh, took
great interest in Whitefield's work, and had him as
their guest in Melville House. This nobleman took
a deep interest in the affairs of the Church to which
he was hereditarily attached, and with the history
of which his own family was closely related.[1]
Whitefield wrote to him in 1741 :—

I have heard of the piety of your lordship's ancestors.
Take courage, my lord, and fear not to follow a crucified Jesus without the camp, bearing His reproach.
Beware of honour, falsely so called. Dare to be
singularly good, and be not ashamed of Jesus or His
Gospel. Look to Christ by faith, and your lordship's
great possessions will not retard, but promote your
progress in the divine life. What sweet communion
will you then enjoy with God in your walks and
gardens ! They will then be a little paradise to your
soul.

At Aberdeen, whither he had gone to preach on
the invitation of the Rev. Mr Ogilvie, he was
attacked by the collegiate minister as a " curate of
the Church of England," and as holding views that
were " grossly Arminian." Whitefield's attitude
was graceful :—

I took no other notice of the good man's ill-timed
zeal than to observe, in some part of my discourse,

---

[1] An Account of Dr Alexander Webster, of the High Church,
Edinburgh, p. 108.

that if the good old gentleman had seen some of my
later writings, wherein I had corrected several of my
former mistakes, he would not have expressed himself
in such strong terms. The people, being thus diverted
from controversy with man, were deeply impressed
with what they heard from the Word of God. All
were hushed and more than solemn, and on the
morrow the magistrates sent for me and begged I
would accept of the freedom of the city.

Leaving Aberdeen on Wednesday, October 13,
Whitefield commenced his return journey to Edinburgh. His journey was characterised by the usual
preaching activity in villages and towns on the
way : on his arrival in Edinburgh he preached and
lectured not fewer than sixteen times in three days.
It is a record of brilliant activity and unwearied
devotion in his Master's service, and Whitefield
traced his strength to a divine source. To his
curate at the Tabernacle, London, he wrote :—

EDINBURGH, *October* 27, 1741.

MY VERY DEAR BROTHER,—Although it is past
eleven at night I cannot miss a post. The Lord is
doing great things here. On Sunday last (October 24)
the Lord enabled me to preach four times, and to
lecture in the evening in a private home. Yesterday
I preached three times, and lectured at night. To-day
Jesus has enabled me to preach seven times : once in
the church, twice at the Girls' Hospital, once in the
Park, once at the Old People's Hospital, and afterwards
twice in a private house. Notwithstanding, I am now
as fresh as when I arose in the morning. Both in the
church and Park the Lord was with us. The girls in

the hospital were exceedingly affected, and so were the standers-by. One of the mistresses told me that she is now awakened in the morning by the voice of prayer and praise : and the master of the boys says that they meet together every night to sing and pray, and that when he goes to their rooms to see if all be safe he generally disturbs them at their devotions. The presence of God at the Old People's Hospital was wonderful. The Holy Spirit seemed to come down like a mighty rushing wind. Every day I hear of some fresh good wrought by the power of God. I scarce know how to leave Scotland. I believe I shall think it my duty to pay the inhabitants another visit as soon as possible. Above £500 have been collected, in money and goods, for the poor orphans. To-morrow I shall leave this place and go through Wales on my way to London.

Such is an account of George Whitefield's first visit to Scotland, and told chiefly from his own words. It is interesting to recall the judgments of those who observed the results of his preaching. Writes one from Edinburgh, November 5, 1741 :—

In the Tolbooth Church [where the Rev. Alexander Webster was minister] there has been at sacrament a hundred more than usual, whereof about thirty young ones had never been admitted before, and of these, eighteen were converted by your ministry.

An Edinburgh minister wrote :—

Since you left Scotland, numbers in different places have been awakened. Religion in this sinful city revives and flourishes. Ordinances are more punctually attended. People hear the Word with gladness, and receive it in faith and love. New meetings for prayer and spiritual conference are being begun everywhere. Religious conversation has banished slander and calumny from several tea-tables. Praise is perfected out of the mouths of babes and sucklings. Some stout-hearted sinners are captivated to the obedience of Christ.

The Rev. Mr Ogilvie wrote regarding Aberdeen that Mr Whitefield had revived in that city

a just sense and concern for the great things of religion. I often think that the Lord sent him here to teach me how to preach, and especially how to suffer. His attachment to no party, but to Christ, appears to me a peculiar excellency in him. While he stayed among us he answered our expectations so much that he has scarce more friends anywhere than here, where at first almost all were against him. The Word came with so much power that I hope several of different denominations will bless the Lord for ever that they ever heard him.

The Rev. Mr Willison of Dundee wrote :—

I look upon this youth as raised up by God for special service, for promoting true Christianity in the world, and for reviving it where it is decayed. I see the man to be all of a piece : his life and conversation to be a transcript of his sermons. *He is singularly fitted to do the work of an evangelist; and I have been long of opinion that it would be for the advantage of the world were this still to be a standing office in the Church.* I have myself been witness to the Holy Ghost falling upon him and his hearers oftener than once ; not in a miraculous, though in an observable manner. Many here are blessing God for sending him to this country,

though Satan has raged so much against it. Though
he is ordained a minister of the Church of England,
he has always conformed to us both in doctrine and
worship, and lies open to conform to us in other
points. God, by owning him so wonderfully, is pleased
to give a rebuke to our intemperate bigotry and party
zeal, and to tell us that neither circumcision nor un-
circumcision availeth anything, but the new creature.[1]

Such testimonies from eyewitnesses in the Church
abundantly prove the far-reaching effects of Whitefield's preaching in Scotland, and bring him before
us as one of God's best gifts to the Church. Well
has Sir James Stephen said : " Whitefield was a
great and a holy man ; among the foremost of the
heroes of philanthropy ; and as a preacher without
a superior or a rival." [2]

## SECOND VISIT, 1742.

Whitefield arrived in Scotland on June 3, 1742,
and his second visit was more remarkable than his
first. As his life and work cannot be fully known
apart from his own letters and those of his corre-
spondents, we will again be indebted to them for a
narrative of the facts. He came to find a general
welcome awaiting him, and his presence was the
means of new quickening.

When he came to Edinburgh the question arose,

---

[1] Tyerman's Life, collected from contemporaneous literature,
vol. i. pp. 527-529.
[2] Essays in Ecclesiastical Biography, vol. ii. p. 88.

Where was he to preach? and the following minute
of the managers of Heriot's Hospital, passed on
June 17, 1742, solved the question :—

The managers agree to erect seats in the Hospital
Park for about two thousand people, part of which
are to be covered with shades and let out to the best
advantage. It is further agreed, that out of the profits
arising from these seats, after paying all charges anent
the same, a sum not exceeding £60 sterling shall be
given to the Rev. Mr George Whitefield, for defraying
his charges during his continuance in this country.[1]

The seats thus erected are described as semicircular
in form: those with shades were let at three
shillings each for the season ; those without shades
at a halfpenny for every time used. A few seats
outside the railing were free, and the back seats
within were to be used by the soldiers gratuitous-
ly.[2] Such was Whitefield's Scottish metropolitan
cathedral.

He spent twelve successive days at Edinburgh,
where he preached twice daily, expounded almost
every night, and visited regularly the three hospitals.[3] It is interesting to have the following
stated by his wife, which testifies not only to
Whitefield's catholicity, but to the catholicity of
the Church of Scotland, notwithstanding all that is
urged against it during this period : " My husband

[1] Scots Magazine, 1742, p. 580.
[2] Tyerman's Life, vol. ii. p. 4.
[3] Weekly History, June 26, 1742.

publicly declared here that he was a member of the
Church of England, and a curate thereof ; and yet
was permitted to receive and assist at the Lord's
Supper in the churches at Edinburgh." [1]

On 15th June he set out for the West of Scotland,
and his visit there was one of the most remarkable
in his life : it led to the great revival of 1742.

*June* 19, 1742.

Yesterday morning I preached at Glasgow to a large
congregation. At mid-day I came to Cambuslang, and
preached at two to a vast body of people ; again at six
and again at nine at night. Such commotions, surely,
were never heard of, especially at eleven o'clock at
night. For an hour and a half there was much weep-
ing, and so many falling into such deep distress, expressed in various ways, as cannot be described. The
people seemed to be slain in scores. Their agonies
and cries were exceedingly affecting. Mr M'Culloch
preached, after I had done, till past one in the morning ; and then could not persuade the people to depart.
In the fields all night might be heard the voices of
prayer and of praise. The Lord is indeed much with
me. I have to-day preached twice already, and am to
preach twice more, perhaps thrice. The commotions
increase.

The parish minister of Cambuslang had been
preparing the people for this revival by his own
teaching, and the following statement regarding it
is given in the Statistical Account, and is from the
pen of the Rev. Dr Clason :—

[1] See letter of date June 16, 1742.

The kirk of Cambuslang being too small, and out of repair, the minister, in favourable weather, frequently conducted the public devotional services of the parish in the open fields. The place chosen was peculiarly well adapted for the purpose. It is a green brae on the east side of a deep ravine near the church, scooped out by nature in the form of an amphitheatre. At present it is sprinkled over with broom, furze, and sloe-bushes, and two aged thorns in twin-embrace are seen growing side by side near the borders of the meandering rivulet which murmurs below. In this retired and romantic spot Mr M'Culloch, for about a year before "the work" began, preached to crowded congregations, and on the Sabbath evenings, after sermon, detailed to the listening multitudes the astonishing effects produced by the ministrations of Mr Whitefield in England and America ; and urged, with great energy, the doctrine of regeneration and newness of life.[1]

He had met Whitefield during his Glasgow visit in 1741 ; and in the following year Whitefield visited Cambuslang with the remarkable results already indicated.[2]

Of the first Communion, celebrated on 11th July 1742, Whitefield writes :—

NEW KILPATRICK, *July* 15, 1742.

Last Friday night I came to Cambuslang to assist at the blessed sacrament. On Saturday I preached to above twenty thousand people. On the Sabbath scarce ever was such a sight seen in Scotland. Two tents were set up,

---

[1] Statistical Account.
[2] See full account in Dr Macfarlane's Revivals of the Eighteenth Century.

and the holy sacrament was administered in the fields. When I began to serve a table the people crowded so upon me that I was obliged to desist, and go to preach in one of the tents, whilst the ministers served the rest of the tables. There was preaching all day by one or another ; and, in the evening, when the sacrament was over, at the request of the ministers, I preached to the whole congregation of upwards of twenty thousand persons. I preached about an hour and a half. It was a time much to be remembered. On Monday morning I preached again to near as many. I never before saw such a universal stir. The motion fled, as swift as lightning, from one end of the auditory to the other. Thousands were bathed in tears—some wringing their hands, others almost swooning, and others crying out and mourning over a pierced Saviour. In the afternoon the concern was again very great. Much prayer had been previously put up to the Lord. All night, in different companies, persons were praying to God and praising Him. The children of God came from all quarters. It was like the Passover in Josiah's time. We are to have another in two or three months, if the Lord will. . . . I am exceedingly strengthened both in soul and body, and cannot now do well without preaching three times a-day.

It had been suggested and agreed to that the Communion should again be celebrated on the 15th of August, and the following ministers assisted on the second occasion : Mr Whitefield ; Mr Webster from Edinburgh ; Mr M'Laurin and Mr Gillies from Glasgow ; Mr Robe from Kilsyth ; Mr Currie from Kinglassie ; Mr M'Knight from Irvine ; Mr Bonar from Torphichen ; Mr Hamilton

from Douglas; Mr Henderson from Blantyre; Mr
Maxwell from Rutherglen; and Mr Adam from
Cathcart.[1]

Whitefield arrived at Cambuslang on August 13,
1742, and spent the next three weeks in the neighbourhood.   His letter to a friend is the best narrative of the period :—

CAMBUSLANG, August 27, 1742.

A fortnight ago I came to this place, to assist at the
sacramental occasion, with several worthy ministers of
the Church of Scotland.   Such a Passover has not been
heard of.   I preached once on the Saturday.   On the
Lord's day I preached in the morning; served five
tables; and preached again, about ten o'clock at night,
to a great number in the churchyard.   Though it
rained very much, there was a great awakening.   The
voice of prayer and praise was heard all night.   It was
supposed that between thirty and forty thousand people
were assembled; and that three thousand communicated.   There were three tents.   The ministers were
enlarged, and great grace was among the people.

On Monday, August 16th, at seven in the morning,
the Rev. Mr Webster (of Edinburgh) preached, and
there was a great commotion; and also in the third
sermon of the day when I preached.

On Thursday, August 19th, I preached twice at
Greenock; on Friday, three times at Kilbride; on
Saturday, once at Kilbride and twice at Stevenston.
On Sunday, August 22nd, four times at Irvine; on
Monday, once at Irvine and three times at Kilmar-
nock; on Tuesday, once at Kilmarnock and four times
at Stewarton; on Wednesday, once at Stewarton and

---

[1] Dr Macfarlane's Revivals, p. 72.

twice at Mearnes ; and yesterday, twice at this place. I never preached with so much apparent success before. The work seems to spread more and more. Oh, my friend, pray and give praise on behalf of the most unworthy wretch that was ever employed in the dear Redeemer's service !

The minister of Cambuslang testified "that upwards of five hundred souls have been awakened," [1] and the following is his account of its fruits :—

Among the particular good fruits already appearing, both in Cambuslang and elsewhere, the following instances seem very encouraging : a visible reformation of the lives of persons who were formerly notorious sinners ; particularly the laying aside of cursing and swearing, and drinking to excess, among those who were addicted to that practice ; remorse for acts of injustice, and for violation of relative duties confessed to the persons wronged, joined with new endeavours after a conscientious discharge of such duties ; restitution, which has more than once been distinctly and particularly inculcated in public since this work began ; forgiving of injuries ; all desirable evidences of fervent love to one another, to all men, and even to those who speak evil of them ; and among those people both in Cambuslang and other parishes, more affectionate expressions of regard than ever to their own ministers, and to the ordinances dispensed by them ; the keeping up divine worship in families, where it was neglected very often by some and entirely by others ; the erecting of new societies for prayer, both of old and young, partly within the parish, where no less than twelve such societies are newly begun, and partly elsewhere,

---

[1] Dr Macfarlane's Revivals, p. 64.

among persons who have been awakened on this occasion ; and, together with all these things, ardent love for the Holy Scriptures, vehement thirsting after the public ordinances, earnest desires to get private instructions in their duty from ministers and others, with commendable docility, and tractableness in receiving such instructions. . . . I would further add that these good impressions have been made on persons of very different characters and ages.[1]

Of the similar work at Kilsyth the minister notices among other effects : " The countenances of others quite changed. There was an observable serenity, a brightness, and openness, so that it was the observation of some concerning them, that they had got new faces." [2]

Similar revivals—some on a more and others ' on a less extensive scale—took place in Glasgow, Edinburgh, Cumbernauld, St Ninians, Gargunnock, Calder, Campsie, Baldernock, Auchterarder, Muthill, Dundee, Crieff, Monzievaird, Nigg, Rosskeen, Nairn, Rosemarkie, Irvine, Coldingham, Easter Logie, Alness, Cromarty, Golspie, Kirkmichael, Avoch, Rogart.[3] The revival was thus far beyond the districts that Whitefield visited, and left its impress on the religious life of the country. Enthusiasm is contagious, and the religious fervour aroused in the west permeated far and wide. The Cameronians denounced the re-

[1] Gillies' Historical Collections, vol. ii. pp. 341, 342.
[2] Mr Robe's Narrative, p. 159.
[3] Gillies' Historical Collections, vol. ii. pp. 339-378.

vival in strong terms; the Seceders ascribed it
to the devil, and appointed the 4th of August
to be observed as a day of fasting and humiliation
through their whole body for the countenance given
to Whitefield, "a priest of the Church of England,
who had sworn the Oath of Supremacy, and ab-
jured the Solemn League and Covenant," and for
"the symptoms of delusion attending the present
awful work upon the bodies and spirits of men
going on at Cambuslang." [1]   Such judgments were
too severe, and failed in generosity, for after every
consideration is made for the abnormal forms that
frequently accompany great religious movements
which stir the hearts of the people to their very
depths, it cannot be denied, in the light of the
evidence afforded by the clergy themselves, that the
movement was productive of wide and permanent
results.   One of the most influential and prominent
of these—the Rev. Dr Webster of the High Church,
Edinburgh — defended it in a pamphlet entitled
'Divine Influence, the true Spring of the Extra-
ordinary Work at Cambuslang, and other places
in the West of Scotland, in a Letter to a Gentleman in the Country.' Whitefield himself was quite
charitable amid the attacks on his work.

The Messrs Erskine and their adherents have appointed a public fast to humble themselves, among
other things, for my being received in Scotland, and

---

[1] Cunningham's History of the Church of Scotland, vol. ii.
p. 317.

for the delusion, as they term it, at Cambuslang and other places ; and all this because I would not consent to preach only for them, till I had light into, and could take the Solemn League and Covenant. To what lengths may prejudice carry even good men ! From giving way to the first risings of bigotry and a party spirit, good Lord deliver us ! . . . O how prejudice will blind the eyes of even good men ! [1]

During his second visit, Scotland contributed £300 to the Orphan House at Georgia.

## Third Visit, 1748.

Whitefield arrived in Scotland on September 14, 1748, and after a preaching-visit of twelve days at Cambuslang and Glasgow, seems to have confined all his labours to Edinburgh. There was some opposition : he said, " I have met with some unexpected rubs, but not one more than was necessary to humble my proud heart." Evidently on account of the strong opposition raised by the Associate Presbytery, many of the clergy were unwilling to countenance him, probably with a view of lessening the ecclesiastical bitterness of the period. The Synod of Perth, he says, " made an Act against employing him." [2] Whitefield had preached in the College Church of

---

[1] Tyerman's Life, vol. ii. pp. 22, 23.

[2] In one of his letters relating to Perth he says, "Some give out that I am employed by the Government to preach against the Pretender, and the Seceders are very angry with me for not preaching up the Scottish Covenant" (Works,

Glasgow for Dr Gillies and in Kirkintilloch for
Dr Erskine, and the matter was discussed along
with other charges in the Synods of Glasgow and
Perth and the Presbytery of Edinburgh.[1]  An
attempt was made to prohibit or discourage him
from preaching in Scottish parish churches.  One
of the ministers who spoke against the motion
said :—

I blush to think that any of our brethren should be-
friend a proposal so contrary to that moderation and
catholic spirit which now is, and I hope ever shall be,
the glory of our Church.  I am sensible many things
in the Church of England need reformation ; but I
honour her, notwithstanding, as our sister-Church.  If
Bishop Butler, Bishop Sherlock, or Bishop Secker were
in Scotland, I should welcome them to my pulpit.  In
this I should imitate Mr Samuel Rutherford, as firm
a Presbyterian as any of us, who yet employed Bishop
Usher.  There is no Law of Christ, no Act of Assembly, prohibiting me to give my pulpit to an Episcopal,
Independent, or Anabaptist minister, if of sound principles in the fundamentals of religion and of sober life.
Our Church expressly enjoins, Act XIII., April 1711,
that great tenderness is to be used to foreign Protestants.  The requiring strangers to subscribe our

---

vol. ii. p. 194).  It is difficult to explain how the first
assertion could be made, unless from some vague report as
to Whitefield's connection by friendship with one of the early
Oxford Methodists—the Rev. John Clayton—who when the
Prince marched through Salford in 1745 fell upon his knees
before him and prayed for the adventurous Chevalier (Tyerman's Oxford Methodists, p. 45).

[1] Memoirs of Whitefield by Dr Gillies, p. 156.

Formula before they preach with us would lay as effectual a bar against employing those of Congregational principles, or Presbyterian non-subscribers, as those of the Church of England.[1]

The motion was lost by 27 to 13, and the following amendment was carried :[2]—

That no minister within the bounds of the Synod should employ ministers or preachers not licensed or ordained in Scotland, till he had sufficient evidence of their licence and good character, and should be in readiness to give an account of his conduct to his own Presbytery when required.[3]

In the East Country on a similar occasion, the Rev. Dr Webster of the Tolbooth, who had already defended Whitefield by pamphlet, spoke thus :—

I shall conclude by observing that the grave opposition made to this divine work by several good men through misinformation or mistaken zeal, and the slippery precipice on which they now stand, may teach

[1] Gillies' Memoirs, p. 176.
[2] Similar resolutions were adopted by the Synod of Lothian and Tweeddale, the Synod of Perth and Stirling, and the Presbytery of Edinburgh (Tyerman, vol. ii. p. 200). The Secessionists met in Edinburgh on November 16, renewed the Covenant, and "solemnly engaged to strengthen one another's hands, in the use of lawful means to extirpate Popery, Prelacy, Arminianism, Arianism, Tritheism, Sabellianism, and George Whitefieldism." The service "was conducted by the Rev. Adam Gibb and his helpers with great solemnity, and the generality of the people evidenced an uncommon seriousness and concern." (Gentleman's Magazine, 1748, p. 523 ; General Advertiser, November 24, 1748.)
[3] Life of John Erskine, D.D., p. 134.

us that it is indeed a dangerous thing to censure without inquiry. It may serve likewise as a solemn warning against a party spirit which so far blinds the eyes. It also gives a nobler opportunity for the exercise of our Christian sympathy towards these our erring brethren, . . . and should make us long for a removal to the land of visions above, . . . where are no wranglings, no strivings about matters of faith, and where, the whole scheme of present government being removed, we shall no more see as through a glass, but face to face, where perfect light will lay a foundation for perfect harmony and love. It is with peculiar pleasure that I often think how my good friend Ebenezer [Erskine] shall then enter into the everlasting mansions with many glorified saints, whom the Associate Presbytery have now given over as the work of Satan. May they soon see their mistake, and may we yet altogether be happily united in the bonds of peace and truth.[1]

Dean Stanley remarks that "these are golden words which no mere enthusiast could have conceived or penned ;" and adds: "This is moderation, if ever there was such on earth. This was in the very depth of the eighteenth century, at the very moment when the Moderate party were beginning to establish their sway." [2] It is pleasant too, amid a time of much ecclesiastical strife, to find words such as those uttered by the Rev. Dr Webster and by the other clergyman (probably Dr Gillies) in the Presbytery of Glasgow : they have a sweetness and a

---

[1] Gledstone's Whitefield, p. 4̶7̶7̶. 2 9 5 - 6.
[2] The Church of Scotland, pp. 137, 138.

light in them that were not by any means characteristic of the period.

Whitefield, notwithstanding the opposition,
preached three times in the Tolbooth Church, and
twice in the Canongate Church, Edinburgh, as well
as about thirty times in the Orphan Hospital Park.
He did not make any collections for his Orphan
Home, evidently with the purpose of giving no
ground of offence.    He returned to his work in
England at the beginning of November.

## Fourth Visit, 1750.

Whitefield reached Edinburgh on July 6, 1750, and
preached in the Orphan Hospital Park.  " People
flock rather more than ever, and earnestly entreat
me not to leave them soon." After preaching
twenty times in Edinburgh, he set out for Glasgow,
and the following is his account of the visit :—

Friends here received me most kindly, and the
congregations, I think, are larger than ever. Yesterday [Sunday], besides preaching twice in the field, I
preached in the College Kirk, being forced by Mr
Gillies.  It was a blessed season.  I have met and
shaken hands with Mr Ralph Erskine.  Oh, when
shall God's people learn war no more ?

The following is his impression of the Scottish
congregations :—

No one can well describe the order, attention, and
earnestness of the Scotch congregations.  They are

unwearied in hearing the Gospel. I left thousands
sorrowful at Glasgow ; and here I was again most
gladly received last night. By preaching always twice,
and once thrice, and once four times in a day, I am
quite weakened ; but I hope to recruit again, and get
fresh strength to work for Jesus.

On August 4, he writes from Berwick :—

I have taken a very sorrowful leave of Scotland. . . .
I shall have reason to bless God to all eternity for this
last visit to Scotland. . . . Many enemies were glad
to be at peace with me. . . . One of the ministers
here has sent me an offer of his pulpit, and I hear of
about ten more around the town who would do the
same.

### Fifth Visit, 1751.

He reached Glasgow on July 18, and preached
there and at Edinburgh each day until August 6.
The following letters to the Countess of Huntingdon
describe his work :—

GLASGOW  *July* 12, 1751.

EVER HONOURED MADAM,— . . . At the desire of
the magistrates [of Irvine] I preached to a great congregation. Since then I have been preaching twice
a-day in this city. Thousands attend every morning
and evening. Though I preached near eighty times
in Ireland, and God was pleased to bless His Word,
yet Scotland seems to be a new world to me. To
see the people bring so many Bibles, and turn to
every passage when I am expounding, is very encouraging.

To the same :—

EDINBURGH, *July* 30, 1751.

The parting at Glasgow was very sorrowful. Numbers set out from the country, to hear the Word, by three or four o'clock in the morning. Congregations here increase greatly. I now preach twice daily to many thousands. . . . Mr Wesley has been there [Mussel-burgh], and intends setting up Societies, which I think imprudent.[1] . . . For near twenty-eight days, in Glasgow and Edinburgh, I preached to near ten thousand souls every day. Ninety-four pounds were collected for the Edinburgh orphans, and I heard of seven or eight students, awakened about ten years ago, who are likely to turn out excellent preachers.

## SIXTH VISIT, 1752.

After a visit to America, he arrived at Edinburgh early in September, and for twenty-eight days preached to audiences there and at Glasgow of "not less than ten thousand each day." His ministry during this and subsequent visits had a powerful influence over the Divinity students. Dr Gillies of Glasgow wrote :—

His preaching had an excellent tendency to destroy bigotry, and to turn men's attention from smaller matters to the great and substantial things of religion. . . . Young people were much benefited by his ministry, and particularly young students. . . . His conversation was no less reviving than his ser-

---

[1] Referring to Wesley's first Scottish visit (April 1751).

D

mons. . . . One might challenge the sons of pleasure, with all their wit, good humour, and gaiety, to furnish entertainments so agreeable. At the same time, every part of it was not more agreeable than it was useful and edifying.

### SEVENTH VISIT, 1753.

Whitefield returned to Scotland on July 20, 1753, and remained until August 7, preaching to as great crowds as ever at Edinburgh and Glasgow. The 'Scots Magazine' narrates :—

Mr George Whitefield arrived at Edinburgh, July 20th ; went thence to Glasgow on the 27th ; returned to Edinburgh, August 3rd ; and set out for London on the 7th. He preached daily, morning and evening, when at Edinburgh, in the Orphan Hospital Park ; and, when at Glasgow, in the Castle Yard, to numerous audiences. In his sermons at Glasgow he declaimed warmly against a playhouse lately erected within the enclosure in which he preached. The consequence was that, before his departure, workmen were employed to take it down, to prevent it being done by ruder hands.[1]

This brought him much misrepresentation, and he defended himself in the following letter, printed in the 'Newcastle Journal' :—

NEWCASTLE, *August* 17, 1753.

GENTLEMEN,—By your last Saturday's paper I find that some Edinburgh correspondent has informed you

---

[1] P. 361.

that when I was preaching at Glasgow on the 2nd
inst., to a numerous audience, near the playhouse
lately built, I inflamed the mob so much against it
that they ran directly from before me and pulled it
down to the ground ; and that several of the rioters,
since then, have been taken up and committed to jail.
But, I assure you, this is mere slander and misinformation. It is true, indeed, that I was preaching
at Glasgow, to a numerous auditory, at the beginning
of this month ; and that I thought it my duty to show
the evil of having a playhouse erected in a trading city
—almost, too, before the very door of the university.
And this, by the help of God, if called to it, I should
do again. But that I inflamed the mob, or that they
ran directly from me, or pulled the playhouse down,
or that the rioters were taken up and put into prison,
is entirely false.

I suppose all this took its rise from the builder
taking down the roof of the house himself. You must
know that the walls of this playhouse were part of
the old palace of the Bishop of Glasgow, and only had
a board covering put upon them during the time of
the players being there. They being gone, the owner
(whether convinced by anything that was said, I cannot tell) began to take off the roof several days before
I left the place ; so that, if there had been any riot,
doubtless I should have seen it.

No, gentlemen, your correspondent may assure himself that I am too much a friend to my God, my king,
and my country, to encourage any such thing. I know
of no such means of reformation, either in Church or
State. The weapons of a Christian's warfare are not
carnal. And therefore, if you please to inform the
public and your Edinburgh correspondent of the mis-

take in to-morrow's paper, you will oblige, gentlemen your very humble servant,

GEORGE WHITEFIELD.

## EIGHTH VISIT, 1756.

Arriving on August 20, he resumed his work at Edinburgh and Glasgow, and continued it for three weeks. He always united philanthropy with his preaching, and the Orphan Hospital at Edinburgh benefited during this visit by £120.[1]

The managers of the Orphan Hospital made him a present of fifty guineas to defray his travelling expenses ; but he returned ten guineas, saying that forty guineas were sufficient to defray the charges, and likewise to pay upwards of £14, which he had laid out here for coarse linen to be sent to his Orphan House in Georgia.[2]

The Magazine continues, that scarcity at home had induced a greater number of Highlanders than usual to come to Edinburgh for harvest-work. The harvest not being ready, they were almost destitute.

Contributions were set on foot to give them two meals a-day at the poorhouse ; and on the evening of September 21, after a sermon suitable to the occasion by Mr Whitefield, a collection was made for them in the Orphan Hospital Park, which amounted to £60, 11s. 4d. sterling, of which half a guinea was given by Mr Whitefield himself.[3]

---

[1] Scots Magazine.       [2] Ibid.       [3] Ibid.

His preaching gave an unquestionable impulse to philanthropic work in Scotland, and everything speaks of the unselfishness of the great preacher.[1]

## Ninth Visit, 1757.

Arriving at Edinburgh on May 11, he continued there for about a month, preaching regularly at the Orphan Hospital Park. Being in Edinburgh during the sittings of the General Assembly, he was warmly received by the Church of Scotland. The Commissioner, Lord Cathcart, and the Moderator, the Rev. Professor Leechman, D.D., of Glasgow University, were kindly disposed to him, and gave him a welcome. He preached morning and evening, and attended every one of the sittings of Assembly; was invited to dine with the Commissioner, and said grace after dinner. His own account is:—

Being the time of the General Assembly (at which I was much pleased), many ministers attended, perhaps a hundred at a time. Thereby prejudices were removed, and many of their hearts were deeply impressed. About thirty of them, as a token of respect, invited me to a public entertainment. The Lord High Commissioner also invited me to his table ; and many persons of credit and religion did the same in a public manner. Thousands and thousands, among whom were a great many of the best rank, daily attended on the Word preached ; and the longer I stayed, the more the congregations and divine influence increased.

---

[1] See Gledstone's Whitefield, p. 517.

Whitefield was thus brought into closer alliance with the Church of Scotland, and his influence was evidently upon the increase both among its people and its ministry. Thomas Rankine, who afterwards became one of Wesley's preachers, was influenced by Whitefield's preaching during this visit.

## TENTH VISIT, 1758.

From August 4 to September 13 he preached frequently at Glasgow and Edinburgh : at the former place £60 was collected after his sermon on behalf of a charitable society, and at Edinburgh £200 for the Edinburgh Orphan Hospital.[1] Surely such is sufficient testimony as to the affection with which the Scottish people venerated him.

## ELEVENTH VISIT, 1759.

He arrived at Edinburgh on June 30, 1759, and spent seven weeks in Scotland, chiefly in Edinburgh and Glasgow. He set out for London on August 14. During his visit to Glasgow he preached ten times on two Sundays alone. Whitefield exhibited his single-mindedness in a very marked way during this visit. He refused, either for himself personally or for his Orphan House, the estate, both money and lands, valued at £7000, of

[1] Scots Magazine.

a Miss Hunter, who offered them to him.[1] Much
of the opposition in the Church arose in unfounded
reports regarding the Georgia Orphan House. They
were absolutely unfounded. Sir Henry Moncreiff
Wellwood wrote :—

They [the people] gave him credit for the purity of
his motives, amidst all the calumnies which were spread
against him. And it can now be affirmed, without
reserve, that whatever opinion may be held with regard
to his conceptions of Christian doctrine, or the form
in which he attempted the work of an evangelist, he
lived to contradict every surmise to the prejudice of
his intentions, and went down to the grave at last with
a character of unblemished and established integrity.[2]

## TWELFTH VISIT, 1762.

At the beginning of November 1761 Whitefield
arrived in Edinburgh, but the incessant strain of
preaching and travelling had already shown evidence
in his physical force. When it is recalled that his
work knew no pause during these many years, and
that through them all he sustained efforts that were
herculean in their extent, it is marvellous that he
could endure so long. But what was impossible to
a life inspired with a vivid and tenacious faith, and
throbbing with an enthusiasm of humanity that
knew no ebbing? When we consider his own

[1] Gledstone's Whitefield, p. 474.
[2] Life of John Erskine, D.D., pp. 102, 103.

testimony, "I would fain die preaching," [1] and his own choice, "A pilgrim life to me is the sweetest on this side eternity," [2] we are in the presence of one who had no thoughts beyond his work, and who loved it with a passionate devotion. Whitefield was only prevented in 1761 entering upon his usual Scottish preaching campaign by the order of "four eminent physicians" in Edinburgh, who recommended rest. "Silence is enjoined me for a while by the Edinburgh physicians. They say my case is then recoverable. The Great Physician will direct."

After a short rest, he resumed his work in England, visited Holland, and attended Wesley's Conference in Leeds, whence he proceeded to Scotland.

*Edinburgh, September 2, 1762.*—I am just this moment returned from Glasgow, where I have been enabled to preach every day, and twice at Cambuslang. Auditories were large.

*Edinburgh, September 9.*—I came here a week ago. Since then I have been helped to preach every day. The kirk has been a Bethel. . . . On Monday, the 13th inst., I shall set off.

### THIRTEENTH VISIT, 1763.

He arrived in Scotland about the middle of March, intending to embark about the middle of April on his sixth visit to America. Illness de-

---

[1] Works, vol. iii. p. 311.     [2] Letter, March 17, 1769.

tained him, and he did not sail till June 4. During this visit he met John Wesley, who was in Scotland also, and in Wesley's Journal we find the following: "I came to Edinburgh on Saturday 21st. The next day I had the satisfaction of spending a little time with Mr Whitefield. Humanly speaking, he is worn out; but we have to do with Him who hath all power in heaven and earth." [1] Whitefield desired "to get upon his throne again," and during the eleven weeks' stay in Edinburgh he was able to preach occasionally notwithstanding his illness.

### FOURTEENTH VISIT, 1768.

His last visit was in June 1768. His popularity was greater than ever. He met in Edinburgh "friends of twenty-seven years' standing." "I am here [in Edinburgh] only in danger of being hugged to death." ;-Preaching from "his throne" to the waiting thousands, he was as a king among men, and all classes hung upon his lips. "Could I preach ten times a-day, thousands and thousands would attend."

"When we are taught," said Dean Stanley, "to think of the Edinburgh of that age as cold and dead, let us remember that it was of it that Whitefield, when he left it, exclaimed, 'O Edinburgh,

[1] See Journal, p. 244.

Edinburgh, surely thou wilt never be forgotten by
me.' " [1] and that same Edinburgh never forgot him.
When, years afterwards, he came to the Scottish
capital again, he was in danger of being hugged to
death by the enthusiastic reception of its citizens,
and he sat, it is said, amongst them "like a king of
men on his throne." [2]

Whitefield continued his labours in England
and America, and he carried across the ocean the
memory of the warm Scottish gratitude. He left
Scotland an exhausted man. "Lord Jesus, I
am weary in Thy work, but not of it." He died
at Newbury Port, America, September 30, 1770,
after a noble service of thirty-four years as an
evangelist.

It is to the glory of the Scottish capital that when
Foote, the actor, brought his play upon the stage
at Edinburgh, two months after Whitefield's death,
and imitated the preacher's appearance and manner
of speaking, the theatre was emptied after the first
night. Public opinion condemned the heartless
caricaturing of one who had always entered the
country as a bearer of good tidings and a messenger
of peace; the Edinburgh pulpits also thundered
out rebukes.[3] Edinburgh assuredly did not forget
Whitefield and his great work.

---

[1] This is the correct version; see Philip's Life and Times of
Whitefield, p. 401.

[2] Stanley's Church of Scotland, p. 138.

[3] Gledstone's Whitefield, pp. 476, 477.

England gave Whitefield birth, and he named himself "a moderate Catholic clergyman of the Church of England," [1] but Scotland gave him a hearty welcome, afforded him a wide field of influence; and Dr Gillies, a minister of the Church of Scotland, wrote his biography, which appeared in 1772. The story of his work is best told by his own letters, which are as sincere, single-minded, and transparent as the man's own nature; their language is the appropriate expression of a soul enthusiastic in a great work and aglow with a great mission. That they are not overstrained is abundantly testified by eyewitnesses whose testimony is beyond question, and who were acquainted with the permanent results of Whitefield's ministry. Dr Gillies thus describes him :—

Mr Whitefield's person was graceful and well proportioned. His stature was rather above the middle size. His complexion was very fair. His eyes were of a dark-blue colour, and small but sprightly. He had a squint with one of them, occasioned either by the ignorance or carelessness of the nurse who attended him in the measles when he was about four years old. His features were in general good and regular. His countenance was manly, and his voice exceeding strong; yet both were softened with an uncommon degree of sweetness. He was always very clean and neat, and often said pleasantly that "a minister of the Gospel ought to be without spot." His deportment was decent

---

[1] Gledstone's Whitefield, p. 196. 4, 97

and easy, without the least stiffness or formality ; and
his engaging polite manners made his company universally agreeable. . . . He was remarkable for his
moderation both in eating and drinking. .`. . Early in
the morning he rose to his Master's work, and all the
day long was employed in a continual succession of
different duties. When he was visited with any distress or affection, preaching, as he himself tells us, was
his catholicon, and prayer his antidote against every
trial. . . . His eloquence was great, and of the true and
noblest kind. He was utterly devoid of all appearance
of affectation. He seemed to be quite unconscious of
the talents he possessed. The importance of his
subject, and the regard due to his hearers, engrossed
all his concern. He spoke like one who did not seek
their applause, but was anxious for their best interests.
. . . He had a strong and musical voice, and a wonderful command of it. His pronunciation was not only
proper, but manly and graceful. He was never at a
loss for the most natural and strong expressions. The
grand sources of his eloquence were an exceeding lively
imagination and an action still more lively. Every
accent of his voice spoke to the ear ; every feature of
his face, and every motion of his hands, spoke to the
eye. . . . One thing remains to be mentioned of an
infinitely higher order—namely, the power of God,
which so remarkably accompanied his labours. It is
here that Mr Whitefield is most to be envied. When
we consider the multitudes that were brought under
lasting religious impressions, and the multitudes that
were wrought upon in the same manner by the ministry
of others, excited by his example, we are led into the
same sentiment with Mr Wesley in his funeral sermon,
"What an honour hath it pleased God to put upon His
faithful servant!"

The account of Mrs Jonathan Edwards, in one of her letters, gives additional features to the portrait :—

He is truly a remarkable man, and during his visit has, I think, verified all that we have heard of him. He makes less of the doctrines than our American preachers generally do, and aims more at affecting the heart. He is a born orator. You have already heard of his deep-toned, yet clear and melodious voice. It is perfect music. It is wonderful to see what a spell he casts over an audience by proclaiming the simplest truths of the Bible. . . . He impresses the ignorant, and not less the educated and refined. . . . He is a very devout and godly man, and his only aim seems to be to reach and influence men the best way. He speaks from a heart all aglow with love, and pours out a torrent of eloquence which is almost irresistible.

Whitefield made fourteen visits to Scotland, and although after 1741 and 1742 there were no such remarkable events as accompanied his preaching at Cambuslang, his later visits were described as re-freshing and stimulating. Their predominant in-fluence was in breaking down party zeal and sec-tarian bigotry ; in emphasising the divine element which transcended all separating barriers. It was an incalculable blessing to the religious life of Scotland to see and hear one who rose above all party shibboleths, and who would preach anywhere if he only felt a new opportunity presenting itself of doing good. It is pleasant, too, to recall that pulpits in the Church of Scotland were open to him, when those in England were closed against him, and he was branded with the then opprobrious name "enthusiast."[1] The real source of the differences that arose in 1748 was want of definite knowledge as to the real objects of his work, and opposition against him directing to the Georgia Hospital, Scottish beneficence, which many thought at the time could be as needfully spent on the charities at home. Whitefield met the opposition by fulfilling its claim, and his preaching both stimulated the religious life of the country and was the means of raising great sums for Scottish humanitarian work, while the victory of his blameless, unselfish character swept away ungrounded suspicions.[2]

From his open pulpit in the Orphan Hospital Park at Edinburgh and at the High Churchyard at Glasgow—where he chiefly preached during his later visits — Whitefield's preaching reached all

[1] In the eighteenth century "enthusiast" was a kind of byword applied in opprobrium and derision. "Its precise meaning differed exceedingly with the mind of the speaker, and with the opinions to which it was applied. It sometimes denoted the wildest and most credulous fanaticism or the most visionary mysticism; on the other hand, the irreligious, the lukewarm, and the formalist often levelled the reproach of enthusiasm, equally with that of bigotry, at what ought to be regarded as sound spirituality, or true Christian zeal, or the anxious efforts of thoughtful and religious men to find a surer standing against the reasonings of infidels and Deists."—The English Church in the Eighteenth Century, by Abbey and Overton, p. 227.

[2] Life of Dr John Erskine, p. 132.

classes of the people[1] — not least in importance,
the students at both universities. He inspired
those who inspired others, and his influence thereby
reached a wide area. At a period when opinion
was a predominating element in the Church, he
emphasised the truth that faith is not acquiescence
in opinions held to be true, but direct contact with
and realisation of spiritual realities ; when a domin-
ant temper in the Church was the metaphysical and
theological one, he directed attention to the repose
of religion—as a divine life within the soul, as a
direct experience. He raised men's thoughts above
the din of the theological battlefield to that serener
air where the divine and the human are reconciled.
His message was much needed, but not less so was
his example. He was an ordained priest of the
Church of England, who preached in Scottish parish
churches, joined in Scottish Communion services,
and even assisted at one in the High Church of
Edinburgh. Such catholicity was supremely needed,
and the continuation of it is the succession of the
true apostolic spirit. It recalled the early years

---

[1] Says Dr Gillies: "His friends in Scotland, among whom
were many of all ranks from the highest to the lowest, were
very constant and steady in their great regard for him, and his
opposers grew more and more mild. But, indeed, Mr Whitefield's whole behaviour was so open to the eyes of the world,
and his character, after it had stood many attacks from all
quarters, came at last to be so thoroughly established, that
several of his opposers in Scotland seemed rather to acquire a
certain degree of esteem for him ; at least they all thought
proper to give over speaking against him."

of the Reformation, when the utmost harmony
and goodwill prevailed among all the Reformed
Churches ; when there was but one Reformed
Church, and the ministers of one Reformed nation
were freely admitted into the pulpits of another ;
when Knox, for example, could minister either in
England, Scotland, or Geneva, and his Church was
wherever Protestantism was.[1]

Whitefield's preaching settled doubt by its transparent earnestness and conviction. The preacher was
single-minded, and his message had the authority
which strong conviction always gives. "All religion," says Mr Leslie Stephen, "historically
speaking, has depended and must depend for the
masses of mankind upon authority. A creed built
on elaborate syllogisms is a creed with ' perhaps ' in
it, and no such creed can command men's emo-
tions."[2] Whitefield's preaching had no " perhaps "
in it, and its authority rested on the preacher's
message finding its vindication in the hearers' experience. It was not so much his grasp of the
truth, as the grasp of the truth upon him, that
made him what he was. It was the being possessed by the truth that enabled him to inspire
others and made him a prophet. And this, added
to a life single-minded in its purpose, devotional
in its spirit,[3] amiable and generous, made him a

[1] Cunningham's Church History of Scotland, vol. i. p. 412.
[2] History of English Thought in the Eighteenth Century, vol.
i. p. 175.
[3] Philip's Life and Times of Whitefield, p. 565.

prophet. He lived in the light of eternity, and
passed from communion with God to his daily
duty ; his preaching awakened and inspired, for the
cardinal principles of the Christian religion were
ever in his heart and on his tongue.[1] It was the
power of the Christian message rediscovered, and
preached with an apostolic fervour: while the
events at Cambuslang were unique,[2] and did not
characterise his later visits, it was acknowledged on
all hands that Whitefield's preaching promoted the
interests of practical religion in the period.[3] It
appealed to all classes, and even David Hume expressed his admiration of it. The letters already
quoted are sufficient testimony to its power : it
created light and diffused life : the marvel is that
with his work in England, Ireland, and America—
in the midst of which his Scottish were as holiday
visits—Whitefield was enabled to maintain it so
long. He was endowed as a great evangelist and
philanthropist, and was an outstanding gift to the
eighteenth century. The opposition he had to en-
counter in England was no less unique than his
own eminence, but Scotland gave him a hearty
welcome : its people were with him, and of the

[1] See Sir James Stephen's Essays in Ecclesiastical Biography,
vol. ii. p. 98.

[2] As has already been stated, Dr Webster and Dr John
Erskine both defended Whitefield's work at Cambuslang, and
even those who opposed it admitted that the converts amounted
to several hundreds (see Life of Dr John Erskine, p. 119).

[3] Erskine's Life, p. 127.

Churches of New England and Scotland he wrote, " There are as many faithful ministers among them as in any parts of the known world." [1]   Whitefield organised no religious societies ; such was the work of John Wesley, of whom it was said by Lord Macaulay " that he had a genius for ecclesiastical government not inferior to Richelieu." [2]

[1] Preface to a Communion Morning's Companion by George Whitefield.
[2] Works, vol. v. p. 333.

# THE REV. JOHN WESLEY.

John Wesley was the son of the Rev. Samuel Wesley, and was born on June 17, 1703, at Epworth, Lincolnshire, where his father was rector from 1696 to 1735. At six years of age he nearly lost his life through the burning of the rectory, and the memory of the event was always potent in his imagination, and impressed itself upon him very vividly. He described himself as "a brand plucked out of the burning." He received, like the other members of the family, a remarkable religious education from his parents, and at eight years of age became a communicant. He entered the Charterhouse School in 1713, and was a pupil there for seven years. He became a commoner at Christ Church, Oxford, on July 13, 1720, and brought with him from the Charterhouse a school exhibition of £40 a-year. In 1725 the thought of taking Orders occurred to him, and during this early period he was much influenced by the 'De Imitatione' and Scougal's 'Life of God

in the Soul of Man'[1]—a book recommended to him
by his mother.   This book, as has already been
noted, had a profound influence upon Whitefield :
it was well known to Charles Wesley ; it also had
an influence over John Wesley that has not been
sufficiently noticed.   His mother recommended the
'Life of God in the Soul of Man' as "an excellent
good book," and "as an acquaintance of mine many
years ago," [2] and John Wesley studied it very carefully during the Christ Church days.   Along with
the 'De Imitatione' it had no little influence at this
critical period of his life in moulding that inward
spiritual view of religion which afterwards was
strengthened by his study of Jeremy Taylor, Law,
and Luther's Preface to the Epistle to the Romans.
Matthew Arnold has said of Wesley that he had
"a genius for godliness," [3] and at this period it
became pronounced.   "I began," he writes, "to
alter the whole form of my conversation and to set
in earnest about a new life.   I set apart an hour or
two a-day for religious retirement ; I communicated
every week ; I watched against all sin whether in
word or deed."   He was ordained deacon by Bishop
Potter in 1725.   He was elected Fellow of Lincoln

---

[1] Wesley afterwards published an abridged edition of
Scougal's work, a third edition of which was issued in 1773.
He also published Scougal's sermons in his Christian Library—
see volume xxiii. pp. 325-456.

[2] Dr Clarke's Wesley Family, vol. ii. p. 103 ; also Life of
Susanna Wesley, by Eliza Clarke, p. 174.

[3] St Paul and Protestantism, p. 16.

College on March 17, 1726, and his connection with it lasted for more than a quarter of a century.[1] In all his books he designates himself as "sometime Fellow of Lincoln College." He mapped out his time methodically. Monday and Tuesday were devoted to Latin and Greek; Wednesday to Logic and Ethics; Thursday to Hebrew and Arabic; Friday to Metaphysics and Natural Philosophy; Saturday to Oratory and Poetry; Sunday to Divinity. In October 1726 he was appointed Greek Lecturer and Moderator of the Classes; the former office, with a salary of £20 a-year, gave him the duty of holding a lecture every week, which all the undergraduates were to attend, on the Greek Testament, with the direct object of teaching Divinity: the latter implied presiding over the Disputations, which were held in the College every day except Sunday.[2] "I could not avoid," says Wesley, "acquiring thereby some degree of expertness in arguing, and especially in discovering and pointing out well-covered and plausible fallacies. I have since found abundant reason to praise God for giving me this honest art." From 1727 to 1729 he was curate to his father, who needed his help, but returned to Oxford in 1728 to be ordained priest.[3] Mr Overton thinks "it is clear that this, the sole experience he ever had in England of work as a parish priest,

---

[1] Overton's John Wesley, p. 15.     [2] Ibid., pp. 15, 16.
[3] Ibid., p. 22.

did not at all commend to him the parochial system."

Dr Morley asked him to return to Oxford for pupils in 1729, which he did, and the epoch-making period of his work dates from his return. He resumed his work as lecturer and moderator, but he found established a little society, or "holy-club" as it was named, which had a profound influence in directing his career and shaping his life-work. During his brother's absence at Epworth, Charles Wesley, who had been a Westminster student at Christ Church for three years, had become impressed with the sense of vital religion, and had resolved to devote himself to a religious life. He gathered around himself a small company of like-minded students, for intellectual and spiritual improvement. On week-days they read the classics, but chiefly the Greek Testament; on Sundays Divinity; they were regular in their attendance on Holy Communion. When John Wesley arrived he found the club started, and soon was at the head of it. Mr Morgan was the first to visit the prisoners in the jail.

In the summer of 1730 [writes Wesley] Mr Morgan told me he had called at the gaol to see a man who was condemned for killing his wife ; and that, from the talk he had with one of the debtors, he verily believed it would do much good if any would be at the pains of now and then speaking with them. This he so frequently repeated, that on the 24th of August

1730 my brother and I walked to the Castle. We were so well satisfied with our conversation there that we agreed to go thither once or twice a-week; which we had not done long before he desired me to go with him to see a poor woman in the town who was sick. In this employment too, when we came to reflect upon it, we believed it would be worth while to spend an hour or two in the week, provided the minister of the parish, in which any such person was, was not against it. But that we might not depend wholly upon our own judgments, I wrote an account to my father of the whole design : withal begging that he, who had lived seventy years in the world, and seen as much of it as most private men have ever done, would advise us whether we had yet gone too far, and whether we should now stand still or go forward.

The father replied favourably :—

Go on, then, in God's name, in the path to which your Saviour has directed you, and that track wherein your father has gone before you. For when I was an undergraduate at Oxford, I visited those in the Castle there, and reflect on it with great satisfaction to this day.

He counselled "walking prudently, but not fearfully," and gaining the approbation of the proper authorities, and signed himself "your most affectionate and joyful father."

John Wesley rejoiced in the approval of his father—indeed the veneration of the whole Wesley family for their parents, their immediate submission to parental advice, their constant trust in counsel during difficulties, are most striking and beautiful features. His father's benediction gave new spirit to the little society, and the members — John Wesley, Charles Wesley, Morgan of Christ Church, Kirkham of Merton College — went on " in spite of the ridicule which increased fast upon them during the winter." They were joined in 1730 by John Gambold of Christ Church, and in 1732 by John Clayton of Brasenose, Benjamin Ingham of Queen's, Thomas Broughton of Exeter, and Westley Hall of Lincoln; in 1733 by James Hervey of Lincoln, John Kinchin, Fellow of Corpus; John Whitelamb of Lincoln, Richard Hutchins of Lincoln, and George Whitefield, servitor of Pembroke, also joined.[1] They were strict churchmen and kept all the fasts of the Church; they communicated every Sunday and every festival; they lived sparingly, and gave, what they denied themselves, to the poor; they visited the poor and sick, the prisoners in the Castle, and the poor debtors in Bocardo;[2] they educated poor children themselves and paid for the education of others. They were called or nicknamed Methodists; and, says John Wesley—

As the name was new and quaint, it clave to them immediately; and from that time both these four young gentlemen, and all that had any religious con-

---

[1] Overton's Life, p. 27.
[2] Wesley's Works, vol. i. p. 42.

nection with them, were distinguished by the name of
Methodists.

He adds :—

The regularity of their behaviour gave occasion to a
young gentleman of the college to say, "I think we
have got a new set of Methodists"—alluding to a set
of physicians who began to flourish at Rome about the
time of Nero, and continued for several ages.

Charles Wesley said that it had reference to the
strict conformity of the method of study and of
practice at which he and his religious friends
aimed.[2] This is also given by John Wesley in
another place as an alternative explanation,[3] while
in his dictionary he defined the word "Methodist"
as "one who lives according to the method laid
down in the Holy Scriptures." The 'De Imitatione,' the 'Holy Living and Dying' of Jeremy
Taylor, the 'Serious Call' by Law, the 'Life of
God in the Soul of Man,' were the favourite manuals of devotion, and John Wesley published a
book of prayers for the use of the brotherhood.[4]
He began rising at four every morning—a practice
which he continued until extreme old age ;[5] avoided
unprofitable friends, whose harmless conversation,

---

[1] Works, vol. vii. p. 402.
[2] Jackson's Life of Charles Wesley, vol. i. p. 19.
[3] Works, vol. viii. p. 339.
[4] A Short History of the Methodists, by W. H. Daniels,
p. 21.
[5] Lecky's England in the Eighteenth Century, vol. ii. p. 551.

he felt, even damped his good resolutions:[1] he studied such works as were persuasive rather than instructive, that warmed, kindled, and enlarged the affections as well as awakened the divine sense in the soul. The personal magnetism of John Wesley was the inspiration of the little society, which existed for ends as spiritual as anything on this side of time can be. Its spirit was intense earnestness and asceticism, and no one of its members was conscious of the deep religious influence it was afterwards to wield in the religious life of the country. They were only conscious of the sincerity of their aims, and notwithstanding the obloquy encountered, pressed towards the realisation of them. John Wesley almost invariably dates the commencement of Methodism from 1729,[2] and its origin was in the meetings founded by Charles Wesley, sustained afterwards and perfected by John Wesley. The spirit of it afterwards took diverse expressions: each member developed it in the way and after the manner that the appointments of life directed him,[3] and we have henceforth to deal chiefly with John Wesley. Two aspects of his mind may be noted at this period, and they are most important in relation to his spiritual development.

1. His desire to model all his doctrine and practice after the manner of the Primitive Church; to get

---

[1] Works, vol. vi. p. 447.    [2] Overton's Life, p. 24.
[3] See excellent account in Mr Tyerman's 'Oxford Methodists.'

beyond the growth of centuries, to the simpler, purer days of the Early Church.

It is a far cry [says Mr Overton] from Ritualism (so called) to Methodism (so called); but it is not fancy, but plain historical fact, that Wesley derived his ideas about the Mixed Chalice, Prayers for the Faithful Departed, and the observance of the Stations, from precisely the same source from whence he derived his ideas about the Class-Meeting, the Love-Feast, the Watch-night, and the tickets of membership; and they date from this period.[1]

He was anxiously studying the history of the Early Church, and seeking there for doctrine and practice, which being in an age nearer the days of Galilee, commended themselves to his intensely spiritual nature. His endeavour was to get beyond later growth and the new forms which institutions and doctrines had assumed to their origins in a time filled with the buoyancy and freshness of a young life.

2. Oxford stamped itself upon Wesley's character, and its atmosphere is felt in his judgments on men, books, and places throughout his journals. It refined his instincts, which were naturally fine, and permeated his mind with the university spirit. It became an inalienable part of him, and gave a rounding to his lovely Christian character. In all his books he designates himself, "Sometime Fellow of Lincoln College, Oxford"; and he carried

[1] Overton's Life, p. 30.

about with him the dignity of one who had received an education at a great college.

All the members of the Oxford brotherhood did noble work in their varied spheres, but even at this early time John Wesley impressed himself as a leader of men (ἀναξάνδρῶν), and the devotion all had for him was a beautiful triumph of his beautiful personality. Wesley had no desire to be a parochial clergyman, but the wishes of his family prevailed, and he consented to accept Epworth if it were given him. His father died in 1735, but the Crown presented the parish to another. Thus he was led to another sphere of work, and became a missionary.

The missionary spirit [says Mr Tyerman] was a passion in the Wesley family when Christian missions to the heathen scarce existed. John Wesley, after being ejected from his church-living in 1622, longed to go as a missionary, first to Surinam and afterwards to Maryland. Samuel Wesley, his son, when a young man of between thirty and forty years of age, formed a magnificent scheme to go as a missionary to India, China, and Abyssinia; and, in the last years of his life, most feelingly laments that he was not young enough to go to Georgia. His sons, John and Charles, now at Oxford, caught his spirit, and, within twelve months after the date of the last letter, actually went. John Whitelamb, his son-in-law, wished to go; but, for some unknown reason, was kept at home.[1]

John Wesley was sent out to Georgia as a missionary by the Society for the Propagation of the Gospel;

[1] Life and Times of the Rev. Samuel Wesley, M.A., pp. 431, 432.

his brother, Charles, went as the secretary to the Governor ; two other young men also went, Benjamin Ingham, the Oxford Methodist, and Charles Delamotte, "who had a mind to leave the world and give himself up entirely to God." This was in 1735. The following is Wesley's own narrative of the voyage :—

Our common way of living was this : From four in the morning till five each of us used private prayer. From five to seven we read the Bible together, carefully comparing it (that we might not lean to our own understanding) with the writings of the earliest ages. At seven we breakfasted. At eight were the public prayers. From nine to twelve I usually learned German, and Mr Delamotte Greek. My brother usually writ sermons, and Mr Ingham instructed the children. At twelve we met to give an account to one another what we had done since our last meeting, and what we designed to do before our next. About one we dined. The time from dinner to four we spent in reading to those whom each of us had taken in charge, or in speaking to them severally, as need required. At four were the evening prayers ; when either the second lesson was explained (as it always was in the morning) or the children were catechised and instructed before the congregation. From five to six we again used private prayer. From six to seven I read in our cabin to two or three of the passengers (of whom there were about eighty English on board), and each of my brethren to a few more in theirs. At seven I joined with the Germans in their public service, while Mr Ingham was reading between the decks to as many as desired to hear. At eight we met again, to exhort and instruct one another. Between nine and ten we went to bed, where neither the roaring of the sea nor the motion of the ship could take away the refreshing sleep which God gave us.[1]

Such was the life of the young missionaries on board ship; and the Moravians, who were among the passengers, impressed Wesley with the simplicity and sincerity of their faith, and opened his mind to further influence at a later stage in his career. "They are," wrote Mr Ingham, "more like the Primitive Christians than any other Church now in the world. . . . In everything they behave themselves with great meekness, sweetness, and humility." It was to converse with these Moravians that John Wesley began on board to learn German, and they made an impression on him by their thoughtfulness for others and their courageous faith which he never forgot, and both of which convinced him of the reality of their religion.

The vessel reached its destination on February 5, 1736, and while Savannah was John Wesley's special sphere, he was also appointed superintendent to the whole colony of Georgia. Charles had a charge at Frederika. They preached and taught and lived on the same high level as at Oxford, but John Wesley's pronounced High Churchism made him unintelligible to the colonists. It brought him into difficulties, and besides, he was somewhat disappointed in his visit: he had gone as a missionary, but on account of the wars

---

[1] Journal, under date October 21, 1735.

of the Indian tribes among themselves, and the
aversion which the Spanish and French had produced among them towards Christianity, he had
been compelled to accept what he had shrunk from
at home, even under the pressure of family influences — the office of a parish priest among the
settlers.[1] His work was not a failure,[2] for Whitefield testifies that the good done was inexpressible;
still Wesley was disappointed in it, for it was not
what he anticipated. His brother Charles and Mr
Ingham had already left Georgia, and John Wesley
with Mr Delamotte took ship from Charlestown
on December 22, 1737, and reached England on
February 1, 1738. Still his visit to Georgia was
important to his spiritual development, in so far
as it brought him into contact with Moravian influence: he was impressed with their primitive
Christianity, and became unsettled in his spiritual
condition: "I went to America to convert the
Indians; but, oh! who shall convert me? I have
a fair summer religion. I can talk well, but let
death look me in the face, and my spirit is troubled.
Alienated as I am from the life of God, I am a
child of wrath, and heir of hell."[3] We cannot take

[1] Overton's Life, p. 54.

[2] While his knowledge of French enabled him to preach to
the French settlers, and his Italian gave him opportunity of
preaching to the Vaudois, he learned the Spanish language that
he might converse with his Jewish parishioners. A parish
clergyman in a difficult parish could surely not be more
faithful.

[3] Tyerman's Life, vol. i. p. 166.

these words literally; for if John Wesley was not a Christian at this stage, who can lay claim to the name? It is the language of intense spiritual earnestness in the presence of the invisible realities : it is the characteristic of a fine spiritual nature, that is always severest upon itself, while it is charitable unto others. And he afterwards modified his view. In reference to the statement that he was not himself converted when he went to convert the Indians, he added, "I am not sure of this." To the words "I am a child of wrath," he added, "I believe not; I had even then the faith of a servant, though not that of a son." In a developing spiritual nature there are moments when inward feeling is not the "most infallible of proofs," and Wesley himself deprecates the too literal interpretation of what was written "in the anguish of my heart to which I gave vent between God and my own soul."

John Wesley was now ripe for the influence which was to prove final in spiritual decision. "I want," he says, "that faith which none can have without knowing it." His conversion now came —at any rate in its final shape. He had come into contact with Peter Böhler, and was enjoined : " Mi frater, mi frater ! excoguenda est ista tua philo-sophia " [1]—" My brother, my brother, that philo-sophy of yours must be purged away." " Preach faith till you have it; and then because you have it, you will preach faith." March 23, 1738 : "I met

[1] Diary, under date March 18, 1738.

Peter Böhler again, who now amazed me more and more by the account he gave of the fruits of living faith—the holiness and happiness which he affirmed to attach to it." Wesley, along with his brother, saw Böhler frequently from February 7, 1738, till May 4, 1738, when Böhler sailed for Carolina, and his edifying conversation led them into two truths — that faith in Christ is inseparably attended (1) by dominion over sin, and (2) by constant peace arising from a sense of forgiveness. As Luther's Epistle to the Galatians had an influence over Bunyan, so his Preface to the Romans had an influence over Wesley.

*May 24, 1738.*—In the evening I went very unwillingly to a society in Aldersgate Street, where one was reading Luther's preface to the Epistle to the Romans. About a quarter before nine, while he was describing the change which God works in the heart through faith in Christ, I felt my heart strangely warmed. I felt I did trust in Christ, Christ alone, for salvation ; and an assurance was given me that He had taken away my sins, even mine, and saved me from the law of sin and death.[1]

He was not finally settled until several months had elapsed,[2] and henceforth no shadow of doubt

[1] Journal. "It is, however, scarcely an exaggeration to say that the scene which took place at that humble meeting in Aldersgate Street forms an epoch in English history. The conviction which then flashed upon one of the most powerful and most active intellects in England is the true source of English Methodism."—Lecky's History in the Eighteenth Century, vol. ii. p. 558.

[2] Overton's Life, p. 61.

ever crossed his horizon, nor did any wavering ever shake the faith which he had known in his own experience as the truth of God.

"I determined, if God should permit, to retire for a short time into Germany."[1] His intention was to see Moravianism in the place of its birth. At Marienborn he met the brotherhood presided over by Count Zinzendorf, and wrote to his brother Samuel:—

God has given me at length the desire of my heart. I am with a Church whose conversation is in heaven ; in whom is the mind that was in Christ, and who so walk as He walked. As they have all one Lord and one faith, so are they all partakers of one spirit—the spirit of meekness and love, which uniformly and continually animates all their conversation.

He also visited Herrnhuth, where a Moravian carpenter, one of the brotherhood, instructed him in the elementary truths : "I would gladly have spent my life here. Oh, when shall this Christianity cover the earth as the waters cover the sea?" He was absent from England on this visit about three months, and although he afterwards parted from the Moravians, and their direct influence over him ceased, yet their indirect influence was in all his later work. The sermon preached at St Mary's, Oxford, on June 11, 1738 (before he went to Germany), may be taken as the manifesto of his position. It was on the text "By grace are ye

[1] Journal, June 7, 1738.

saved through faith," and he upheld salvation by
faith as a threefold deliverance—(1) from the guilt
of all past sin ; (2) from servile fear; (3) from the
power of sin. The Christian is pardoned ; has the
witness of the Spirit ; is born again and lives without sin. Such was Wesley's message, that created
a great Church and awakened the religious life of
the country : it was a renewal of the Reformation ;
and in the providence of God, his remarkable education in the rectory of Epworth, his own moral
earnestness, his study of a pious literature, his contact with like-souled companions, the discipline of
his life, and the contact with Peter Böhler and the
Moravians, as well as the fixing of his study on the
early days of the Church, were the means by which
he was led to the position, from which he never
wavered. Of him it was true in a unique sense,
" I believed, and therefore have I spoken." The
people found in him their religious leader, and he
flashed into their hearts his own belief and earnestness. His faith sustained him amid opposition,
and enabled him to realise a service unparalleled in
its activity. In 1738 began the incessant round of
itinerant labours in the British Isles, which he
maintained until his death in 1791.

The mere figures which represent John Wesley's
itinerant labours are enough [says Mr Overton] to take
one's breath away. . . . Wesley was not the mere
preacher. . . . He had to organise and visit numerous societies : he kept himself well abreast of the

literature of the day by a wide and varied course of
reading : he was a most indefatigable writer and
compiler ; a frequent though most unwilling contro-
versialist ; a reformer of practical abuses, and an
ardent philanthropist.[1]

For more than fifty years [says Mr Leslie Stephen]
Wesley was the autocratic chief of his society, and, not
content with administration from a distance, personally
inspected, at frequent intervals, every part of the
machinery which he had organised.   He travelled on
his ceaseless round of duty some 4500 miles annually ;
he preached two or more sermons a-day ; and it is
calculated that in fifty-two years he travelled 225,000
miles, and preached over 40,000 sermons.   The sermons were occasionally delivered to audiences of 20,000
persons, and at the age of eighty-six (August 23, 1789)
he records an address delivered to a congregation of
25,000.   Though he doubts whether all could hear
the feat, considered as a mere exhibition of physical energy, is something stupendous.   He arose every
morning at four, allowing himself only six hours of
sleep, though we are told that he possessed the fac-
ulty, common to nearly all great workers, of falling
asleep at a moment's notice.   He often rode seventy
miles a-day, and generally read as he rode, avoiding
stumbling, as he tells us, by riding with a slack rein.
On his eighty-fifth birthday he ascribes his health to
his constant exercise and change of air, to his powers
of sleeping, to early rising, and regular preaching
during sixty years at 5 A.M., and to his having had
little pain, sorrow, or anxious care during his life.[2]

----

[1] Life, pp. 87, 88.
[2] History of English Thought in the Eighteenth Century,
vol. ii. pp. 410, 411.

It was only an absorbing faith that could be the inspiration of such a work, and Wesley throughout his long and busy life was strengthened by a two-fold consciousness that he was doing work to which God had called him, and doing it with God's visible blessing.[1] "The best of all is, God is with us," was the underlying comfort of his life, sustaining him in the midst of his labours with its deep, calm peace. "In the world ye shall have tribulation, but in Me ye shall have peace," was his life-secret and daily experience.

John Wesley was the eighteenth-century Luther, and he shines out in history as the rediscoverer of the Christian message, and the Reformer of the Church. Recent historians have traced the low tone of the Church of England in the eighteenth century to five causes—(1) its outward prosperity ; (2) the influence and policy of Sir R. Walpole (*quieta non movere*) ; (3) the controversies of her own and previous generations ; (4) political complications ; (5) want of synodal action ; [2] and all historians repre-sent its condition as very dark during the period.

Overwhelming evidence [says Dean Farrar] exists to prove what was the preaching of that day, and what was the condition of the Church and people of England. How dull, how soulless, how effete, how Christless was

---

[1] Dean Farrar in 'Contemporary Review,' March 1891, p. 349.

[2] The English Church in the Eighteenth Century, by Abbey and Overton, pp. 280-284.

the preaching! How vapid, how Laodicean was the general character of the Church! How godless, how steeped in immorality was the general condition of the nation! Wesley was the first man who revived the spirit of religion among the masses of the people, and who roused the slumbering Church. His was the voice that first offered the great masses of the people hope for the despairing, and welcome to the outcast.[1]

Wesley brought new life to the Church of the period, which may be described in Leighton's words as a fair carcass without a spirit, but his teaching also saved England from political anarchy. His message was a return to Christ, a rediscovery of what had been lost, a reaffirmation of the Christianity of the apostles.

1. His message was the assertion that God is not only the God of the past, but the Revealer in the present; the living, inspiring, redeeming God to-day. And so it drove out of the field by the irresistible argument of experience the philosophy of Deism, which asserted that God was dwelling apart and had no direct relationship to the human soul: so it opposed the theology, which made the work of the Spirit historical — a feature of the past — speaking to men from long-vanished centuries, or from a sealed book. Wesley believed that the Comforter was "to abide for ever,"[2] that He was witness-bearing in the soul to-day; that He was giving light and life to all open souls.

[1] Centenary Sermons and Addresses, pp. 183, 184.
[2] Stoughton's History of Religion in England, vol. vi. p. 121.

In the assertion of that truth lay the uniqueness
of his ministry and the secret of his influence.

2. His guide in matters of faith and conduct
was the Bible, illuminated and interpreted by the
living Spirit.

At any price, give me the Book of God! I have
it : here is knowledge enough for me. Let me be *homo
unius libri.* Here then I am, far from the busy ways
of men. I sit down alone : only God is here. In His
presence I open, I read, His book ; for this end, to
find the way to heaven. Is there a doubt concerning
the meaning of what I read ? Does anything appear
dark or intricate ? I lift up my heart to the Father
of Lights, " Lord, is it not Thy Word ? ' If any man
lack, let him ask of God.' Thou 'givest liberally, and
upbraideth not.' Thou hast said, ' If any man be willing to do Thy will, he shall know !' I am willing to
do, let me know Thy will." I then search after and
consider parallel passages of Scripture, " comparing
spiritual things with spiritual." I meditate thereon
with all the attention and earnestness of which my
mind is capable. If any doubt still remains, I consult
those who are experienced in the things of God ; and
then the writings whereby, being dead, they yet speak ;
and what I thus learn, that I teach.[1]

3. As to doctrine, he states :—

Our main doctrines, which include all the rest, are
three : that of repentance, of faith, and of holiness.
The first of these we account, as it were, the porch
of religion ; the next, the door ; the third, religion
itself.

---

[1] Preface to Sermons.

(*a*) True faith and holiness are as inseparable in experience as justification and sanctification.

The moment we are justified by the grace of God through the redemption that is in Jesus, we are also born of the Spirit; but in order of thinking, justification precedes sanctification. We first conceive His wrath to be turned away, and then His Spirit to work in our hearts. Justification implies only a relative, the new birth a real, change. God in justifying us does something *for* us; in begetting us again, He does the work *in* us. By justification, instead of enemies we become children; by sanctification, instead of sinners we become saints. The first restores us to the favour, the other to the image, of God. Justification, in short, is equivalent to pardon, and the very moment we are justified, sanctification begins. In that instant we are born again.

(*b*) Another prominent feature in Wesley's teaching is the new birth. It is the work of God in us —the renewal of the sinful nature—the change, " whereby the earthly, sensual, devilish mind " is turned into the " mind which was in Christ Jesus."

(*c*) There are other two prominent aspects in Wesley's preaching—(1) the doctrine of Christian Perfection, and (2) of Assurance. As to the former he said :—

I never meant any more by perfection than the loving God with all our heart, and serving Him with all our strength. But I dare not say less than this.[1]

---

[1] Tyerman's Life, vol. ii. p. 233.

On another occasion he wrote :—

What is Christian perfection ? The loving God with all our heart, mind, soul, and strength. This implies that no wrong temper remains in the soul ; and that all the thoughts, words, and actions are governed by pure love.[1]

This doctrine led to much controversy, but Wesley never interpreted it as "sinless perfection" : it was to him loving God with all our heart, and serving Him with all our strength ; but it did not involve freedom from ignorance, or from error, or temptation, or infirmities.[2] It was in this sense only that Wesley used the Scriptural term perfection ; it was to him synonymous with dominion over sin, not with sinlessness. He fought against misapprehension regarding it, and warned his followers that they must wait for entire sanctification or perfection

Not in careless indifference, or indolent inactivity ; but in vigorous, universal obedience, in a zealous keeping of all the commandments, in watchfulness and painfulness, in denying ourselves, and taking up our cross daily ; as well as in earnest prayer and fasting, and a close attendance on all the ordinances of God. If any man dream of attaining it any other way, yea, or of keeping it when it is attained, he deceiveth his own soul. It is true we receive it by simple faith ; but God does not, will not, give that faith, unless we seek it with all diligence in the way which He hath ordained.[3]

---

[1] Tyerman's Life, vol. ii. p. 346.     [2] Overton's Life, p. 82.
[3] Wesley's Works, vol. xi. p. 378 *et seq.*

While Wesley never believed that he had attained
this degree of perfection himself, it was the humility
of his greatness that he frequently believed those
who maintained that they had. As to Assurance,
it was wrapt up to Wesley's thought in a heart-
felt faith. Seating religion in the heart, he regarded it as necessary that with the gift of pardon
the soul should possess a certain sense of it.
"Faith implies assurance; an assurance of the
love of God to our souls, of His being now reconciled to us, and having forgiven all our sins."[1]
In old age he modified his opinion, and did not
hold it absolutely necessary that assurance was
necessary as a proof of salvation.

When [he wrote] fifty years ago, my brother Charles
and I, in the simplicity of our hearts, taught the people
that unless they *knew* their sins were forgiven they
were under the wrath and curse of God, I marvel they
did not stone us. The Methodists, I hope, know better
now. We preach assurance, as we always did, as a
common privilege of the children of God, but we do
not enforce it under pain of damnation denounced on
all who enjoy it not.[2]

The change of heart Wesley believed to be instan-
taneous: it was as the awakening from a sleep by
a flash of divine light: it was as the snapping of
a chain.

The forgiveness of sins is one of the first unseen
things whereof faith is an evidence. And if you are

---

[1] Earnest Appeal.  [2] Overton's Life, p. 84.

sensible of this, will you quarrel with us concerning an indifferent circumstance of it? Will you think it an important objection that we assert that this faith is usually given in a moment?[1]

(*d*) As to the sacraments, Wesley regards them not as bare signs, but as direct means of grace.

Baptism [he says] is the outward sign of this inward grace (the New Birth), which is supposed by our Church to be given with and through that sign to all infants and to those of riper years, if they repent and believe the Gospel.[2] The benefits of receiving the Holy Communion are—(1) the forgiveness of our past sins, and (2) the present strengthening and refreshing of our souls. The grace of God given herein confirms to us the pardon of our sins, and enables us to leave them. Christ's Body and Blood is the food of our souls: it gives strength to perform our duty, and leads us on to perfection. Whoever, therefore, goes from the Holy Table when all things are prepared, either does not understand his duty, or does not care for the dying command of his Saviour, the forgiveness of his sins, the strengthening of his soul, and the refreshing it with the hope of glory.[3]

In 1745 a volume of hymns on the Lord's Supper was published by John and Charles Wesley, to which they prefixed a brief spiritual treatise of Dr Brevint entitled 'The Christian Sacrament and Sacrifice.' The manual was widely circulated, and passed through many editions; it expresses their

[1] Earnest Appeal, p. 24.    [2] Overton's Life, p. 78.
[3] The Eucharistic Manuals of John and Charles Wesley, edited with Introduction by W. E. Dutton, pp. xiv, xv.

views on the sacrament, and impresses upon the Societies the importance of frequent communion.[1] Their position is the same as that of the Scottish Reformers :—

We utterlie dampne the vanitie of those that affirme Sacramentis to be nothing else but naked and bair signes. No, we assuredlie belove, that by Baptisme we ar ingrafted in Christ Jesus to be maid partakers of His justice, by the whiche our synes are covered and remitted ; and also, that in the Supper, rychtlie used, Christ Jesus is so joyned with us, that He becumis the verray nurishement and foode of our saullis.[2]

It may be said that Wesley fought out in his own experience a development similar to that of Luther ; justification by faith was to both of them the test of a living Church, and with regard to the sacrament their position was identical. Wesley redis-covered the principle of the Reformation principle, and in this sense we can say with the Rev. Hugh Price Hughes :—

All modern religious history is summed up in the two momentous facts that Ignatius Loyola has cap-tured the Catholic Churches, and that John Wesley has captured the Evangelical Churches. Jesuitism and Methodism—these are the two ultimate forms of intense, logical, thorough-going Christianity. Absol-ute subjection to the Christ—there is no other alter-native for the enthusiastic "out-and-out" Christian

---

[1] Jackson's Life of Charles Wesley, vol. i. p. 421.
[2] Knox's Works, vol. ii. p. 114.

of the twentieth century. Absolute subjection to a Creed is no longer possible. Men are becoming too much in earnest for any illogical compromise.[1]

Wesley made his faith real to the masses of the people ; his work was an evangelism—an effort that signally succeeded in reviving the Reformation, and awakening the Church from the lethargy into which, after the brighter days of Puritanism, it had fallen.[2] If he was brought into controversy, it was from necessity and not from choice ; he endeavoured always to be true to Archbishop Potter's words, and recalled them in old age with gratitude :—

Near fifty years ago a great and good man, Dr Potter, then Archbishop of Canterbury, gave me an advice for which I have ever since had occasion to bless God. " If you desire to be extensively useful, do not spend your time and strength in contending for or against such things as are of a disputable nature, but in testifying against open, notorious vice, and in promoting real essential holiness."[3]

Dean Stanley frequently emphasises this as the supreme object of Wesley's life,[4] and states it in

---

[1] Nineteenth Century, March 1891, p. 479.

[2] Principal Cairns' Address in Centenary Volume, p. 426.

[3] Stanley's Addresses and Sermons delivered in America, p. 47.

[4] Dean Stanley records the saying of the old Scottish Methodist, who on his deathbed regretted his denunciation of the heresies of the rival sects on either side of the street where he lived. " The street I'm now travelling in, lad, has nae sides ; and if power were given me, I would preach purity of life mair, and purity of doctrine less, than I did."—Dean Stanley's Life, vol. ii. p. 538.

the words of Alexander Bruce,[1] that "his main, fundamental, overpowering passion was not the promotion of any particular dogma or any particular doctrine, but the elevation of the whole Christian world in the great principles of Christian holiness and morality."[2] That he strove towards and succeeded in this great mission arose from the fact that he was a prophet with a message, true to his own spiritual experience, and finding its response in the hearts of thousands. His Christian work was inspired and sustained by his strong belief, and he was evangelical in the largest, simplest sense of the word—viz., that in an artificial age he returned to the literal teaching of the Gospel.[3] From 1739, when he began field-preaching,[4] to 1791, he declared his great message and pursued his great ideal, but it cannot be overlooked that one of his greatest helps was the power of sacred song.

> "A verse may find him who a sermon flies,
> And turn delight into a sacrifice."

"Perhaps no other Church" (like the Methodist), says Dr Stoughton, "has ever lived, and moved, and had its being in such an atmosphere of sacred song."[5] And just here is another point of similarity between

---

[1] Latest Edition of Southey's Life.
[2] American Addresses, p. 46 ; Life, vol. ii. p. 538.
[3] John Wesley, by Julia Wedgwood, p. 139.
[4] The Living Wesley, by Dr Rigg, p. 166.
[5] History of Religion in England, vol. vi. p. 141.

the movement headed by Luther and that by the
Wesleys—both were accompanied by a great outburst of religious poetry. "The whole people,"
wrote a Romanist at the time, "is singing itself
into this Lutheran doctrine." "Luther did as
much," said Coleridge, "for the Reformation by
his hymns as by his translation of the Bible."[1]
The hymns of John and Charles Wesley—especially of the latter—instilled their burning faith,
devotion, and aspiration into the hearts of the
people, and it is in no small degree due to the
influence of these hymns that the evangelism was
so successful. "Suspiria vatum solatium ecclesiæ."
Charles Wesley was the "sweet singer" of the
religious revival.

His hymns [says Mr Green] expressed the fiery convictions of its converts in lines so chaste and beautiful
that its more extravagant features disappeared. The
wild throes of hysteric enthusiasm passed into a passion for hymn-singing, and a new musical impulse was
aroused in the people which gradually changed the face
of public devotion throughout England.[2]

It has been estimated that during Wesley's lifetime there were published not fewer than 6600
hymns from the pen of Charles Wesley alone.[3]
They also collected and furnished tunes;[4] "why
should the devil," John Wesley said, "have all the

---

[1] Prescott's Hymn and Hymn-Writers, p. 68.
[2] A Short History of the English People, vol. iv. p. 1614.
[3] Tyerman's Life, vol. i. p. 397.
[4] John Wesley was conducting worship, and his sense of

best tunes?" These hymns reached the hearts of the people, and many of them are in the hymn-books of all the Churches to-day. The Wesleys were teachers and poets, but it was John Wesley's distinctive work to be the founder of societies throughout England, Ireland, and Scotland. The motto of such was, "Strengthen one another": their object was to bring to bear upon the life of the whole the life of each; to give a sphere of influence to the awakened life so that the strong might help the weak, and the spiritually mature the immature. The last thing he desired was separation from the Church; his societies aimed at filling up what was wanting in the English Church, that there might be realised all that a Christian Church should be.[1] They were intended to strengthen the Church by advancing Scriptural holiness; they met at hours non-canonical, and were regarded by Wesley as streams feeding the spiritual life of the Church. Their object was to build up in Christian doctrine and fellowship; and they were similar to the Exercise in the Scottish Reformed Church, to which prominence was given in the First Book of Discipline. Wesley recognised the necessity of an itinerating ministry; so did the

harmony was ruffled by the discordant voice of an old woman.

"My good sister, you are singing out of tune."

"My heart is singing, sir," was the prompt reply.

"Then sing on, my sister."—Christopher's Poets of Methodism, p. 16.

[1] John Wesley, by Julia Wedgwood, p. 247.

early Scottish Reformers, although they afterwards
endeavoured to have a pastor settled in every parish :
it is also interesting to observe that their " Exercise "
and Wesley's societies were somewhat identical.
Both were an abandonment of sacerdotal tradi-
tions ; both were an assertion of the priesthood of
the Christian people. The Scottish Exercise was
a kind of general or congregational assemblage,
which was held once a-week, with the object of
bringing the members of the Church together on
a social basis for mutual edification, " that the
Kirk have judgment and knowledge of the graces,
gifts, and utterances of every man within their
body ; the simple and such as have somewhat profited shall be encouraged daily to study and to
prove in knowledge, and the whole Kirk shall be
edified. . . . Every man shall have liberty to utter
and declare his mind."[1] Wesley's religious societies
—with their class-meetings, their band-meetings,
love-feasts, quarterly meetings, watch-night services,
their lay assistants or helpers—were intended to
realise the same purpose. The Scottish Reformers
and he were practically at one, and both received
their inspiration from the same model in apostolic
times. We know that Wesley, when a young man,
was much impressed by the words of a serious man
at Wroote : " You wish to serve God and go to
heaven. Remember you cannot serve Him alone ;

[1] The Apostolic Ministry in the Scottish Church, by Principal Story, p. 258.

G

you must therefore find companions or make them ; the Bible knows nothing of solitary religion." He was impressed with the meetings held at Epworth, when his father was at Convocation,[1] by his talented mother, Susanna Wesley, who has been called the real founder of the Methodists.[2] He recognised the impulse to the spiritual life which the Oxford holy club gave to his companions and himself, and he could not doubt that such would be helpful to the Church in general. All such predispositions were strengthened by his study of the Primitive Church, and it was there that he recognised the authority for his movement which achieved so much for the cause of vital religion.

I could not but observe,—This is the very thing which was from the beginning of Christianity. In the earlier times those whom God had sent forth "preached the Gospel to every creature." And the οἱ ἀκροάται, "the body of hearers," were mostly either Jews or heathens. But as soon as any of them were so convinced of the truth as to forsake sin and seek the Gospel salvation, they immediately joined them together, took an account of their names, advised them to watch over each other, and met those κατηχουμένοι, "catechumens" (as they were then called), apart from the great congregation, that they might instruct, rebuke, exhort, and pray with them, and for them, according to their several necessities.[3]

---

[1] Diary, vol. i. pp. 361-363.
[2] Life, by Julia Wedgwood, p. 49.
[3] Works, vol. viii. p. 250.

The object of the societies was to revive the spirit of religion throughout the land ; to advance "Scriptural holiness": their meetings were to be apart from Church hours, and were constituted to bring new warmth and impact to the Church.

I met [he wrote in 1786] the classes at Deptford, and was vehemently importuned to order the Sunday service in our room at the same time as that of the Church. It is easy to see that this would be a formal separation from the Church. We fixed both our morning and evening service, all over England, at such hours as not to interfere with the Church ; with this very design—that those of the Church, if they chose it, might attend both one and the other. But to fix it at the same time was obliging them to separate either from the Church or us ; and this I judge to be not only inexpedient, but totally unlawful for me to do.

Three months later he added :—

If you are resolved you may have your service in church hours ; but, remember, from that time you will see my face no more. This struck deep, and from that hour I have heard no more of separating from the Church.

The places where Wesley's influence was most felt were the largely-populated commercial centres and the country villages—not least of all the mining districts. Fashionable resorts and university cities were not much affected by him. Refined gentleman and scholar as he was, he loved to work among the poor.

Wesley and Whitefield [says Charles Kingsley], and many another noble soul, said to Nailsea colliers, Cornish miners, and all manner of brutalised fellows living like the beasts that perish : " Each of you— thou, and thou, and thou — stand apart and alone before God.  Each has an immortal soul in him, which will be happy or miserable for ever, according to the deeds done in the body.  A whole eternity of shame or of glory lies in you—and you are living like a beast." And in proportion as each man heard that word and took it home to himself, he became a new man and a true man.[1]

Wesley [says Dr Rigg] devoted his labours chiefly to districts of the country where the population was large ; where there was free opportunity for them to follow his ministry, if they had a mind to do so, and where he would have it in his power, night after night, and visit after visit, at not too long intervals, to follow up his work by blow after blow, by stroke upon stroke. He gave little labour or attention to fashionable places of resort.[2]

It was amid the neglected wastes that he accomplished his most successful work ; it was there that he became the evangelist of the masses ; it was from the dark corners of the earth that he won the brightest trophies for the Redeemer's kingdom, and formed his converts into societies, the primary aim of which was to strengthen one another.

His officers were called by him " lay assistants or helpers "; their office was—

In the absence of the minister (that is, a regular

---

[1] Roman and Teuton, p. 238.    [2] The Living Wesley, p. 228.

clergyman), (1) to expound every morning and evening; (2) to meet the united society, the bands, the select society, and the penitents once a-week; (3) to visit the classes once a-quarter; (4) to hear and decide all differences; (5) to put the disorderly back on trial, and to receive on trial for the bands or society; (6) to see that the stewards, the leaders, and the schoolmasters faithfully discharge their several offices; (7) to meet the leaders of the bands and classes weekly, and the stewards, and to overlook their accounts. . . . They no more take upon them to be priests than to be kings. They take not upon them to administer the sacraments — an honour peculiar to the priests of God. Only, according to their power, they exhort their brethren to continue in the grace of God.

It was in 1741 that Wesley began to employ lay preachers, and it was on the advice of his mother that he first sanctioned them; the order arose from the stress of circumstances, and was reluctantly permitted by Wesley. He hedged it by the strictest precautions: every preacher had to be a "local" before becoming an "itinerant," and Wesley ruled them by a firm hand, although there was a paternal gentleness in his government. He inspired their devotion, but he ruled their zeal: he termed his itinerants "preachers" or "helpers," while the superintendent of a circuit was called "the assistant."[1] It is interesting to find here another resemblance between Wesley's system and that of the early Scottish Reformers. The following is his defence of the order :—

---

[1] Overton's Wesley, p. 134.

I am bold to affirm that these unlettered men have help from God for the great work of saving souls from death. But, indeed, in the one thing which they profess to know, they are not ignorant men. I trust there is not one of them who is not able to go through such an examination, in substantial, practical, experimental divinity, as few of our candidates for holy orders, even in the university, are able to do. In answer to the objection that they are laymen, I reply, The scribes of old, who were the ordinary preachers among the Jews, were not priests; they were not better than laymen. Yea, many of them were incapable of the priesthood, being not of the tribe of Levi. Hence, probably, it was that the Jews themselves never urged it as an objection to our Lord's preaching. That He was no priest after the order of Aaron, nor, indeed, could be, seeing He was of the tribe of Judah. Nor does it appear that any objected this to the apostles. If we come to later times, was Mr Calvin ordained? Was he either priest or deacon? And were not most of those whom it pleased God to employ in promoting the Reformation abroad, laymen also? Could that great work have been promoted at all, in many places, if laymen had not preached? In all Protestant Churches ordination is not held a necessary prerequisite of preaching; for in Sweden, in Germany, in Holland, and, I believe, in every Reformed Church in Europe, it is not only permitted, but required, that, before any one is ordained, he shall publicly preach a year or more *ad probandam facultatem*. And, for this practice, they believe they have an express command of God : " Let those first be proved, then let them use the office of a deacon, being found blameless" (1 Tim. iii. 10). Besides, in how many churches in England does the parish clerk read one of the lessons, and in some the whole service of the Church, perhaps every Lord's day? And do not other laymen constantly do the same thing in our very cathedrals? which, being under the inspection of the bishops, should be patterns to all other churches. Nay, is it not done in the universities themselves? Who ordained that singing man at Christ Church; who is likewise utterly unqualified for the work, murdering every lesson he read: not endeavouring to read it as the Word of God, but rather as an old song?[1]

Wesley thus found a reason for his action in the examples of the Primitive and Reformed Churches; but his mother's words could not be without their influence, and they came at a crisis. John Nelson and Thomas Maxfield had begun lay preaching in Yorkshire and London, and Wesley, hearing of the irregularity, hurried to London to stop it. His mother, living in the house near the Foundry, said : "John, take care what you do with respect to that young man [Maxfield], for he is as surely called to God to preach as you are. Examine what have been the fruits of his preaching, and hear him yourself."[2] Wesley did so, and the Rubicon was crossed.

In the choice of his preachers Wesley recognised three things as necessary—character, gifts, grace; and over them and the societies (which were completed by the institution of a Conference, 1744, and held annually ever afterwards) he was supreme and absolute ruler. The minutes are interesting in

[1] Tyerman's Life, vol. i. p. 370.     [2] Ibid., p. 369.

themselves, and as manifesting the development of the movement. Wesley united two opposites—a genius for ruling and a constant openness to influence wherever it commended itself to his reason; one of the most interesting features in his life for over half a century was his government, almost autocratic, and the devotion he inspired among his preachers. The letters they wrote to him are permeated with a lovely personal religion, and a childlike devotion and implicit obedience to their leader.[1]

By these societies, and the earnest religious fervour they called forth; by these lay preachers, local and itinerant,[2] whom he inspired with quenchless enthusiasm; by his own personal superintendence over them all, his unique personality, and his own itinerant labours extending for over half a century, and exhibiting an apostolic fervour and a strength almost superhuman in their range; by the library of healthy Christian literature, which he edited and spread among the people; by his own and his brother's soul-stirring hymns; by his own preaching, and his apostolic life, which manifested faith as a reality to the world,—John Wesley pro-

[1] See Jackson's Library of Christian Biography, 12 vols.
[2] It has been said, " When the school of heraldry shall make for Methodist preachers a coat-of-arms, it will surely have a man on horseback in its field; but if the artist would be true to history, the itinerant must have an open book before him, resting on the horn of his saddle."—A Short History of the Methodists, by W. H. Daniels, A.M., p. 132.

duced a remarkable change in the religious life of the country, and so permeated all the Churches with his zeal that his influence may be said to pulse through them still. Luther is his only peer, and the Churches that bear their honoured names are the direct fruits of their work; but they both leavened other Churches far and wide, which testify equally to their influence. "During the nineteenth century," says Dr Marshall Lang, "the atmosphere of the Churches of Christendom has been transformed. It has risen from zero to blood-heat."[1] It is only historically true to say that much of the religious fervour, belief, catholicity, and enthusiasm of humanity have come from John Wesley and the religious movement he created and inspired. The Churches are all rich with his memory, but richer with his inspiring and quickening example; thousands have seen in him a faith which years could not dim nor opposition lessen. His is a splendid, dauntless figure, full of inspiration to all who love and admire devotion. "The Evangelical movement, the Oxford movement, even the recent enthusiasm of the Salvation Army," says Dean Farrar, "are traceable to his example, and to the convictions which he inspired."[2] "The Salvationists," said the late Bishop Lightfoot, "taught by Wesley, have learnt, and have taught to the Church again, the lost

---

[1] Expansion of the Christian Life, p. 209.
[2] Contemporary Review, March 1891, p. 353.

secret of the compulsion of human souls to the Saviour."

Wesley awakened the Church by inspiring the enthusiasm of humanity, and organising an awakened people; he held out a welcome to the despairing, a welcome to the outcast, and, like his Master, sought and saved the lost; his work has been carried on by Churches inspired by the spirit that possessed him. Wesley influenced every subsequent generation by deeply and permeatively influencing his own; his influence spread by contagion, and was continued by the succession of spiritual character; his movement was purely religious, and any explanation attributing it to personal ambition is not for a moment to be considered. He aroused a religious force in the nation, and thus awakened the Church of England, as well as inspired philanthropic and missionary movements, which, widened and broadened since his day, owe to him their initial start and *vis vivida*. He lessened the evils that accompany the growth of industrialism, which went forward with great rapidity in his day; he counteracted the inflammable elements that were massed together, and he did so by bringing to bear upon the visible chaos the power of spiritual forces. Well for England was it that this transition to industrialism was, in the words of a great historian, " preceded by a religious revival which opened a new spring of moral and religious energy among the poor, and at the same time gave a powerful impulse to the philanthropy of the rich." [1]

He not only made the Methodists good Christians, he also made them good citizens. "Fear God, honour the king," was an outstanding principle in his creed. In doing so to his age, and in leavening the thousands of his followers by it, he saved England from a revolution that might have been similar to that in France. Says Mr Lecky :—

Religion, property, civil authority, and domestic life were all assailed, and doctrines incompatible with the very existence of government were embraced by multitudes with the fervour of a religion. England, on the whole, escaped the contagion. Many causes conspired to save her, but among them a prominent place must, I believe, be given to the new and vehement religious enthusiasm which was at that very time passing through the middle and lower classes of the people, which had enlisted in its service a large proportion of the wilder and more impetuous reformers, and which recoiled with horror from the anti-Christian tenets that were associated with the Revolution in France. [2]

Loyalty and patriotism were parts of Wesley's religion ; many of his followers were soldiers, and it was said that there were no better soldiers in the army than the Methodists. [3] If the true problem of religion be to save men from practical atheism in life and anarchy in politics, John Wesley's teaching

[1] Lecky's England in the Eighteenth Century, vol. ii. pp. 637, 638.

[2] *Ut antea*, pp. 635, 636.        [3] Overton's Life, p. 143.

and practice signally succeeded. He exercised his
vast influence in favour of both, and the power of
his personality was absolute among his followers.
In his 'Calm Address to the Inhabitants of England' he tells the Methodists that "though many
who go under that name hate the king and all his
ministers only less than they hate an Arminian,
he will no more continue in fellowship with them
than with thieves, drunkards, and common swearers."
In 1789, in extreme old age, he preached a thanksgiving sermon at Bristol on "the grand day of
rejoicing for his Majesty's recovery." He protested
against smuggling :—

Neither sell nor buy anything that has not paid the
duty. Defraud not the king any more than your
fellow-subject. Never think of being religious unless
you are honest. What has a thief to do with religion?
. . . A smuggler is a thief of the first order, a highwayman or pickpocket of the worst sort. Let not any
of those prate about religion! Government should
drive these vermin away into lands not inhabited!
. . . That detestable practice of cheating the king
is no more found in our societies. And since that
accursed thing has been put away, the work of God
has everywhere increased.

Wesley's politics were an application of his religious beliefs; while he had the vision of eternity,
he had also the vision of a city of God on earth—
while of heaven, yet in time.

The Wesleyan revival was a great missionary
movement. Beginning as a home mission and a care

for the neglected wastes, it led to foreign missionary enterprise, for both are different aspects of
the same spirit and are not to be separated from
each other. John Wesley created and inspired in
the eighteenth century the enthusiasm of humanity,
and both his and Whitefield's example gave it a
mighty impulse. It was the outcome of the religious revival, fostered by them. The Archbishop
of Canterbury has said, "The time was not far off
when it would be felt that no Christian was living
a Christian life who did not care for the preaching
of the Gospel to the heathen." [1]  John Wesley was
an embodiment of the missionary spirit, and his
work had no small power in diffusing it far and
wide. The missionary enthusiasm was coeval with
Methodism, and it has broadened ever since.

Such is a short account of John Wesley's life,
belief, and work ; his movement was deepest felt
in England and Ireland, but it entered Scotland as
a spiritual force within the Church. There is the
John Wesley of Scottish Church history, and there
is the John Wesley within Scottish Church history,
and if the first does not seem to have accomplished
much on Scottish soil, the second has been deep and
pervasive. Before dealing with the second we have
to deal with the first, and it is interesting and instructive, for he has left a Journal,[2] in which there is

[1] Grosvenor House Address, July 3, 1898.
[2] "Walpole, Wesley, and Johnson (Boswell I mean), three
very different men whose lives extend over the same times, and

to be found a record of his Scottish visits. Although they form but a very small part of his herculean labours, they are filled with interest, and to his record men will turn, not only as the narrative of a brave endeavour to spread "Scriptural holiness," but as a work casting light upon the Church history of the period. His remarks on the country, Scottish history, churches, men, and books are all interesting, as giving the impressions of an impartial eyewitness, and they ought to be more widely known. His Journal is the work of spiritual genius, looking at things in its own clear light. "Few men," says Mr Leslie Stephen, "have left more vivid portraits of their own personality than that which is embodied in Wesley's Journals,"[1] and it is true to say that his short but fascinating account of his Scottish visits will grow in interest with the flight of years. It is free from sectarian partisanship, and is the work of the greatest religious personality that visited and preached in Scotland last century. Whitefield is a man possessed with one overmastering conception—the work of an evangelist; he has little or nothing to say of anything else. Wesley's interest was no less earnest, but it had a very wide horizon, and his Diary tells of many things beyond the

whose diverse ways of looking at the world they live in make a curious study. I wish some one would write a good paper on this subject."—Letters of Edward Fitzgerald to Fanny Kemble, p. 29.

[1] History of English Thought in the Eighteenth Century, vol. ii. p. 410.

history of Methodism on Scottish soil. Whitefield formed no organisation in Scotland, but his preaching was an inspiring force within the Church. Wesley, on the other hand, did not affect Scotland to nearly the same extent by his preaching, which was of a different order from that of Whitefield. It had nothing rhetorical or dramatic about it; it had no melting pathos, but was strong, calm, deliberative, full of conviction logically expressed.[1] Wesley's preaching has been compared to a strong, steady, all-pervading current; Whitefield's to a rushing and resistless wind;[2] and Whitefield's pulpit power affected Scotland in a way that Wesley's did not. In Wesley's, light was the outstanding feature; in Whitefield's, heat; and, as was to be expected from his Calvinism, Whitefield was more successful than Wesley, for his teaching was more akin to the theological temper of the country during the eighteenth century. Yet it cannot be overlooked, and it is to the credit of the country, that during the long period when Wesley received opposition of the most discreditable kind in England and Ireland and Wales, he was everywhere received in Scotland with a dignity and a courtesy which were due to him as a Christian gentleman, scholar, and teacher. He was received always with respect, and his reception speaks much for the civilisation of the people, as well as for their spiritual percep-

---

[1] Stoughton's History of Religion in England, vol. vi. p. 289.
[2] Tyerman's Oxford Methodists, p. 326.

tion. Methodism did not take deep root in Scotland, as far as extent was concerned, in the eighteenth century; but this was chiefly due to theological differences, to the severe reticence and aversion of the people to emotion in religious matters, and to their attachment, both hereditary and acquired, to Presbytery as the embodiment of their religious struggles, and as the expression of their national faith.

The sense of nationality [says Dr Stark], strengthened by the long and bitter struggles which they had long ago to make for its maintenance, tended to lead the Scottish people to look askance at anything which had the brand of the other side of the Border, and was different from their own chosen and beloved Presbyterianism.[1]

In Scotland [says Mr Lecky] the Methodist movement was much less important than in other parts of the island. It had not there to dispel the same ignorance or the same apathy, and it found a people accustomed to a higher standard of dogmatic preaching than in England.[2]

It is a curious instance [says Mr Overton] of the predominance of temperament over training that Wesley was more successful in Ireland than he was in Scotland. According to the principles of the majority of the Irish, Wesley was a pestilent heretic ; according to those of the Scotch, a true evangelist. But in Ireland feeling ruled over intellect, in Scotland intellect ruled over feeling. Of all things, John Wesley disliked contro-

---

[1] The Lights of the North, p. 246.
[2] History of the Eighteenth Century, vol. ii. p. 606.

versy ; and if the Scotch were not controversial, they were nothing.[1]

A prominent Wesleyan historian, Dr Stevens, says :—

In no part of Europe had the Reformation more thoroughly wrought its work among the common people. An intelligent, frugal, and religious population, they needed less than any other the provocations of zeal which are usually furnished by new sects. Wesley marvelled at their insusceptibility to Methodism ; but Methodism at this time was more important as a general moral movement, pervading the whole Churches, and the whole public mind, than as a sectarian development, more or less organised. In the former sense it did a good work in Scotland. . . . If Methodism regrets its little progress in Scotland, it may at least console itself that there is less reason for this regret than in any other country in the world.[2]

A Scottish critic has said by way of explaining the scanty growth :—

Some of the reasons to be alleged are subjects of congratulation. The religious condition of the Scots in the days of Wesley and Whitefield was immeasurably different from that of the masses of English miners and artisans and labourers who at first so brutally mobbed the early Methodist preachers. The great Church of Scotland was also soon to have its own awakening, and to put off its own offshoots of

----

[1] Life, p. 114.
[2] The History of the Religious Movement of the Eighteenth Century called Methodism, vol. ii. p. 117.

evangelical enterprise. Had these not taken place the mission of Methodism might have been somewhat more needed.[1]

Though Methodism across the Tweed [says Mr Tyerman] has never had the same success as it had in England, yet it would be untrue to say that its efforts have been a failure. Besides, there have been causes for the difference. In England, Wesley and his assistants found the masses ignorant ; in Scotland, they had to battle with a partially enlightened prejudice. In England, the great body of the people were without a creed ; in Scotland, the people were priest-ridden. In England, the itinerant plan was not objected to ; in Scotland, it has always been a bugbear.[2]

If Wesley failed in forming a great number of societies north of the Tweed, it is to be recalled that the Scottish Reformers did not produce a permanent organisation on the same lines. The similarity between their creed and polity and Wesley's is very striking. Their superintendents with dioceses corresponded with Wesley's superintendents and circuits ; their insistence on justification by faith, personal religion, and the sacraments as means of grace, was identical with Wesley's views ; their meetings for "prophesying" corresponded with Wesley's class-meetings ; many of their churches were served by itinerants, as Wesley's were, but it was only the stress of circumstances that required it, and, adopted as a temporary expedient,

---

[1] Wesley Centenary in Scotsman, March 2, 1891.
[2] Life and Times of John Wesley, vol. ii. p. 119.

itinerancy was within thirty years given up, and a
settled pastorate for every parish adopted. Wesley,
on the other hand, would not adapt his movement
to the Scottish demand for a settled ministry as
the Scottish Reformers had ultimately to do, and
willingly did. Now, it is interesting to observe
that what Wesley retained the Scottish Reformers
surrendered—viz., the meetings for prophesying,
corresponding to the class-meeting, and the itinerant
ministry. The first does not seem to have been
adapted to the religious reticence of the Scottish
people, and passed into a more formal meeting " in
which the minister gradually assumed the lead, if
he did not indeed monopolise the whole function ";[1]
the latter could not take the place of an ordained,
settled pastorate in each parish. Probably this,
with the previous statements, may explain the com-
paratively small number of the Methodist societies
in Scotland, notwithstanding the fact that they were
promoted by such a spiritual splendour as John
Wesley, who appealed to the Scottish love of goodness by his apostolic life. Wesley did not succeed
where the Scottish Reformers failed,[2] but, unlike
them, he did not meet Scottish needs far enough.

On the other hand, it is impossible to read
Knox's 'History of the Reformation in Scotland,'
and not to see that, apart from the mere visible

---

[1] Principal Story's Apostolic Ministry in the Scottish Church,
p. 259.
[2] See Dr M'Crie's Life of Knox, vol. ii. pp. 6, 7.

historical forces that brought the Reformation about, the real pervasive work among the people was to a considerable extent effected by means of religious societies. Knox, being a prominent agent in the drama, is of course explicit in his emphasis of the greater events; but he tells us enough to justify the position that there were numerous religious societies throughout the country, and that in the quickening they imparted, and the interest they aroused, the Reformation found a strong ally. The Lollards disseminated their reformed faith in the fifteenth century by societies chiefly in Kyle; and in the sixteenth century, prior chiefly, but also subsequent to 1560, these societies had a wider scope. In the reading of Knox's narrative the references are apt to be overlooked, but they are filled with interest. Here are specimens of them. Of 1538 Knox writes :—

This thaire tyranny notwithstanding, the knowledge of God did wonderouslie increase within this realme, partlie by reading, partlie by brotherlye conference, which in those dangerouse dayis was used to the comforte of many.[1]

In 1558 he writes :—

The brethrein assembled thameselfis in such sorte, *in companyes* synging psalmes, and praising God, that the proudast of the ennemies war astonied.[2]

The young Reformed Church was served by the friends of the Reformation, who were all laymen,

[1] Knox's Works, vol. i. p. 61.    [2] Ibid., p. 261.

with the exception of Robert Hamilton,[1] who afterwards became minister of St Andrews. In 1558
Knox narrates regarding the spiritual earnestness of
the movement, that it was concluded—

That the Brethren in everie toune at certane tymes
should assemble togidder, to Commoun Prayeris, to
Exercise and Reading of the Scripturis, till it should
please God to give the sermone of Exhortatioun to
some, for comforte and instructioun of the rest. . . .
And for that purpose, by commoun electioun, war
eldaris appointed, to whome the hole brethren pro-
missed obedience ; for at that tyme we had na pub-
lict ministeris of the Worde : onlie did certane zelous
men (amonges whome war the Lard of Dun, David
Forress, Maister Robert Lokharte, Maister Robert
Hammylton, Williame Harlay, and otheris) exhorte
thare brethrein according to the giftes and graces
granted unto thame.[2]

Again of 1558 he narrates :—

It is thought necessare that doctrin, preacheing,
and interpretatioun of Scriptures, be had and used
privatlie in qwyet houssis, without great conventionis
of the people tharto, whill afterward that God move
the Prince to grant preacheing be faithfull and trew
ministeris.[3]

These instances from among many are sufficient
to prove the power which the religious societies
and the lay preachers exercised in the Scottish
Reformation ; and although the office of the elder-

---

[1] Knox's Works, vol. i. p. 300, note.
[2] Ibid., pp. 299, 300.     [3] Ibid., pp. 275, 276.

ship had a more primitive source, it was an early
institution in the Scottish Reformed Church, and
became an official recognition of a class that had
even done more than the clergy (as a body) to
bring the Reformation about.  In Scotland it was
pre-eminently a lay movement, and it is chiefly
because Presbytery from the first in Scotland recognised the lay element in its government, rested
upon the people for its support, and was always
in the line of their liberties, that it has ever since
been the ecclesiastical polity of the majority in the
country, and has been the form in which any strong
secession from the Establishment expressed itself.
It is interesting, however, to observe this as another
similarity between Presbytery in Scotland and Methodism in England, that both did their constructive
work in religion by means of the religious societies;
both rested their claims finally upon the religious
instincts of the people, and both equally rested in
their implicit trust on the universal priesthood of
Christian believers.   These religious societies were
also strong in Scotland during the Covenanting
period, so that it seems historically true to say
that, besides other elements in common, the Scottish Church had anticipated and to a considerable
extent embodied John Wesley's unique work in
England.   This, with the theological differences of
the eighteenth century, may be the chief *immobilis
inertia* that retarded the progress of Methodism
in the period.

There was another. Scotland had not the large town centres of population that England during the same period had, and it was among the large populations in England, as has already been indicated, that Methodism did its greatest work. After the Rebellion of 1745 in Scotland had passed away, a period of national torpor in religion and politics had begun : Moderatism was a sign of the age, and was an expression of its spirit. A reaction had set in after the prolonged national struggles, too, of the Covenanting periods, and their objects being attained, men somewhat felt at rest. The nation was in a chrysalis stage ; was chiefly agricultural, very little industrial : commercial enterprise was only beginning to look around for channels through which its energy might flow. There were not the congested populations as in England ; the burghs generally were attached to the Church of Scotland, and the country parishes had the efficient system of school education fostered by the Church, and an equally efficient pastoral oversight, known last century as the " ministerial catechising," which if impossible to be realised in the towns and burghs, was realised in the country parishes. This kept a popular Church in touch with the people : if the Church had not been afflicted with patronage, it would have had a far greater expansion from within ; but, as it was, the Church was in touch with the people, and so, neither from the point of view of population nor of inefficient pastoral work, was a great occasion offered to John Wesley in the eighteenth century. "Non-resident pastors" were unknown in Scotland, and ecclesiastical abuses were prevented by its Church courts. Dissatisfied Presbyterians found refuge in the Scottish Secession, headed by the Erskines and their friends; the sense of nationality, too, was strong, and was not favourable to influences from the Church of England. Wider catholicity prevails now, but it did not then, and influences from England were jealously and suspiciously watched. Such were the circumstances amid which Wesley came to Scotland in 1751, ten years after Whitefield's first visit; his great work in England had been warmly appreciated by many of the Scottish clergy as early as 1745,[1] and along with Whitefield he had published in 1738, with a preface, the Autobiography of Thomas Halyburton, Professor of Divinity at St Andrews,[2] a book widely circulated and well known last century.

Wesley was thus well known in Scotland before 1751, and well might it be so, for he had been engaged for thirteen years with his work in England, Wales, and Ireland. His object in coming to Scotland was, in the words of a Wesleyan historian, " to make a stand against the overflowing of Arianism and Socinianism in that kingdom."[3] In the words

[1] Moore's Life of Wesley, vol. i. pp. 92-95.
[2] Jackson's Library of Christian Biography, vol. i.
[3] Myles' Chronological History of the People called Methodists, p. 65.

of another : " Wesley, accompanied by Christopher
Hopper, one of the first preachers, crossed the Border
and introduced Methodism into Scotland ; a measure
to which he appears to have been specially urged by
the abounding of Arianism and Socinianism in that
country." [1]   Such views were considered prevalent
within the Church, and some holding high places
were regarded as imbued with the scepticism of
Hume. [2]   Wesley's mission in Scotland, as elsewhere, was the elevation of Christian living, and
he resolved to enter into no controversy—if such
could be avoided in Scotland.

Charles Wesley thought that Scotland afforded
no scope for Methodist work at the period, and
Whitefield said to John Wesley :—

You have no business there, for your principles are
so well known that if you spoke like an angel, none
would hear you ; and if they did, you would have nothing to do but to dispute with one and another from
morning to night.

Wesley replied :—

If God sends me, people will hear.   And I will give
them no provocation to dispute ; for I will studiously
avoid controverted points, and keep to the fundamental truths of Christianity ; and if any still begin to
dispute, they may, but I will not dispute with them. [3]

1 Smith's History of Wesleyan Methodism, vol. ii. p. 71.
2 Dr Lindsay Alexander's Life of Dr Wardlaw, p. 43.
3 Southey's Life, vol. ii. p. 243.

## First Visit to Scotland, 1751.

His visit was made in accordance with the wish of Captain (afterwards Colonel) Gallatin, who was then quartered at Musselburgh. Wesley, accompanied by one of his preachers, arrived at Musselburgh on April 24, 1751. On his journey he was impressed by the "air of antiquity" and "oddness" about the Scottish towns; arriving at Musselburgh, curiosity brought abundance of people together, who gave him a respectful hearing and "remained as statues from the beginning of the sermon to the end."[1] The following day he rode to Edinburgh, which at that day appeared to him "as one of the dirtiest cities he had ever seen," Cologne not excepted. He returned to Musselburgh and preached at six o'clock. All received his words in love; prejudice was swept away; he was invited to stay for some time, and a preaching-place would be prepared for him. He would gladly have complied, but engagements in the South prevented, and he left on the 26th. He consented to send them Mr Hopper the next week, who returned and for a fortnight preached morning and evening at Musselburgh, and thus Methodism planted its first society on Scottish soil. Wesley was impressed with the freeness and openness of the people, who raised not dispute of any kind, nor asked any questions concerning his opinions.[2] A little party of gentle-

[1] Appendix, p. 230.   [2] Ibid.

men from Edinburgh attended his second service at Musselburgh, and Scotland was henceforth included in his journeys.

### SECOND VISIT, 1753.

Riding through Dumfries (where he admired two elegant churches), Thornhill, Leadhills, Lesmahagow, he arrived at Glasgow on April 17, 1753, and was the guest of the Rev. Dr Gillies of the College Church, by whose invitation he had come. Dr Gillies was a man of wide catholicity and toleration : he was the lifelong friend of Whitefield and wrote his life : to Wesley he was a kind of Scottish Fletcher of Madeley. As he took an important position in the Scottish evangelical revival last century, a short account of his life here may be interesting.

John Gillies, D.D. (1712-1796). He was born in 1712 at the manse of Careston, near Brechin, where his father was parish minister, and after prosecuting his literary and divinity courses, and being engaged as tutor in several Scottish families, was ordained minister of the College Church, Glasgow, July 29, 1742. This charge he served for fifty-four years. It is said of him that besides preaching three times every Sunday, he lectured in his church three times each week to crowded audiences, and published for some time a weekly paper, as well as regularly visited and catechised

his parish.[1]   Dr Gillies is still known for a work
entitled 'Historical Collections relating to the
Success of the Gospel,' 2 vols., Glasgow, 1754;
an Appendix was added in 1761, and a Supplement in 1786.   Another work was, 'Devotional
Exercises on the New Testament,' published in
1769.   He also published 'Exhortations to the
Inhabitants of the South Parish of Glasgow,' 2
vols., 1750; 'Life of the Rev. Mr George Whitefield,' 1772; 'Essays on the Prophecies relating to
the Messiah,' 1773; 'Hebrew Manual for the use of
Students'; 'Psalms of David with Notes,' 1786;
'Milton's "Paradise Lost" illustrated by Texts of
Scripture,' 1778; "Life of John Maclaurin" for
Maclaurin's 'Sermons and Essays,' 1755.[2]   Dr
Gillies was distinguished as a hard worker in his
parish, and as a student in the field of literature;
but in the eighteenth century he anticipated much
of the catholic spirit and toleration of the late Dean
Stanley, and recognised charity as the genial atmosphere that best nourishes the religious life, and
recognises inward resemblances beyond outward di-
vergences.   Dr John Erskine wrote of him in 1796:
"Dr Gillies saw and approved what was excellent
in men, whose sentiments in politics, and even in
religious matters less essential, greatly differed from
his.   Strict in examining his own heart and life,

[1] Account by Dr John Erskine, Edinburgh, p. 86.
[2] Stephen's and Lee's Dictionary of National Biography,
vol. xxi. pp. 367, 368.

he viewed with candour the conduct of others." [1]
We have already seen that Dr Gillies was an ally
of Whitefield, and in 1753 he was the means of
bringing John Wesley to Glasgow. Wesley was a
guest at his house for a week, and during his stay
assisted in the most important of Dr Gillies' books—
the 'Historical Collections.' In vol. ii. (pp. 55-106)
will be found extracts from Mr Wesley's 'Journal,'
and (pp. 106-136) extracts from Mr Whitefield's ;
throughout vol. i., on the other hand, will be found
extracts from books published in Wesley's Christian
Library, so that his help in this important work was
very considerable.

Wesley preached at the prison and also in the
open air ; but it is interesting to observe that, at a
time when the churches in England were closed to
him, he was invited to preach in the College Church
of Glasgow : he accepted the invitation, and did so
several times. "Who would have believed five-
and-twenty years ago, either that the minister would
have desired it, or that I should have consented to
preach in a Scotch kirk ?" [2] Many of the students
were among his hearers, and he was impressed with
the reverence of the large congregations.

The behaviour of the people at church, both morning
and afternoon, was beyond anything I ever saw, but
in our congregations. None bowed or curtsied to each

---

[1] Supplement to Historical Collections, p. 84.
[2] Appendix, p. 232.

other either before or after the service ; from the
beginning to the end of which none talked, or looked
at any but the minister.   Surely much of the power of
godliness was here, when there is so much of the form
still.[1]

There were no adversaries but a " poor seceder," and
the people of Glasgow gave Wesley a warm welcome.
Wesley evidently was the means of introducing
hymns, which in those days were not generally
acceptable to the Scottish congregations.   " After
the sermon Mr Gillies concluded with the blessing.
He then gave out, one after another, four hymns,
which about a dozen young men sung.   He had
before desired those who were so minded to go
away ; but scarce any stirred till all was ended."[2]
As far as evidence goes, Wesley was a pioneer in
introducing hymns into the worship of a Scottish
parish church ; during the period of Wesley's visits
the authorised publications were the metrical Psalms
(still in use) with the Paraphrases added in 1745.[3]

[1] Appendix, p. 233.                [2] Appendix, p. 232.
[3] "In 1564," says Mr Prescott, "two years after the publication of Sternhold and Hopkins' version, the General Assembly
of the Kirk ordered the use of the Psalms in metre.   This was,
in the main, that old version with certain additions.   The
next century, at the Revolution, the Long Parliament recommended for the consideration of the General Assembly at
Edinburgh the Psalter which had been compiled by one of the
members of the House of Commons, Francis Rouse, as well as
the Scotch Psalter then in use.   A Committee of the Kirk
Assembly produced, in 1649, on this basis, the ʻParaphrase of
the Psalms,' which was ordered to be used throughout Scotland.
This was adopted on May 1st, 1650, and there it is now. . . .
In 1745 some ʻParaphrases' of other portions of the Bible were ad-

There was throughout the period, and long after it,
a rigid adherence to the metrical version, and any
attempt to introduce " human hymns " was strongly
opposed. Soon after Wesley's departure, Dr Gillies,
in a letter to him, wrote :—

The singing of hymns here meets with greater opposition than I expected. Serious people are much divided.
Those of better understanding and education are silent ;
but many others are so prejudiced that they speak
openly against it, and look upon me as doing a very
sinful thing. I beg your advice, whether to answer
them only by continuing in the practice of the thing,
or whether I should publish a sheet of arguments from
reason and Scripture, and the example of the godly.
Your experience of dealing with people's prejudice
makes your advice of the greatest importance. I bless
the Lord for the benefit and comfort of your acquaintance ; for your important assistance in my ' Historical
Collections' ; and for your edifying conversation and
sermons in Glasgow.[1]

Wesley was a strenuous advocate of the use of
hymns in public worship,[2] and he met with strong prejudice against them in the Scotland of the eighteenth
century. The ' Church Hymnary ' contains twenty-
two hymns of Charles Wesley, and several hymn-
translations by John Wesley. These hymns express
the deepest in the religious life.

mitted by a Committee of the General Assembly into the Scotch
Psalter."—Christian Hymns and Hymn-Writers, pp. 127, 128.
    [1] Whitehead's Life of Wesley, vol. ii. p. 273.
    [2] Hymns and Hymn-Writers, by Rev. Duncan Campbell,
B.D., p. 42.

*May 22, 1755.*—His Journal states : Mr Wardrope, minister of Bathgate in Scotland, preached at the Orphan-house in the evening, to the no small amazement and displeasure of some of his zealous countrymen."

## THIRD VISIT, 1757.

He rode through Dumfries, Thornhill,[1] and arrived at Glasgow on June 1, 1757, where he was the guest again of Dr Gillies. He preached near the Infirmary to a large congregation — on other occasions to several thousands, at such an early hour as seven in the morning. He refers to the College and Cathedral,[2] and the lovely, fruitful, cultivated plain as seen from the Cathedral spire. He was busy in preaching and meeting the members of the religious societies : " After preaching I met as many as desired it, of the members of the praying societies. I earnestly advised them to meet Mr Gillies every week ; and at their own meetings not to talk loosely, and in general (as their manner had been) on some head of religion, but to examine each other's hearts and lives." [3]  He arrived at Musselburgh on the 6th, and preached in the poor-house " to a large and deeply attentive congregation." Two-thirds of the society " knew in whom they believed " ; " the national shyness and stubbornness were gone, and they were as open and teachable as little children." Between forty and

---

[1] Appendix, p. 234.     [2] Appendix, p. 235.
[3] Appendix, p. 236.

fifty dragoons were present. On Wednesday he rode to Dunbar, where he found a little society, "most of them rejoicing in God their Saviour." [1] He preached also at Berwick-on-Tweed and Kelso, where he began his service by a Scotch psalm, and gathered a large congregation. Engaged as he was in the work of an evangelist, he did not lose his interest in literature on his journey, and notes: "To-day 'Douglas,' the play which has made so much noise, was put into my hands. I was astonished to find it is one of the finest tragedies I ever read. What pity that a few lines were not left out! and that it was ever acted at Edinburgh!" [2] On his third visit he spent eleven days in Scotland.

In 1757 he published 'A Sufficient Answer to "Letters to the Author of Theron and Aspasio" in a Letter to the Author.' The author to whom Wesley addressed his answer was the Rev. John Glass or John Sandeman, the founders of a religious sect called the "Glassites" or "Sandemanians." Wesley's answer was a defence of his friend the Rev. James Hervey on the subject of saving faith, in opposition to the Glassite or Sandemanian theory that faith is an assent to the truthfulness of the Gospel history.[3] "Palæmon" is generally agreed to have been Mr Sandeman.[4]

---

[1] Appendix, p. 236.    [2] Appendix, p. 237.
[3] Tyerman's Life, vol. ii. p. 293.
[4] A Defence of Theron and Aspasio, by James Hervey, p. 214.
Benjamin Ingham, one of the members of the Oxford Society and an early friend of Wesley's, became "the York-

## FOURTH VISIT, 1759.

His route was the same as on the former visits, and he preached at the same places. Dr Gillies was as sympathetic as ever, and consented to superintend the little divided society.

I found the little society which I had joined here two years since had soon split into pieces. In the afternoon I met several of the members of the praying societies, and showed them what Christian fellowship

---

shire Evangelist" (Tyerman's Oxford Methodists). In 1759 he read Sandeman's 'Letters on Theron and Aspasio' and Glass's 'Testimony of the King of Martyrs,' and was impressed by them. "He deputed," says Dr Stevens, "two of his preachers to Scotland to learn more fully the views of their authors. At Edinburgh they met Sandeman, and Glass at Dundee. They returned converts to the Sandemanian principles, and immediately spread discontent and disputes among the societies. Ingham's authority could not control the partisan violence which soon broke out. He called in the assistance of his friends. The Countess of Huntingdon wrote them letters. Whitefield felt deeply for them, 'wept and prayed,' and used his influence to save them. Ingham attempted to excommunicate the disturbers, but it was an endless task. The whole order was wrecked and sunk. Thirteen societies only remained from more than eighty which had flourished with all the evidences of permanent prosperity. . . .

"The fate of Ingham's societies is one of the best vindications of Wesley's wisdom as an ecclesiastical legislator. The dispersion of these societies, however, left some good results. Many of them were merged in the Wesleyan or dissenting bodies, especially in the class of Scotch Presbyterians called Daleites."—The History of the Religious Movement of the Eighteenth Century, vol. i. p. 300.

was, and what need they had of it. About forty of
them met me on Sunday 27, in Mr Gillies's kirk, immediately after evening service. I left them determined to meet Mr Gillies weekly, at the same time
and place. If this be done, I shall try to see Glasgow
again ; if not, I can employ my time better.[1]

Dr Gillies was a beautiful personality, who
transcended the narrow spirit of his age, and
invited Wesley's help at a time when Wesley's
spiritual genius was not recognised. Would that
he had not been such a solitary figure ! His was
the type that the Church supremely needed.

## Fifth Visit, 1761.

Wesley passed through Moffat and arrived at
Edinburgh on April 28, 1761. He preached at
Edinburgh and disarmed prejudice.[2] This was the
first occasion when he crossed the Forth and
carried Methodism into the northern counties. He
arrived at Aberdeen and sent to the Principal and
Regent, desiring leave to preach in the College
Close. The request was courteously met, and
as it was raining he was requested to take the
College Hall, and added forty new members to
the already existing society of fifty members.[3] As
was his wont, Wesley attended the parish church

---

[1] Appendix, p. 239.            [2] Appendix, p. 240.
[3] Tyerman, vol. ii. p. 404.

on the Sunday, where he heard two "useful" sermons by the Principal and Professor of Divinity : a "huge multitude" afterwards gathered together in the College Close, and received the truth in love.

He visited King's College on the Monday, which he regarded "as not unlike Queen's College, Oxford"; he met there a large company of ladies and gentlemen and was requested to address them. He did so, and the word "fell as dew on the tender grass."[1] In the Library of Marischal College he met the Principal, the Very Rev. George Campbell, D.D., and the Divinity Professor, the Rev. Alexander Gerard, D.D.,[2] who both invited him to their houses. · A large crowd awaited his preaching at the evening service on the Monday, as well as on the following evening, when the

[1] Appendix, p. 241.

[2] I am indebted for those names to the courtesy of the Rev. Professor Cowan, D.D., Aberdeen. He describes the Principal of the period as "the illustrious George Campbell," who was the author of 'Dissertations on Miracles,' in answer to Hume ; 'Philosophy of Rhetoric' ; 'Lectures on Ecclesiastical History.' Alexander Gerard, D.D., was the author of the 'Essay on Taste.' It is to the glory of these distinguished men that they welcomed Wesley at a time when opposition in England was bitter against him, and it was probably due to their influence that he preached so frequently in the College Church at Aberdeen. Wesley says of the Principal: "I accepted the Principal's invitation, and spent an hour with him at his house. I observed no stiffness at all, but the easy good breeding of a man of sense and learning." Of the Professor, "He invited me to his lodgings, where I spent an hour most agreeably."— Appendix, pp. 241, 242.

Principal, all the professors, and some of the magistrates were present. "I set all the windows open, but the hall, notwithstanding, was as hot as a bagnio. But this did not hinder either the attention of the people or the blessing of God."[1] On the Wednesday he was the guest of the Rev. Mr Ogilvie, one of the ministers of Aberdeen. "A more open-hearted, friendly man I know not that I ever saw." Of the clergy themselves he adds, "I have scarce seen such a set of ministers in any town of Great Britain or Ireland."[2] Verily, Principal, professors, clergy, magistrates, and people in Aberdeen extended a welcome worthy of their visitor!

Throughout Wesley's life it was no uncommon thing — it was his regular practice — to preach at 5 A.M. or 7 A.M. to his people, and in these days of forenoon and evening services, it is interesting as well as instructive to find that his vigorous little society at Aberdeen had regular services at the following hours: every Sunday at 7 A.M. and 6 P.M.; Tuesdays, Thursdays, and Saturdays at 5 A.M. and 7 P.M.; Mondays, Wednesdays, and Fridays they met at 6 P.M. for private examination.[3] Has the greater comfort of the present day made us less earnest in our religious quests? or has the greater stress and strain of to-day forced later hours upon us "for the assembling of ourselves together"? Verily Wesley's followers were, like their great

---

[1] Appendix, p. 242.    [2] Ibid.

[3] Scots Magazine for 1763, p. 421.

leader, in earnest, and the morning glow brought
fervour to their religious life.

Wesley spent five days at Aberdeen, and into
them compressed a noble record of work. He
then left for Monymusk on the invitation of Sir
Archibald Grant, who was one of his Aberdeen
hearers. Engaged as he was in his apostolic labours,
his eye was still open to all things around him, and
he rejoices in the stately house of Monymusk, with
its walks and gardens; the steep mountains, the
clear river, the lovely valley; he notices the improvement carried out by Sir Archibald in plough-
ing up the waste ground and planting millions of
trees.[1] The following is his reference to the service,
with its hearty praise, in a Scottish parish last
century, when he preached :—

About six, went to the church [at Monymusk]. It
was pretty well filled with such persons as we did not
look for, so near the Highlands. But if we were surprised at their appearance, we were much more so at
their singing. Thirty or forty sang an anthem after
sermon with such voices as well as judgment that I
doubt whether they could have been excelled at any
cathedral in England.[2]

---

[1] Appendix, p. 242.  "He is said to have planted about
48,000,000 trees on the property ; . . . he was the first to
engage in those agricultural improvements that may be said to
have almost changed the face of the North of Scotland."—
Church and Priory of Monymusk, by the Rev. W. M. Macpher-
son, B.D., pp. 275, 277.

[2] Appendix, p. 242.

He reached Edinburgh on 9th May, and, although tired, "would not disappoint the congregation," and "God gave me strength according to my day." On the Saturday evening and the Sunday he preached three times "even to the rich and honourable," and "I bear them witness, they will endure plain dealing, whether they profit by it or not."

He admired lovely Edinburgh and Princes Street —"far before any in Great Britain"—although he has words of criticism on the civic authorities of 1761.[1] His remarks on Holyrood Palace and Queen Mary will also be read with interest.[2] After preaching at Musselburgh, Haddington, North Berwick, Dunbar, and Berwick-on-Tweed, he returned to his great work in the South. Wesley was "one of the unresting, unhasting men," who embodied in his life the gospel of work,[3] and was too busy to fret.

"I hear a voice you cannot hear,
Which says I must not stay ;
I see a hand you cannot see,
Which beckons me away."

---

[1] Appendix, p. 243.  [2] Ibid.

[3] Of John Wesley, Johnson said : "He can talk well on any subject." "John Wesley's conversation is good, but he is never at leisure. He is always obliged to go at a certain hour. This is very disagreeable to a man who loves to fold his legs, and have out his talk, as I do."—Boswell's Life of Samuel Johnson, vol. i. pp. 333, 261.

## Sixth Visit, 1763.

As on the former occasion, he did not visit Glasgow, but went direct to Edinburgh, where he preached, and thence through Forfar to Aberdeen, which extended another warm welcome.

Surely never was there a more open door. The four ministers of Aberdeen, the minister of the adjoining town, and the three ministers of Old Aberdeen, hitherto seem to have no dislike, but rather to "wish us good luck in the name of the Lord." Most of the town's people as yet wish us well, so that there is no opposition of any kind. O what spirit ought a preacher to be of, that he may be able to bear all this sunshine!

He preached in the College Close to "a multitude of people," and again in the College Hall. "What an amazing willingness to hear runs through this whole kingdom."

His visit was brief, and he soon returned to Edinburgh.

*Sunday, May 29.*—I preached at seven in the High School Yard at Edinburgh. It being the time of the General Assembly, which drew together not the ministers only, but abundance of the nobility and gentry, many of both sorts were present; but abundantly more at five in the afternoon. I spake as plain as ever I did in my life; but I never knew any in Scotland offended at plain-dealing. In this respect the North Britons are a pattern to all mankind.[1]

---

[1] Appendix, p. 245.

He rode thence to Dunbar, where he is persuaded "much good will be done, if we have zeal
and patience."

## SEVENTH VISIT, 1764.

Arriving at Dunbar on May 24th, 1764, Wesley
preached there and at Haddington, the Calton
Hill and High School Yard of Edinburgh. He
gives his impressions of the General Assembly in
1764.[1] He travelled northwards to Dundee, "where
poor and rich attended" his sermon; "but the
misfortune is, they know everything, so they learn
nothing." At Brechin he is interested in a strange
disorder, and possessing, as he did, a strong sense of
the supernatural, cannot account for it on purely
natural grounds.[2] At Aberdeen he preached in the
College Close, and on the Sunday for the first time
in the College Kirk to a crowded audience; again
in the evening at the College Close. At Monymusk
he preached in the parish church, where the church
was pretty well filled, though upon short notice—
"Certainly this is a nation swift to hear and slow
to speak," though not "slow to wrath."[3] At Old
Meldrum, twelve miles distant from the city, many
from Aberdeen attended. At Inverness he preached
in the High Church, which was filled, and the
parish ministers showed "most cordial affection;

[1] Appendix, p. 246.    [2] Appendix, pp. 247, 248.
[3] Appendix, p. 249.

were it only for this day, I should not have regretted the riding a hundred miles." [1]   He was
invited to preach in a neighbouring parish, but a
near engagement only permitted him to preach in
the High Church of Inverness.

I think the church was fuller now than before ; and
I could not but observe the remarkable behaviour of
the whole congregation after service.   Neither man,
woman, nor child spake one word all the way down
the main street ; indeed the seriousness of the people
is less surprising when it is considered that for at least
a hundred years this town has had such a succession
of pious ministers as very few in Great Britain have
known.[2]

His northern journey was a triumphal march.
At Nairn the parish kirk bell was rung and a large
congregation assembled, and here again the Scottish
congregation impressed him.   " O what a difference
is there between South and North Britain !   Every
one here at least loves to hear the Word of God ;
and none takes it into his head to speak one uncivil word to any for endeavouring to save their
souls." [3]   He visited Forres, Elgin, Strathbogie,
" where the whole family at our inn, eleven or
twelve in number, gladly joined with us in prayer
at night : indeed so they did at every inn where
we lodged ; for among all the sins they have imported from the English, the Scots have not yet

---

[1] Appendix, p. 250.                                    [2] Ibid.
[3] Appendix, p. 251.

learned, at least not the common people, to scoff at sacred things." He returned from Aberdeen, where he preached twice, through Dundee to Edinburgh, where after preaching, as was always his custom, at non-canonical hours, he attended Holy Communion at St Cuthbert's Parish Church, Edinburgh ; of the service he gives a narrative which will be read with interest.[1]

Wesley's seventh visit to Scotland was a record of hard work, and of favourable receptions from all classes in the country. In Edinburgh, however, there was a Scottish lady who joined his society, and who afterwards became one of his strongest Scottish supporters and a lifelong friend — Lady Maxwell.[2] D'Arcy Brisbane, youngest daughter of Thomas Brisbane, Esq. of Brisbane, Largs, married Sir Walter Maxwell, fourth Baronet of Pollok and son of John Maxwell of Blanarthill, who on the death of John Maxwell of Pollok succeeded to his honours and estate. In little more than two years after her marriage she lost her husband by death, and her only child six weeks after ; she was left a widow at nineteen

[1] Appendix, pp. 252, 253.

[2] For biographies of Lady Maxwell, see Sir William Fraser's Maxwells of Pollok, vol. i. pp. 412-417.   A Christian Sketch of Lady Maxwell, by Robert Bourne (1819).   Life by Rev. John Lancaster, 2 vols. 1822. — New edition, revised and abridged by the Rev. William Atherton.   Life in Wesleyan Methodist Magazine for 1816 (Nos. for October, November, December).   Homes, Haunts, and Friends of John Wesley, p. 129.

years of age.[1]  "God brought me to Himself by affliction," she wrote in her diary.[2]

She was one of the persons of high eminence who joined Wesley's audiences in Edinburgh, and became acquainted with him in 1764. She became a member of the Wesleyan Society in Edinburgh about this time, and continued a member of it till the close of her life, although she generally communicated with the Church of Scotland, and remained a member of St Cuthbert's, Edinburgh. It is said of her that from twenty-three to fifty-five years of age she attended the preaching of the Gospel at five in the morning.[3] She subdued the strong prejudices of education and country,[4] and adhered to Wesley's cause during the bitter Calvinistic controversies that raged throughout the latter part of his life. On July 2, 1770, Lady Maxwell established a school in Edinburgh for the purpose of giving education and Christian instruction to poor children. She classed herself with the most zealous and active patrons of Sunday-schools, and had no small influence in spreading them over the country. She contributed towards the support of several divinity students in Edinburgh, when she found their circumstances were such as to require assistance. She was the lifelong friend of Lady Henrietta Hope, and Lady Glen-

[1] See Sir William Fraser's Memoirs of the Maxwells of Pollok, vol. i. pp. 412-417.
[2] Bourne's Sketch of Lady Maxwell, p. 17.
[3] Ibid., p. 47.          [4] Atherton's Life, vol. i. p. 71.

orchy, who wrote of her: "She is indeed one among a thousand. Of all I have ever known, she is the most upright Christian. . . . I have often found an hour's conversation with her act as a cordial."[1] Lady Glenorchy left her in her will with the charge "of finishing Hope Chapel at Bristolwells, and of aiding those of Carlisle, Workington, and the other chapels and institutions;"[2] this she undertook, and shortly before her death accomplished. Lady Maxwell was the devoted friend of Wesley in Scotland, and gave him the same support in the North as Mary Bosanquet of Cross Hall and Lady Mary Fitzgerald did in the South.[3]

In her 'Diary and Correspondence' will be found many interesting letters on religious topics to Wesley, whom she regarded as her counsellor and guide. Her diary is characterised by a beautiful Christian spirit, that had attained the highest elevation, repose, and joy in Christian experience. There breathes throughout it a refined spirituality and mysticism. Lady Maxwell was one of those who in earlier days would have been canonised by the Church. The ascent of her life towards God was well expressed in her own words :—

The veil that covers unseen things from mortal eyes

---

[1] Dr Jones' Life of Lady Glenorchy, pp. 118, 125.
[2] Ibid., p. 518.
[3] See The Homes, Haunts, and Friends of John Wesley, pp. 126-130.

grows more transparent. I got clearer views of the eternal world ; of the happiness of its blessed inhabitants.[1] The more God gives me of the world, the more clearly He makes me see its emptiness ; it recedes, it disappears, it lessens in my view.[2] Evermore, O my God, do Thou thus guide and overrule my determinations both in heart and life, till Thy love has made an entire conquest.[3]

Her life was a carrying out of her early resolution—" I see God requires my whole heart, and He shall have it."[4]

Lady Maxwell remained a member of Wesley's society until her death in 1810, and from 1764 to 1791 some of Wesley's most interesting letters were written to her, while she wrote most helpful letters to him in the midst of his apostolic labours. Shortly before his death, and when age had begun to lessen his vigour, the venerable man seems to have been much strengthened by the sympathy and kind words of his Scottish friend. March 2, 1791 (when eighty-eight years of age), Wesley wrote to Lady Maxwell : " I really love to write to you, as I love to think of you. And sometimes it may please Him, who sends by whom He will send, to give you some assistance by me. Your letters have frequently been an encouragement and a comfort to me. Let them never, my dear friend, be intermitted during the few days I have to stay below."[5]

Such is a short account of this remarkable

[1] Atherton's Life, p. 326.  [2] Ibid., p. 296.
[3] Ibid., p. 133.  [4] Ibid., p. 16.  [5] Ibid., p. 99.

Scottish lady, of whom we will hear more in the course of the subsequent narrative. Wesley's letters to her recall Rutherford's to his friends. The first was written to her two months after he left Scotland in 1764.

LONDON, *August* 17, 1764.

MY DEAR LADY,—Since I had the pleasure of yours, I have hardly had an hour that I could call my own, otherwise I would not have delayed writing so long, as I have a tender regard for you, and an earnest desire that you should be altogether a Christian. I cannot be content with your being ever so harmless, or regular in your behaviour, or even exemplary in all externals. You have received the fear of God already; but shall you stop here? God forbid. This is only the beginning of wisdom. You are not to end there Fear shall ripen into love. You shall know (perhaps very soon) that love of God which passeth knowledge. You shall witness the kingdom of God within you, even righteousness, peace, and joy in the Holy Ghost. It is no small instance of the goodness of God toward you, that you are conscious of your want of living faith. And this goodness herein is more remarkable, because almost all your neighbours would set you down for a right good believer. O beware of these flatteries. Hold fast to the convictions which God has given you. Faith—living, conquering, loving faith—is undoubtedly the thing you want; and of this you have frequently a taste to encourage you in pressing forward. Such is the tender mercy of Him that loves you ! Such His desire, that you should receive all His precious promises ! Do not think they are afar off. Do not imagine you must stay long months, or years, before you receive them. Do not put them off a day, an hour. Why not now? Why should you not look up this instant, and see, as it were, Jesus Christ evidently set forth, crucified before your eyes? O hear His voice, " Daughter, be of good cheer! thy sins are forgiven thee!" "Say not in thy heart, Who shall go up into heaven, or who shall go down into the deep!" No! "The word is nigh thee, even in thy mouth, and in thy heart." "Lord, I believe! Help my unbelief!" Joy in the Holy Ghost is a precious gift of God; but, yet, tenderness of conscience is a still greater gift. And all this is for you—just ready.

> "The speechless awe, that dares not move,
> And all the silent heaven of love."

I am no great friend to solitary Christianity. Nevertheless, in so peculiar a case as yours, I think an exception may be admitted. It does seem most expedient for *you* to retire from Edinburgh, at least for a season, till God has increased your strength. For the company of those who know not God, who are strangers to the religion of the heart, especially if they are sensible, agreeable persons, might quite damp the grace of God in your soul.

You cannot oblige me more than by telling me all that is in your heart. There is no danger of your tiring me. I do not often write so long letters as this; but when I write to *you*, I am full of matter. I seem to see you just before me — a poor, feeble, helpless creature, but just upon the point of salvation : upright of heart (in a measure), full of real desires for God, and emerging into light. The Lord take you whole! So prays, my dear lady, your affectionate friend,

JOHN WESLEY.

EIGHTH VISIT, 1765.

Wesley's work during this visit was most uneventful in its general details, but it was very necessary on account of a certain publication that had
appeared in Scotland, with a preface by the Rev.
Dr John Erskine of Greyfriars, Edinburgh. "My
coming," he writes,[1] "was quite seasonable (though
unexpected) as those bad letters, published in the
name of Mr Hervey, and reprinted here by Mr
John Erskine, had made a great deal of noise."

James Hervey (1714-1758) was one of the very
earliest links connecting the Methodist movement
with literature.[2]   He was born at Hardingstone
near Northampton, 26th February 1714, and studied
at Lincoln College, Oxford, where he joined the
Methodist Society presided over by Wesley.   From
1743-1758 he was rector of Weston-Favell—his
father's parish.   He died at the early age of forty-
four.   He has been thus described :—

A more gentle, pious, unworldly spirit than that of
James Hervey it is difficult to conceive.  He was never
known to be in a passion : he made a solemn vow to
dedicate all the profits of his literary work to pious
uses, and scrupulously performed it.  He was naturally
disinclined to controversy, though from a sense of duty
he threw himself into the hottest and most unsatis-

---

[1] Appendix, p. 253.
[2] Lecky's Eighteenth Century, vol. ii. p. 551.

K

factory of all controversies. The simplicity of his
character is a strange contrast to the artificiality of
his best known writings ; but in his correspondence
and his sermons he uses a simpler and therefore a
more pleasing style. His popularity as a writer never
led him to take a false view of his own powers : when
it was at its height he frankly confessed that he was
not a man of strong mind, and that he had not power
for arduous research.[1]

The best of his known works (all Calvinistic in
tone) are his 'Meditations and Contemplations'
(1746), including his famous 'Meditations among
the Tombs,' 'Contemplations on the Night' (1747),
and 'Theron and Aspasio,' with which we have
here to do. Hervey's aim is well expressed in his
'Theron and Aspasio.' "Let us," says one of the
speakers in the dialogue, "endeavour to make religious conversation, which is in all respects desirable, in some degree fashionable." And so he
adopted dialogue as the best means for expressing
his message, and as the means of consecrating conversation itself. "I can hardly," he says, "name a
polite family where the conversation ever turns on
the things of God. I hear much frothy chit-chat,
but not a word of Christ. And I am determined
not to visit those companies where there is not
room for my Master as well as for myself."[2]

'Theron and Aspasio' was published in 1755,
but previous to publication Hervey sent the work

---

[1] Leslie Stephen's Dictionary, vol. xxvi. p. 283.
[2] Tyerman's Oxford Methodists, p. 325.

to Wesley for revisal. Wesley revised the first
three dialogues, and "sent them back with a few
inconsiderable corrections."[1] Hervey replied, "You
are not my friend if you do not take more liberty
with me." Wesley promised that he would, and
alterations were made of a more important character.[2]
Some of his alterations must have offended Hervey,
for when the work was nearly ready for the press
the old college friends had become somewhat alienated. Writing to Lady Shirley, Hervey says:
"Mr John Wesley takes me very roundly to task
on the score of predestination, at which I am much
surprised. Because a reader, ten times less pene-
trating than he is, may easily see that this doctrine
(be it true or false) makes no part of my scheme;
never comes under consideration; is purposely and
carefully avoided." Hervey's book was well received and widely read: Wesley was quite fair in
his remarks upon it, but took exception to a phrase
which he did not like—"imputed righteousness."
"'The imputed righteousness of Christ' is a phrase
not Scriptural. It has done immense harm. I
have had abundant proof that the frequent use of
this unnecessary phrase, instead of 'furthering
men's progress in vital holiness,' has made them
satisfied without any holiness at all; yea, and encouraged them to work all uncleanness with greedi-
ness."[3] The book excited great interest in Scotland,

---

[1] Tyerman's Oxford Methodists, p. 290.
[2] Works, vol. x. p. 305.     [3] Ibid., p. 306.

where the "Marrow controversy" was still fresh:
Sandeman in his 'Letters on Theron and Aspasio'
both approved and disapproved; Dr Witherspoon
of Beith published a pamphlet to show that Hervey's
doctrine of imputed righteousness does not weaken
the obligations to holiness of life.[1]  Wesley, as has
been already indicated, replied to the first (p. 129).

In 1756 Wesley wrote to Hervey several letters,
giving his criticisms on the whole work, and for some
inexplicable reason, probably through the influence
of those who were Wesley's enemies, Hervey did not
reply.   Wesley published in 1758 this critique in
'Preservative against Unsettled Notions in Religion.'
Hervey felt deeply wounded : "He is so unfair in
his quotations, and so magisterial in his manner,
that I find it no small difficulty to preserve the
decency of the gentleman, and the meekness of the
Christian, in my intended answer.   May our divine
Master aid me in both these instances, or else not
suffer me to write at all."   Hervey began a reply to
Wesley, under the influence of Wesley's theological
antagonist, the Rev. William Cudworth.  Wesley
wrote to his old friend as follows, notwithstanding
the alienation, and the letter must be inserted to
make what followed clear :—

LONDON, *November* 29, 1758.

DEAR SIR,—A week or two ago, in my return from
Norwich, I met with Mr Pierce of Bury, who informed
me of a conversation which he had a few days before.

---

[1] Tyerman's Oxford Methodists, pp. 297, 298.

Mr Cudworth, he said, then told him, "that he had prevailed on Mr Hervey to write against me, who likewise, in what he had written, referred to the book which he (Mr Cudworth) had lately published."

Every one is welcome to write what he pleases concerning me. But would it not be well for you to remember that, before I published anything concerning you, I sent it to you in a private letter?—that I waited for an answer several months, but was not favoured with one line?—that when at length I published part of what I had sent you, I did it in the most inoffensive manner possible: in the latter end of a larger work, purely designed to *preserve* those in connection with me from being tossed to and fro by various doctrines! What, therefore, I may fairly expect from my friend is, to mete to me with the same measure; to send to me, first, in a private manner, any complaint he has against me; to wait so many months; and, if I give you none, or no satisfactory answer, then to lay the matter before the world, if you judge it will be to the glory of God.

. . . O leave not your old well-tried friends! The new is not comparable to them. I speak not this because I am *afraid* of what any one can say or do to *me;* but I am really concerned for *you.* An evil man has gained the ascendant over you, and has persuaded a dying man, who had shunned it all his life, to enter into controversy, as he is stepping into eternity! Put off your armour, my brother! You and I have no moments to spare. Let us employ them all in promoting peace and goodwill among men. And may the peace of God keep your heart and mind in Christ Jesus! So prays, your affectionate brother and servant,

J. WESLEY.[1]

---

[1] Tyerman's Oxford Methodists, p. 320.

Hervey died before his reply was finished, and certainly before it received its final revision.[1]  The manuscript was submitted to Cudworth, who was anxious to have it published.  Hervey on the evening before his death expressed a desire to the contrary—"As it is not a finished piece, I desire you will think no more about it."[2]  He died on Christmas 1758, and six years after his death (notwithstanding the request of Hervey) the letters were published surreptitiously, without the printer's name, and with a brief preface signed "Philolethes." The following year Hervey's brother published another edition entitled 'Eleven Letters from the late Rev. Mr Hervey to the Rev. Mr John Wesley, containing an Answer to that Gentleman's Remarks on "Theron and Aspasio."'  Wesley could not allow this publication to remain unanswered, and in 1765 he printed 'A Treatise on Justification, extracted from Mr John Goodwin; with a Preface, wherein all that is material in Letters just published under the name of the Rev. Mr Hervey is answered.'[3]

[1] Tyerman's Life of Wesley, vol. ii. p. 527.      [2] Ibid., p. 528.

[3] "Hervey's brother gave Cudworth leave 'to put out and put in' whatever he thought expedient.  Cudworth's Anti-nomian sentiments led him to abhor Wesley's opinions; he caricatured them relentlessly by his interpolations of Wesley's pages, and sent forth in Hervey's name the first and most reckless and odious caveat against Methodism that ever emanated from any one who had friendly relations to it.  It was republished in Scotland, and tended much to forestall the spread of Methodism there.  Wesley felt keenly the in-justice and heartlessness of this attack, but his sorrow was mitigated by the knowledge that most of the abuse in the

The appearance of the 'Eleven Letters' was most unfortunate; they were, in the first place, written at a time of misunderstanding and alienation between the two great men; they were not desired to be published by the author, and "the authentic edition hardly differs a hair-breadth from the surreptitious one." [1] In England the publication led to the Calvinistic controversy, which raged so long and bitterly, and in which Wesley had the noble help of his friend the saintly Fletcher of Madeley; [2] in Scotland Wesley's doctrines were denounced, and a bitter storm aroused. Wesley felt the matter deeply. "And is this thy voice, my son David? Is this thy tender, loving, grateful spirit? No, 'the hand of Joab is in all this.' . . . Peace or war, ease or pain, life or death, is good, so I may but 'finish my course with joy,' and the ministry which I have received of the Lord Jesus, to testify the Gospel of the grace of God."

The 'Eleven Letters' were printed by the Rev. Dr John Erskine in Scotland, with a preface, in 1765. Kershaw, one of Wesley's itinerants, replied in 'An Earnest Appeal to the Public, in an honest, amicable, and affectionate reply.' Dr Erskine, the leader of the Evangelical party in

publication was interpolated, and that Hervey, who had delighted to call him his 'friend and father,' knew him too well to have thus struck at him from the grave."—Dr Stevens' History of Methodism, vol. ii. p. 284, 285.

[1] Oxford Methodists, p. 331.

[2] See Fletcher's Works, vols. i. and ii., and Tyerman's Life.

Scotland, rushed into controversy again in 'Mr
Wesley's Principles Detected, or a Defence to the
Edinburgh Edition of "Aspasio" vindicated; in
answer to Mr Kershaw's "Appeal."' Dr Erskine
was a saintly and, notwithstanding his pronounced
Calvinistic views, a kindly man; but his preface
was characterised by intemperate language against
Wesley, and was very bitter.[1] What can be now
said of the following?—

The publisher never received the least provocation
from any of the Methodists; nay, has been treated by
them with unmerited respect; many of them he es-
teems and loves for the truth's sake which is in them,
and shall be with them for ever. Of the sincere piety
of some of their teachers, nay, even of their sound
principles, he would think favourably. But when he
reflects that one is at the head of their societies who
has blended with some precious Gospel truths a medley
of Arminian, Antinomian, and enthusiastic errors, he
thinks it high time to sound an alarm to all who
would wish to transmit to posterity the pure faith once
delivered to the saints, seriously to consider what the
end of these things may be. Damnable heresies,
superstitious rites, and the wildest fanaticism may
gradually gain ground; and opinions and practices
take place the mention of which would shock many,
it is hoped the greatest part of people in this country,
at present attached to Methodism. If men are once
brought to believe that right opinion is a slender part
of religion, or no part at all, there is scarce anything
so foolish or so wicked which Satan may not prompt

---

[1] See Life of John Erskine, D.D., pp. 249-265.

them to, by transforming himself into an angel of light.[1]

Wesley did not reply ; his aim was not controversial, but to elevate the religious life of the country and deepen personal religion ; he only felt it appropriate to be with his little religious societies in the time of misunderstanding.

It is to be regretted that bitter words were written against Wesley by Dr Erskine ; that he was wounded by letters " published in the name of Mr Hervey "; that the spirit of controversy was aroused throughout the country, so fatal to the growth of the religious life which Wesley had solely at heart. " Religion must have repose." [2] Wesley's preachers felt their difficulties doubly increased. One writes :—

We then spent our time and strength about the meaning of words, instead of promoting the fear and love of God.[3]

Another wrote from Dundee :—

Before I left the place there were near a hundred joined in our society. About this time Mr Erskine published Mr Hervey's letters, with a preface equally bitter. O the precious convictions these letters destroyed ! They made me mourn in secret places. Mr Erskine being much esteemed in the religious world, and recommending them through the whole kingdom, our enemies made the advantage of them. These made the late Lady Gardiner leave us, after

---

[1] Preface, p. 6.     [2] Memorials of Edwin Hatch, D.D., p. 322.
[3] Early Methodist Preachers, vol. i. p. 211.

expressing a thousand times in my hearing the great profit she received by hearing our preaching. Many were then brought to the birth, but by those letters their convictions were stifled. What a pity good men should help to destroy the real work of God in the hearts of men.[1]

A third wrote :—

One great obstacle in my way was, a new edition of the 'Eleven Letters,' ascribed to Mr Hervey, had just come out, prefaced by a minister in Edinburgh, a man much esteemed in Scotland. These letters fully answered their design. They carried gall and worm-wood wherever they came. So that it was a sufficient reason for every one to keep his distance, because I was connected with Mr Wesley. I laboured to keep as clear as possible of controversy, dwelling chiefly upon repentance, faith, and the new birth.[2]

Still, " he who fears God," says Leighton, " knows no other fear," and Wesley was undaunted.


NINTH VISIT, 1766.

When at Edinburgh he visited the General Assembly, and records his impressions of it.[3]    At Dundee[4] he endeavoured to lessen prejudice and to

[1] Vol. ii. p. 145.    [2] Vol. v. p. 29.    [3] Appendix, p. 255.
[4] During 1765 Thomas Olivers was Wesley's evangelist at Glasgow, and during 1766 at Dundee (Minutes, pp. 49, 75). He was the author of the well-known hymn "The God of Abraham praise," of which James Montgomery declares, "There is not in our language a lyric of more majestic style." The following is the account of its origin : The son of a Wesleyan minister said a few years ago, "I remember my father telling

meet the objections taken against him in Scotland.[1] At Aberdeen he preached in the College Kirk, and at Monymusk in the parish church. At Glasgow Dr Gillies was as helpful as ever, and was occasionally present at the little society. Wesley seems to have preached there in the College Church : " I perceived the Scots, if you touch but the right key, receive as lively impressions as the English."

His remarks on the Scottish Reformation will be read with interest.[2]

On the Solway Firth he had a dangerous adventure.[3]

The minutes of the Leeds Conference (1766) have the question : " When should we enforce the rules of the Society in Ireland and Scotland ? Without delay. Only show them the reasonableness of it in Scotland, and they will conform to anything."[4]

me that he was once standing in the aisle of City Road Chapel during a conference in Wesley's time. Thomas Olivers, one of the preachers, came down to him and said, ' Look at this ; I have rendered it from the Hebrew, giving it, as far as I could, a Christian character, and I have called on Leoni the Jew, who has given me a synagogue melody to suit it ; here is the tune, and it is to be called " Leoni." ' " Dr Julian, to verify this story, communicated with the late Rabbi Adler, and discovered that the hymn is really a free rendering, with Christian colouring, of the " Hebrew doxology which rehearses in metrical form the thirteen articles of the Hebrew creed drawn up by Maimonides (1130-1205). It is still chanted on Friday evening in every synagogue of the British empire to the melody known to us as ' Leoni.' "—Hymns and Hymn-makers, Campbell, pp. 49, 50.

[1] Appendix, p. 256.     [2] Appendix, p. 259.
[3] Appendix, p. 259.     [4] Minutes, p. 58.

## TENTH VISIT, 1767.

Wesley was again impressed with a feature of the Scottish nation that he expresses more than once : "I must say for the Scots in general, I know no men like them for bearing plain dealing"; yet in desiring plain preaching, he did not approve of scolding preaching :—

I was sorry to find both the society and the congregations smaller than when I was here last. I impute this chiefly to the manner of preaching which has been generally used. The people have been told frequently and strongly of their coldness, deadness, heaviness, and littleness of faith, but very rarely of anything that would move thankfulness. Hereby many were driven away, and those that remained were kept cold and dead.[1]

Wesley was always interested in those questions relating to that mysterious borderland where mind and body blend, and with his strong belief in, and personal experience of, the spiritual and supernatural acting upon the natural and physical, was open to receive evidence from all quarters, even the humblest. He united intellectual and moral majesty with docility of spirit, and a capability of considering every such case brought before him —some may think too deferentially. In this journey, as in the former and subsequent ones, such cases were before his notice,[2] and Wesley did not

[1] Appendix, p. 261.          [2] Ibid.

regard it as superstitious to believe that purely physical phenomena were capable of explaining them. Some may say he had too much credulity, but belief did not lessen his great capability for work, or make him dreamy in his creed. On the Sunday we find him preaching three times in Edinburgh, and on the following Monday visiting as many as he could, sick and well, and endeavouring to confirm them ; in the evening preaching at seven and nine, concluding about twelve ; next morning off to Dunbar, "if possible to arouse some of the sleepers." It is a marvel : his own life was the best evidence of a soul fed from unseen rills of strength.

## Eleventh Visit, 1768.

Religion [it has been said] may be demonstrated from two sides—reason and experience, logic and life —and hence we have apologetical literature and biographical literature ; but surely the latter is not inferior to the former in power and conclusiveness. The thousands of honest men and women who have had experience of the things of God, who have tested the truth of Christ in all life's chequered scenes—these are witnesses for the defence of the faith, certainly not inferior to Pearson, Butler, and Hooker. Here Methodist literature has rendered great service to the Church of Christ — it has been a witnessing Church in a very eminent degree, telling out what it has felt and seen of the grace of God.[1]

---

[1] Wesley : The Man, his Teaching, and his Work, p. 267.

Its founder made this the object of his life, and throughout his journeys in Scotland we find him asserting religion, not as an opinion or a theory of the here and the hereafter, but as a life within the believer's life.[1]

I spoke to most of the members of the society [at Glasgow]. I doubt we have few societies in Scotland like this; the greater part of those I saw not only have found peace with God, but continue to walk in the light of His countenance. Indeed that wise and good man Mr G—— has been of great service to them, encouraging them by all possible manner to abide in the grace of God.

Dr Gillies of the College Parish, Glasgow, was a great worker (p. 124) and a beautiful catholic spirit. Like Wesley, he recognised worth in those who might differ from him in doctrine, and it is no small honour to his memory that he was among the very earliest of Wesley's Scottish friends, and that he recognised the great movement of which Wesley was the inspirer.

Wesley left Glasgow for Perth,[2] where he was well received; proceeded to Aberdeen, where he found a society "truly alive, knit together in peace and love."[3] He preached again in the College Kirk, and in the evening at the Castle Gate. Wesley only received violence in Scotland on one occasion, and in this respect his Scottish visits

[1] Appendix, p. 262.  [2] Ibid.
[3] Appendix, p. 263.

form a pleasant contrast to his English receptions. "A large number of persons were all attention ; but there were many rude, stupid creatures round about them, who knew as little of reason as of religion. I never saw such brutes in Scotland before. One of them threw a potato, which fell on my arm ; I turned to them and some were ashamed." [1] After six days' work in Aberdeen he returned South, preaching at Brechin, Dundee, Perth, Edinburgh, Dunbar. His impressions of the Queen Mary controversy,[2] Scone Palace,[3] and Holyrood,[4] will be read with interest.[5]

Two other features in this Scottish visit deserve to be noticed. At the close of 1767 the Earl of Buchan died, and he had always taken an interest in and felt a benefit from Wesley's preaching. His last words were, " Happy, happy, happy ! " His Countess-Dowager, a lady of deep piety, appointed Wesley, with other two, as her domestic chaplains.[6] This was done through the intervention of Lady Huntingdon, to whom Wesley wrote the following :—

[1] Appendix, p. 264.     [2] Appendix, pp. 263, 264.
[3] Appendix, p. 265.     [4] Ibid.
[5] *January, 11, 1768.*—" 'This week I spent my scraps of time in reading Mr Wodrow's ' History of the Sufferings of the Church of Scotland.' It would transcend belief, but that the vouchers are too authentic to admit of any exception. O what a blessed governor was that good-natured man, so called, King Charles the Second ! Bloody Queen Mary was a lamb, a mere dove, in comparison of him ! "—Diary, vol. iii. p. 296.
[6] Tyerman's Life, vol. iii. p. 2.

LONDON, *January* 4, 1768.

MY DEAR LADY,—I am obliged to your ladyship, and to Lady Buchan, for such a mark of your regard as I did not at all expect. I purpose to return her ladyship thanks by this post.

That remark is very striking as well as just : If it is the Holy Spirit that bears witness, then all speaking against that witness is one species of blasphemy against the Holy Ghost. And when this is done by those who profess to honour Him, it must in a peculiar manner grieve that blessed Spirit. Yet I have been surprised to observe how many, who affirm salvation by faith, have run into this ; running full into Mr Sandeman's notion that faith is merely an assent to the Bible ; and not only undervaluing, but even ridiculing, the whole experience of the children of God. I rejoice that your ladyship is still preserved from that spreading contagion, and also enabled plainly and openly to avow the plain, old, simple, unfashionable Gospel.

Wishing your ladyship many happy years, I remain, my dear lady, your very affectionate servant,

JOHN WESLEY.

Wesley when in Scotland wrote and probably preached his famous sermon on "The Good Steward." He emphasises the message of all things—soul, body, talents, goods—as a trust for which man is to render account. The sermon was published under the title, "The Good Steward. A Sermon by John Wesley, Chaplain to the Right Honourable the Countess-Dowager of Buchan."

Again, during this visit, he sought an interview

with the Rev. Dr John Erskine, who had written
the intemperate preface to Hervey's Letters against
him, and the following extracts from a letter to the
Rev. Mr Plenderleith of Edinburgh, describing it,
are interesting :—

I had for some time given up the thought of an
interview with Mr Erskine, when I fell into the company of Dr Oswald. He said, " Sir, you do not know
Mr Erskine. I know him perfectly well. Send and
desire an hour's conversation with him, and I am sure
he will understand you better." I am glad I did send.
I have done *my* part, and am now entirely satisfied. I
am likewise glad that Mr Erskine has spoken his
mind. I will answer with all simplicity, in full confi-
dence of satisfying *you*, and all impartial men.

He objects (1) That I attack predestination as subversive of all religion, and yet suffer my followers in
Scotland to remain in that position.

Much of this is true. I did attack predestination
eight-and-twenty years ago, and I do not believe now
any predestination which implies irrespective reproba-
tion. But I do not believe it is *necessarily subversive*
of all religion. I think hot disputes are much more so.
Therefore I never willingly dispute with any one about
it ; and I advise all my friends, not in Scotland only,
but all over England and Ireland, to avoid all conten-
tions on this head, and let every man remain in his
own opinion. Can any man of candour blame me
for this ? Is there anything *unfair* or *disingenuous*
about it ?

He objects (2) That I " assert the attainment of sinless perfection by all that are born of God." I am
sorry that Mr Erskine should affirm this again. I
need give no other answer than I gave before, in the

L

seventh page of the little tract I sent him two years ago. I do not maintain this. I do not believe it. I believe Christian perfection is not attained. by any of the children of God till they are what the apostle John terms *fathers;* and this I expressly declare in that sermon which Mr Erskine so largely quotes.

He objects (3) That I "deny the imputation of Christ's active obedience." Since I believed justification by faith, which I have done upwards of thirty years, I have constantly maintained that we are pardoned and accepted wholly for the sake of what Christ hath both *done* and *suffered* for us. Two or three years ago Mr Madan's sister showed him what she wrote down of a sermon which I had preached on this subject. He entreated me to write down the whole and print it, saying it would satisfy all my opponents. I was not so sanguine as to expect this : I understand mankind too well. However, I complied with his request : a few were satisfied ; the rest continued just as they were before.

As long as Mr Erskine continues in the mind expressed in his Theological Essays, there is no danger that he and I should agree any more than light and darkness. *I love and reverence him, but not his doctrine.* I dread every approach to antinomianism. I have seen the fruit of it over the three kingdoms. I never said that Mr Erskine and I were agreed. I will make our disagreement as public as ever he pleases ; only I must withal specify the particulars. If he *will* fight with me, it must be on this ground ; and then let him do what he will, and what he can.

One cannot escape the feeling that Wesley had been somewhat harshly treated ; but probably Dr Erskine would have replied in the same noble terms with which Wesley spoke of him: "I love and reverence him; but not his doctrine."

## TWELFTH VISIT, 1770.

At Glasgow he spent two days "with much satisfaction." At Edinburgh he was grieved at the result of the controversy raised, and "that the children of God should so zealously do the devil's work." At Perth he had encouraging meetings, and pleasant fellowship with the ministers. At Inverness he was well received by the senior minister, "a pious and friendly man," and preached twice in the parish church: at Nairn he also preached in the parish church: at Aberdeen in the College church. At Arbroath "the whole town seems moved; the congregation was the largest I have seen since we left Inverness; and the society, though but of nine months' standing, is the largest in the kingdom, next to that of Aberdeen."[1] He was impressed both with the abbey ruins and the town.[2] At Dundee the ministers "are bitter enough." At Edinburgh he found the society smaller, preached in Lady Glenorchy's Chapel, the High School Yard, and his own chapel. He ended his visit at Musselburgh and Dunbar.

In the Life of Lady Glenorchy, containing extracts from her diary and correspondence, are several references to Wesley's visit. Lady Glenorchy, in

---

[1] Appendix, p. 269.　　　　　[2] Ibid.

union with her friend Lady Maxwell, and probably
at her suggestion, had about this period opened a
place of worship in Edinburgh at which ministers
of all denominations, who held essential truths,
might preach.[1] This chapel was situated in Nid-
dry's Wynd, and was opened on March 7, 1770.[2]
Many were opposed to it, but among the supporters
of the movement was the Rev. Dr Webster of the
Tolbooth, Edinburgh, who was as friendly to Wesley as he had been to Whitefield,[3] and who joined
Lady Maxwell every Sunday evening in worship at
Mr Wesley's chapel, then in the Calton.[4] Dr Webster was a pronounced Calvinist, but was liberal in
his views and conduct toward those who differed in
opinion from him.

*February 2, 1770.*—This morning [says Lady Glen-
orchy] I met with Dr Webster at Lady Maxwell's to
consult about the chapel. It is determined I am to
seek an English Episcopal minister to supply it ; and
to give one day in the week to the Methodists.[5]

The religious meetings [says her biographer] to be
held in St Mary's Chapel, appear to have been reg-
ulated by a plan laid down by Lady Glenorchy and
Lady Maxwell, with the assistance of Dr Webster ;
and divine service was intended to be performed by
Presbyterians, Episcopalians, and one day in the week
by Mr Wesley's preachers. The chapel was not to be

---

[1] Life, by Dr Jones, p. 131.  [2] Ibid., p. 155.
[3] See An Account of Dr Alexander Webster, by Grace
Webster.
[4] Dr Jones' Life of Lady Glenorchy, p. 132.  [5] Ibid., p. 133.

occupied in canonical hours ; but there was worship in it on the Lord's day at seven in the morning, in the interval between the morning and afternoon services in the churches, which was then much longer than now, and in the evenings, and in some of the evenings of the week-days.[1]

It was probably in connection with this arrangement that Wesley preached in Lady Glenorchy's chapel on Sunday morning, May 13, 1770 ; and during his visit he had interviews with Lady Glenorchy and Dr Webster, "who always heard Mr Wesley when in Edinburgh, as well as occasionally his preachers."[2] May 12, 1770, the Diary states :—

This morning the Rev. Dr Webster and Mr Wesley met at my house and had a long conversation together. They agreed on all doctrines on which they spoke except those of God's decrees, predestination, and the saints' perseverance, which Mr Wesley does not hold. After Mr Wesley was gone Dr Webster told me, in a fair and candid way, wherein he disapproved of Mr Wesley's sentiments. I must (according to the light I now have, and always have had, ever since the Lord was pleased to awaken me) agree with Dr Webster.[3]

Notwithstanding this difference, Lady Glenorchy desired Wesley to procure for her school a schoolmaster, which he did, and at the beginning of the following year a minister, when he appointed the Rev. Richard De Courcy, of Trinity College, Dublin,

---

[1] Dr Jones' Life of Lady Glenorchy, p. 133.
[2] Ibid., p. 155.    [3] Ibid., p. 156.

who had obtained deacon's orders, and had officiated as a curate.  This was in February 1771, but
two letters to Lady Maxwell at this period show
that the great Calvinistic controversy from 1770,
in which Wesley was so fiercely attacked, was not
confined to England.

LONDON, *January* 24, 1771.

MY DEAR LADY,—Although Mr Macnab[1] is quite
clear as to justification by faith, and is in general a
sound and good preacher, yet I fear he is not clear of
blame in this.  He is too warm and impatient of contradiction, otherwise he must be lost to all common-
sense, to preach against final perseverance in Scotland.
From the first hour that I entered the kingdom, it was
a sacred rule with me never to preach on any controverted point—at least, *not in a controversial way.*
Any one may see that this is only to put a sword into
our enemies' hands.  It is the direct way to increase
all their prejudices, and to make all our labours fruit-
less. . . .                                      JOHN WESLEY.[2]

*February* 26, 1771.

MY DEAR LADY,—I cannot but think the chief reason
of the little good done by our preachers in Edinburgh
is the opposition which has been made by the ministers
of Edinburgh, as well as by the false brethren from
England.  These steeled the hearts of the people against
all the good impressions which might otherwise have
been made ; so that the same preachers, by whom God
has constantly wrought, not only in various parts of
England, but likewise in the northern parts of Scot-

---

[1] One of his preachers.  Minutes, p. 103.
[2] Lady Maxwell's Life, p. 72.

land, were in Edinburgh only useless. They felt a damp upon their spirits : they had not their usual liberty of speech ; and the word they spoke seemed to rebound upon them, and not to sink into the hearts of the hearers. At my first coming I usually find something of this myself ; but at the second or third time of preaching it is gone.

I think it will not be easy for any one to show us either that Christ did not die for all, or that He is not willing as well as able to cleanse from all sin, even in this present world. If your steady adherence to these great truths be termed bigotry, you have no need to be ashamed. You are reproached for Christ's sake, and the spirit of glory and of Christ shall rest upon you. Perhaps our Lord may use you to soften some of the harsh spirits, and to preserve Lady Glenorchy, or Mr De Courcy, from being hurt by them.—I am, my dear lady, your affectionate servant,

JOHN WESLEY.[1]

These letters are sufficient to show the condition of affairs in Scotland, and the battle Wesley had to fight for the larger view of divine truth that is preached to-day, and of which he was then the most outstanding pioneer. It must have been to him a time of anxiety, for De Courcy joined the Calvinistic party, and with them was left in sole possession of the chapel.[2] Lady Glenorchy's Diary states :—

*Taymouth, June 28, 1771.*—Before I left Edinburgh I dismissed Mr Wesley's preachers from my chapel, as, from some writings of Mr Wesley which fell into my

---

[1] Lady Glenorchy's Life, p. 228.
[2] Tyerman's Life of Wesley, vol. iii. p. 65.

hands, and from the sentiments of some of his preachers
of late officiating there, I found that they held doctrines
that appear to be erroneous. First, They deny the
doctrines of imputed righteousness, election, and the
saints' perseverance, which I think are clearly revealed
in Scripture. Secondly, I found that none of our
Gospel ministers would preach in the chapel if they
continued to have the use of the pulpit; so that, by
receiving them, I should exclude those who were sound
in the faith, and thereby frustrate the end I had in
view in opening the chapel, which was to have all who
preached pure evangelical doctrine to preach there,
of any sect or denomination whatsoever. Thirdly, I
found by experience that my own soul had been hurt,
and kept from establishment in the faith, by hearing
some of the preachers, and I judged that others might
be hurt by them also.[1]

Notwithstanding all this, Lady Maxwell remained
a supporter of John Wesley, and a friend of Lady
Glenorchy, who died on November 11, 1771, and
left her sole executrix and manager of her chapels
and schools.

### THIRTEENTH VISIT, 1772.

*April* 17.—" Being Good Friday, I went to the
Episcopal chapel, and was agreeably surprised : not
only the prayers were read well, seriously and distinctly, but the sermon, upon the sufferings of
Christ, was sound and unexceptionable. Above
all, the behaviour of the whole congregation, rich

[1] Life, p. 239.

and poor, was solemn and serious." [1]    At Glasgow
he spoke against "the miserable bigotry for opinions and modes of worship."    He extended his labours to Greenock and Port-Glasgow,[2] and returned
to Glasgow, where he had pleasant fellowship with
Dr Gillies and other three Scottish ministers.    At
five in the morning he had a large congregation,
"with the gay and fashionable among them." [3]
At Perth he preached twice on the Sunday, and
had a kind reception from two of the Perth ministers.    He preached at Dunkeld, Brechin, and in
the College Church of Aberdeen ; on his return
journey at Arbroath, Dundee, Edinburgh, Ormiston, Leith.    During his ten days' stay at Edinburgh
his activity knew no decline : he was suffering
from hydrocele, and three medical men held a
consultation regarding his health, yet that very
day he opened a new chapel at Leith, and two
days afterwards started for Newcastle, preaching
on the way at Dunbar.    His old age was a perpetual youth, and if in any life the words of the
prophet had a fulfilment it was surely in Wesley's :
"They that wait upon the Lord shall renew their
strength ; they shall soar with wings like eagles ;
they shall run, and not be weary ; they shall walk,
and not faint."    When at Dunbar he visited the
Bass Rock, "which, in the horrid reign of Charles
the Second, was the prison of those venerable men

---

[1] Appendix, p. 272.        [2] Appendix, pp. 272, 273.
[3] Appendix, p. 273.

who suffered all things for a good conscience."[1]
As he notes details of surroundings, he is still more
impressed with the moral atmosphere of the place,
with its memories of great struggles. "How many
prayers did the holy men confined here offer up in
that holy day! And how many thanksgivings
should we return for all the liberty, civil and religious, which we enjoy!" He visited also Tantallon
Castle and the Roman camp.[2]

His remarks on the first volume of Dr Robertson's
'History of Charles V.'[3] and on Beattie's 'Enquiry
after Truth' are racy and interesting.[4]

Reference is made in the Journal (p. 277) to the
"Circular Letter":—

I had designed [he says] to preach (as usual) at
Provost Dixon's, in Haddington, in the way to Dunbar.
But the Provost too had received light from the "Cir-
cular Letter," and durst not receive these heretics.

Another indirect reference is:[5]—

I dined at the minister's, a sensible man, who
heartily bid us God speed. But he soon changed his
mind. Lord H——n informed him that he had received a letter from Lady H——, assuring him that
we were "dreadful heretics, to whom no countenance
should be given."

The "Circular Letter" was one of the products
of the fierce Calvinistic controversy, and was sent

[1] Appendix, p. 278.          [2] Ibid.
[3] Appendix, p. 274.          [4] Appendix, p. 275.
          [5] Appendix, p. 276.

far and wide throughout the country. It was a proposal to have a meeting at the same time as Wesley's Conference at Bristol in 1771, of those who disapproved of Wesley's Minutes of 1770: "As the same are thought injurious to the very fundamental principles of Christianity, it is further proposed, that they go in a body to the said Conference, and insist upon a formal recantation of the said Minutes, and, in case of a refusal, that they sign and publish their protest against them." The letter was a piece of extravagant and needless assumption, and did not meet with much support, although it evidently produced hesitancy far and wide among the people, and was felt even in Scotland.

Wesley and his friends at the Conference in 1771 met the doctrinal points raised in a noble Christian spirit, and disclaimed the doctrinal interpretation put upon his Minutes, as well as satisfied all the fears of the Christian conscience that had been aroused during the period. And as the matter had become public and required a statement, his saintly friend, Fletcher of Madeley, who united brilliant intellectual force and logical power with a piety that is only to be equalled in spiritual splendour with that of St Francis of Assisi, published Vindications. Every one will respond to these beautiful words, and to the defence which they give of the Christ-like devotion and service of Wesley :—

O, sir, have we not fightings enough without to employ all our time and strength? Must we also declare war and promote fightings within? Must we catch at every opportunity to stab one another? What can be more cutting to an old minister of Christ than to be traduced as a dreadful heretic, in printed letters sent to the best men of the land, through all England and Scotland, and signed by a person of your rank and piety? While he is gone to a neighbouring kingdom to preach Jesus Christ, to have his friends prejudiced, his foes elated, and the fruit of his extensive ministry at the point of being blasted? . . . Of the two greatest and most useful ministers I ever knew, one is no more.[1] The other, after amazing labours, flies still, with unwearied diligence, through the three kingdoms, calling sinners to repentance. Though oppressed with the weight of near seventy years, and the cares of near thirty thousand souls, he shames still, by his unabated zeal and immense labours, all the young ministers in England, perhaps in Christendom. He has generally blown the Gospel trumpet, and rode twenty miles, before most of the professors who despise his labours have left their downy pillows. As he begins the day, the week, the year, so he concludes them, still intent upon extensive services for the glory of the Redeemer and the good of souls. And shall we lightly lift up our pens, our tongues, our hands against him? No; let them rather forget their cunning. If we *will* quarrel, can we find nobody to fall out with but the minister upon whom God puts the greatest honour?[2]

While Wesley received this noble defence south of the Border, notwithstanding all the cry of " heretic "

[1] Whitefield, died September 30, 1770.
[2] Works of Fletcher of Madeley, vol. i. pp. 62, 63.

that was loudly sounded north of the Border, two Scottish towns presented Wesley with their freedom and enrolled him as an honorary burgess. It was a public acknowledgment of the venerable man, and reflects honour on the towns that had the catholicity to confer it.

*April 28, 1772.*—In the evening I preached once more at Perth to a large and serious congregation. Afterwards they did me an honour I never thought of —presented me with the freedom of the city. The diploma ran thus :—

" Magistratuum illustris ordo et honorandus senatorum coetus inclytae civitatis Perthensis, in debiti amoris et affectus tesseram erga Johannem W——y, immunitatibus praefatae civitatis, societatis etiam et fraternitatis aedilitiae privilegiis donarunt.

*" Aprilis die 28 anno Sal. 1772."* [1]

---

[1] "The diploma," says Mr Moore, "was struck off from a copper-plate upon parchment ; the arms of the city and some of the words were illuminated, and flowers painted round the borders, which gave it a splendid appearance."—Life of Wesley, vol. ii. p. 254. The translation is :—

"The illustrious order of Magistrates, and the honourable Court of Senators (Aldermen) of the famous city of Perth, as a proof of their well-merited esteem and affection for John Wesley, Master of Arts, late Fellow of Lincoln College in Oxford, have invested him with the immunities of the above-mentioned city, and with the privileges of the society and brotherhood of a burgess.

*" At Perth the 28th day of April 1772."*

It is to be observed that Wesley modestly omits in his Diary the reference to " Artium Magistrum, nuper Collegii Lincoln-iensis, Oxoniae, Socium."—Moore, vol. ii. p. 253.

I question [adds Wesley] whether any diploma from the city of London be more pompous or expressed in better Latin.[1]

*May 6, 1772.*—The magistrates here also [Arbroath] did me the honour of presenting me with the freedom of their corporation. I value it as a token of their respect, though I shall hardly make any further use of it.[2]

## FOURTEENTH VISIT, 1774.

At Glasgow he preached on May 13th and 14th to people on the Old Green, "the greatest part of whom hear much, know everything, and feel nothing,"[3] and this physical effort notwithstanding a constitution far advanced in years, and weakened by a recent operation. He heard two sermons in the church on Sunday, "which contained much truth, but were no more likely to awaken one soul than an Italian opera."[4] He preached in the evening an open-air sermon to a multitude of people assembled on the Green.[5] On the following Monday he preached morning (at seven) and afternoon in the parish church of Port-Glasgow, in the evening at Greenock. He was again at the Glasgow Green on Tuesday (17th May), at Edinburgh on the 18th, and Perth on the 19th, and regrets that the morning

[1] Appendix, p. 274.  [2] Appendix, p. 276.
[3] Appendix, p. 279.
[4] Wesley published an abridgment of Scougal's 'Life of God in the Soul of Man,' and a third edition of it appeared in 1773.
[5] Appendix, p. 279.

preaching had been given up there.[1]  The burial
service is now read or a prayer offered generally at
the grave, but it was not so in the eighteenth century ; and to Wesley, accustomed to the beautiful
service of the Church of England, it seemed neither
reverent nor becoming : [2]—

O what a difference is there between the English
and the Scotch method of burial !  The English does
honour to human nature, and even to the poor remains that were once a temple of the Holy Ghost !
But when I see in Scotland a coffin put into the earth,
and covered up without a word spoken, it reminds me
of what was spoken concerning Jehoiakim, "He shall
be buried with the burial of an ass." [3]

At Perth he preached on the 21st and 22nd ; but
here, as elsewhere, the people had strong opinions,
and were more open to debate than to suffer exhortation.  "The generality of the people here are so
wise that they need no more knowledge, and so good
that they need no more religion." [4]  He records his
impressions of a tract on the "Gowry Conspiracy," [5]

[1] Appendix, p. 280.                    [2] Ibid.
[3] It is interesting to compare with Wesley's impression of a
Scottish funeral that of the Rev. Rowland Hill.  Says his bio-
grapher : "At Hawick he saw for the first time a Scotch
funeral, conducted without a prayer or the presence of a
minister, and observed to a bystander, 'Your funerals are soon
over.'  A loquacious old woman told him prayers were no use
to the dead.  This he admitted, but suggested that the people
of Scotland lost an excellent opportunity of doing good to the
living if they could do nothing for the dead."—Life by the
Rev. Edwin Sidney, A.M., p. 186.
[4] Appendix, p. 281.                    [5] Ibid.

on Lord Kames' Essays,[1] Dr Reid's Essay.[2] He preached further north, at Aberdeen and Arbroath, and returned to Edinburgh, where on Sunday he preached twice, besides being at Ormiston in the morning. Wesley was subjected at Edinburgh to a trying experience :[3] *Wed., June* 8.—"I took my leave of our affectionate friends, and in the evening preached at Dunbar."[4]

Wesley's great difficulty in Scotland was the objection to an itinerant ministry.[5]  The use and wont of Scotland were against it.  It was true for an outstanding religious splendour such as Wesley, "the world is my parish"; yet for the daily work of the Church it is no less true that daily needs assert the necessity for a permanent ministry, with its counter-principle "the parish is my world," provided the need for a larger vision combined with it is not forgotten.  Scottish experience and demands were well expressed by the words of Dean Stanley :—

There is some value in a pastor growing up amongst his people, a pastor who has seen successive generations growing up around him—when to the influence of his preaching is added the far greater and more spiritual influence of a long life of good example,

---

[1] Appendix, p. 281.   One of Wesley's publications in 1774 was 'Thoughts upon Necessity.'  In it he states, "I cannot believe the noblest creature in the visible world to be only a fine piece of clockwork."

[2] Appendix, p. 283.            [3] Appendix, pp. 283, 284.

[4] Appendix, p. 284.

[5] Wesleyan Methodism, by Isaac Taylor, pp. 62, 244.

known and loved by the fathers and children of all the homes that are gathered within reach of the parish church. Yet we ought all to feel that there is, nevertheless, such a thing as the necessity of enlightening and refreshing these more stationary pastorates by the introduction of new influences, new hopes, new instruments, such as John Wesley had in mind when he conceived his design of itinerant preachers.[1]

Wesley's presence brought new inspiration, but the Scots evidently were asserting their desire for fixed pastorates. One of Wesley's letters, written in 1774, indicates this as well as Wesley's answer to the claim.

I have written [says he in a letter of date October 16, 1774] to Dr Hamilton, that Edinburgh and Dunbar must be supplied by one preacher. While I live, itinerant preachers shall be itinerants ; I mean, if they choose to remain in connection with me. The society at Greenock are entirely at their own disposal ; they may either have a preacher between them and Glasgow, or none at all. But more than one between them they cannot have. I have too much regard both for the bodies and souls of our preachers to let them be confined to one place any more. I have weighed the matter, and will serve the Scots as we do the English, or leave them.[2]

The following is an interesting account of Wesley, given by one of his Edinburgh preachers, Joseph Benson, to whom the above letter was addressed :—

I was constantly with him for a week ; I had the

---

[1] American Addresses, p. 44.
[2] Wesley's Works, vol. xii. p. 395.

opportunity of examining narrowly his spirit and conduct ; and, I assure you, I am more than ever persuaded he is a *None-such*.   I know not his fellow,
first, for abilities, natural and acquired ; and, secondly,
for his incomparable diligence in the application of
those abilities to the best of employments.   His lively
fancy, tenacious memory, clear understanding, ready
elocution, manly courage, indefatigable industry, really
amaze me.   I admire, but wish in vain to imitate, his
diligent improvement of every moment of time ; his
wonderful exactness even in little things ; the order
and regularity wherewith he does and treats everything he takes in hand ; together with his quick de-
spatch of business, and calm, cheerful serenity of soul.
I ought not to omit to mention, what is very manifest
to all who know him, his resolution, which no shocks
of opposition can shake ; his patience, which no length
of trials can weary ; his zeal for the glory of God and
the good of man, which no waters of persecution or
tribulation have yet been able to quench.   Happy
man !   Long hast thou borne the burden and heat
of the day, amidst the insults of foes and the base
treachery of seeming friends ; but thou shalt rest from
thy labours, and thy works shall follow thee ! [1]


## Fifteenth Visit, 1776.

Wesley was now seventy-three years of age, and
his last seven visits to Scotland are marvels of
activity.   His diary gives a record of twenty-two
days' work, and it is almost inexplicable when we
recall that it was done in the days of no railways.

[1] Methodist Magazine, 1825, p. 386.

Wesley generally rode, but in his later years he
used a carriage. The venerable apostle's old age
was indeed a perpetual youth, sustained by invisible
rills of spiritual strength, from waiting upon God.

His impressions and notes of St Andrews in 1776
will be read with interest.[1]  Of course it was to be
expected that, trained in Oxford with its resident
life, he would not be able to understand or sympa-
thise with the Scottish University system : " In the
English colleges every one may reside all the year,
as all my pupils did ; and I should have thought
myself little better than a highwayman if I had not
lectured them every day in the year but Sundays." [2]

Wesley interpreted some passages of the Old
Testament too literally, and once thought that to
give up the belief in witchcraft was to give up
belief in the Bible.[3]  A great man, while moulding
and guiding his age, is sometimes conditioned by it,
and we read :—

I read over Mr Pennant's 'Journey through Scotland,' a lively as well as judicious writer ; but I cannot

---

[1] Appendix, pp. 288, 289.

[2] Appendix, p. 289.  Wesley reports the date of St Regulus'
Tower, but the date is too early.  Dr Joseph Robertson, followed by other authorities, places it between the years 1127
and 1144 : what Wesley adds regarding the Tower may be true
regarding the early Celtic chapel at St Andrews, which was
visited by St Columba and St Cainnech at the close of the
sixth century (Skene's Celtic Scotland, vol. ii. p. 137).

[3] The Bible : its Meaning and Supremacy, by Dean Farrar,
p. 180.

give up to all the Deists in Great Britain the existence of witchcraft, till I give up the credit of all history, sacred and profane. And at the present time I have not only as strong, but stronger proofs of this, from eye and ear witnesses, than I have of murder ; so that I cannot rationally doubt of one any more than the other.[1]

In this respect many other great men were, in the period, like him.

## Sixteenth Visit, 1779.

The places visited were nearly the same as in the former journey. We find the venerable man, ladened with the weight and the honour of seventy-six years, preaching in the open air by the river-side at Glasgow, "to a huge multitude of serious people."[2] The following Thursday, after preaching on his journey, he preached at Aberdeen and rejoiced in a people "that can feel as well as hear." Next day he was at Inverness and Inverurie, where he preached " to a considerable number of plain country people, just like those we see in Yorkshire. My spirit was much refreshed among them." He was always thoughtful for others, and on his way to Strath-bogie we find the following instance of it. " Mr Brackenbury was much fatigued, so I desired him to go into the chaise, and I rode forward to Keith,"[3] Wesley's chaise was also his study, and contained

---

[1] Appendix, p. 288.    [2] Appendix, p. 290.
[3] Appendix, p. 291.

his writing-desk ; and although travelling, he was always at work, editing his 'Christian Library' or writing articles for his Magazine, or guiding and counselling his preachers or people. If genius is the power to do hard work, then John Wesley is unique, for every hour had to him a duty. On Sunday, 6th June, he preached in the parish church of Keith ; at Forres he was the guest of Sir Ludovic Grant. He conducted prayers in his house : "Thus ended this comfortable day ! So has God provided for us in a strange land."[1] The minister of Nairn gave him a hearty welcome, and on Tuesday the 8th he preached in the parish church, which was full from end to end. "I have seldom seen a Scotch congregation so sensibly affected ; indeed it seemed that God smote rocks, and brake the hearts of stone in pieces."[2] At Inverness he spent nearly two days, counselling and helping his society : "In the morning we had an affectionate parting, perhaps to meet no more."[3] He commenced his return journey on the 9th, preaching in the course of it, and reached Edinburgh on the 16th, where he laboured for four days.

The Minutes of Wesley's Conference, held at London in 1779, contain the following directions to his preachers in Scotland :—

What can be done to revive the work in Scotland ?
*A*. 1. Preach abroad as much as possible.

---

[1] Appendix, p. 292.       [2] Ibid.       [3] Ibid.

2. Try every town and village.
3. Visit every member of every society at home.
4. Let the preachers at Dundee and Arbroath never stay at one place more than a week at a time.
5. Let each of them once a quarter visit Perth and Dunkeld, and the intermediate villages.[1]

During his stay at Edinburgh in 1779, Wesley had a call from Boswell, who was anxious to consult him on a curious matter in which he was interested. Boswell says :—

I wished to be made acquainted with Mr John Wesley ; for though I differed from him in some points, I admired his various talents and loved his pious zeal. At my request, therefore, Dr Johnson gave me a letter of introduction to him.

" To the Reverend Mr JOHN WESLEY.

" SIR,—Mr Boswell, a gentleman who has been long known to me, is desirous of being known to you, and has asked this recommendation, because I think it very much to be wished that worthy and religious men should be acquainted with each other.—I am, sir, your most humble servant,          SAM. JOHNSON.

" *May* 3, 1779."

Mr Wesley [Boswell adds] being in the course of his ministry at Edinburgh, I presented this letter to him, and was very politely received.[2]

---

1 Minutes, p. 141.          2 Life of Johnson, vol. v. p. 85.

## Seventeenth Visit, 1780.

This visit was a short one, and uneventful. It was limited to the Edinburgh neighbourhood, and the references to Holyrood,[1] Roslin Castle and Chapel, and Queen Mary[2] are very interesting.

## Eighteenth Visit, 1782.

He preached again at Dunbar : while at Edinburgh he was the guest of Lady Maxwell at Saughton Hall, and addressed her neighbours, as well as the school which she supported. The *ambitiosa paupertas* interests him.[3] The reticence of the Scottish people in religious matters—oftenest most silent when most impressed—grieved him, as it has many another. " I seldom speak anywhere so roughly as in Scotland, and yet most of the people hear and hear, and are just as they were before." Although seventy-nine years of age, he continued his preaching tour to Dundee, Arbroath, and Aberdeen, where he heard pleasant news of his work prospering in the north. In Newburgh, a small fishing village in Aberdeenshire, " not only men and women, but a considerable number of children, are either rejoicing in God, or panting after Him."[4] He was four days at Aberdeen, and on his return journey to Edinburgh, where he arrived on the 12th,

---

[1] Appendix, p. 295.             [2] Ibid.
[3] Appendix, p. 296.            [4] Appendix, p. 297.

preached at Arbroath and Dundee. His work at Edinburgh rejoiced him. He went to Kelso on the 14th, where he was the guest of Dr Douglas : the need for the stimulus of fellowship in religion strikes him as *the* needful, and he adds, " How shall they keep awake, unless they ' that fear the Lord speak often together ' ? "

At Kelso he fell head foremost down the stair, but escaped unhurt. " Does not God give His angels charge over us," the saintly man adds, " to keep us in all our ways ? "

Probably at this time he had among his hearers Sir Walter Scott, then a boy, who wrote to Southey, in a letter dated Abbotsford, April 4, 1819 :—

When I was about twelve years old I heard Wesley preach more than once, standing on a chair in Kelso churchyard. He was a most venerable figure, but his sermons were vastly too colloquial for the taste of Saunders. He told many excellent stories. One I remember which he said had happened to him at Edinburgh. " A drunken dragoon," said Wesley, " was commencing an assertion in military fashion, ' G—d eternally d—n me,' just as I was passing. I touched the poor man on the shoulder, and when he turned round fiercely, said calmly, ' You mean, " God bless you." ' " In the mode of telling the story he failed not to make us sensible how much his patriarchial appearance and mild, yet bold, rebuke overawed the soldier, who touched his hat, thanked him, and, I think, came to chapel that evening.[1]

---

[1] Lockhart's Life, vol. vi. pp. 45, 46.

Wesley's activity has no parallel. On his eightieth birthday (June 28, 1782) he adds :—

I entered into my eightieth year ; but, blessed be God, my time is not "labour and sorrow." I find no more pain or bodily infirmities than at five-and-twenty. This I still impute—1. To the power of God, fitting me for what He calls me to. 2. To my still travelling four or five thousand miles a-year. 3. To my sleeping night or day, whenever I want it. 4. To my rising at a set hour (4 A.M.) And 5. To my constant preaching, particularly in the morning.[1]

And yet until 1790 he still faced the colder climate in Scotland ; and at eighty years of age visited Holland, where he was well received. The following year he adds :—

I have this day [June 28, 1783] lived fourscore years, and, by the mercy of God, my eyes are not waxed dim; and what little strength of body or mind I had thirty years since, just the same I have now. God grant I may never live to be useless ! Rather may I

"My body with my charge lay down,
And cease at once to work and live." [2]

NINETEENTH VISIT, 1784.

Wesley arrived at Edinburgh on April 24, 1784, and his activity is noteworthy.

On the 25th he attended sermon at the Tolbooth Church, preached at Lady Maxwell's house at four in the afternoon, and at six in the evening in his

[1] Diary at date.          [2] Diary at date.

own chapel. " I am amazed at this people. Use the most cutting words, and apply them in the most pointed way, still they *hear*, but *feel* no more than the seats they sit upon." [1] On Monday, in the evening, on Tuesday and Wednesday, morning and evening, he preached at Glasgow ; on the Thursday he preached at four in Glasgow and in the evening at Edinburgh. On the 30th he preached at Perth —" the sweetest place in all North Britain, unless perhaps Dundee " — and at five o'clock the next morning (May 1), afterwards pressing on to Dundee, where he preached in the evening. On the 3rd he reached Arbroath, and was delighted with his little society. On the 4th he was at Aberdeen, where he grieves over his preachers giving up the morning services, and exhorts them to restore the morning work and to stay less in the one place. " Many were faint and weak for want of morning preaching and prayer-meetings, of which I found scarce any traces in Scotland." [2] Thursday, 6th May, " We had the largest congregation at five which I have seen since I came into the kingdom." He immediately afterwards set out for Old Meldrum, where he was the guest of Lady Banff, and preached twice in the district. He preached at Keith on the evening of the 7th and the morning of the 8th May ; arriving at Elgin in the afternoon, he pressed onwards towards Forres, where he gave a helpful visit to Sir Ludovic Grant, and preached twice the fol-

[1] Appendix, p. 298.  [2] Appendix, p. 300.

lowing Sunday. On Monday, 10th May, he set out
for Inverness, and to aid the horses "walked about
twelve miles and a half of the way through heavy
rain. But, blessed be God, I was no more tired
than when I set out from Nairn." [1] He preached at
Inverness on the evening of the 10th, and at 5 A.M.
and in the evening on the 11th. There is a solemn
pathos in the words of the venerable man : "We
had then a solemn parting, as we could hardly expect
to meet again in the present world." On the 12th
he was again at Sir Ludovic Grant's house, and
preached at Elgin twice—on this and the following
evening.

On Friday, 14th, he read prayers and preached in
the Episcopal church at Banff about two, and at ten
in Lady Banff's dining-room at Fort-glen. On the
15th he arrived at Aberdeen, and on the way was
interested in reading Fingal's poems. [2] On Sunday
the 16th he preached at Newburgh in the morning ;
at Trinity Chapel, Aberdeen, in the afternoon ; and
at five in the evening in his own chapel. On the
17th he was at Arbroath ; on the 18th he preached
at Dundee. On the 19th he was at Melville Castle
as the guest of the Leven family, and preached there
in the evening. [3] On the 21st he was at Edinburgh,

---

[1] Appendix, p. 302.      [2] Appendix, p. 303.

[3] Alexander, Earl of Leven, was the King's Commissioner to
the General Assembly of the Church of Scotland from 1741 to
1753 ; David, Earl of Leven, and afterwards Earl of Leven and
Melville, was Commissioner from 1783 to 1801 (Acts of the
General Assembly, pp. 1204, 1205).

and found many in his society "alive to God."[1]
On the 22nd he addressed the scholars in the school
supported by his friend and helper, Lady Maxwell.
On Sunday, 23rd, he attended service at the Tolbooth Church in the morning, at the old Episcopal
chapel in the afternoon, and preached in the evening.
On the 24th and 25th he preached at Dunbar; on
the 26th at Berwick-on-Tweed; on the 27th at
Kelso.[2]   This is a marvellous record of work for one

[1] Appendix, p. 304.

[2] Two Seceding ministers at Kelso (Appendix, p. 305) did not
behave generously towards Wesley, but it is interesting to record
the following kindly action done by Wesley towards a Secession
congregation in Edinburgh.   The Bristo Street Church, Edinburgh, disagreed on the appointment of a minister, and the
minority desired the Rev. Dr James Hall: they sought the
right to worship in Wesley's chapel.   Says the late Rev. Principal Cairns in his Centenary Letter: "It was in the Low
Calton, under the shadow of where the present Post - Office
stands, but in a humble block of buildings vulgarly called the
'Saut-Backet,' from its resemblance to a wooden salt-cellar still
used in some parts of Scotland.   There the Seceders were
allowed by the Methodists to worship at a separate hour, paying a rent of half a guinea each Sabbath, and 'ten pounds
besides for liberty to set [let] the seats.'   This continued for
one year or more, from 1785 till the end of 1786, when these
Seceders went off to the new church built by them in Rose
Street, where Dr Hall came to minister.   Now the interesting
thing is that all these arrangements, as to the use of this
Methodist chapel, were made with the knowledge and con-
currence of John Wesley himself, six years before his death,
and when the whole Connexional property was still in his
hands.   How little could he have foreseen that this Presbyterian separation was to grow up into three large and flourishing
congregations—Rose Street, Broughton Place, and Palmerston
Place—all in Edinburgh, each with a high name in connection
with Christian work at home and abroad."—Centenary Sermons
and Addresses, p. 426.

who was at the time nearly eighty-two years of age : the more marvellous when it is recalled that the Scottish visits were but as little breaks in the life of one who knew not what a holiday was apart from his work, and who sustained it at the same high level of activity for over fifty years, writing, corresponding, superintending at the same time.

One cannot read the narratives of the later journeys without observing the tender feeling expressed at the partings, especially at Inverness, the most northerly point that he reached. Wesley prepared for what must very soon come to one so far advanced in life; and on February 28, 1784, executed his deed of declaration, which a few days afterwards was enrolled in the High Court of Chancery.[1] In 1784 Coke and Ashbury were ordained as superintendents for the Methodists in America, and with regard to ordinations for Scotland his Diary states :—

*1785. August 1.*—Having with a few select friends weighed the matter thoroughly, I yielded to their judgment, and set apart three of our well-tried preachers—John Pawson, Thomas Hanby, Joseph Taylor—to minister in Scotland.

At the Conference of 1786 he ordained two others.

A year later [says Mr Tyerman] five others were ordained : in 1788, when Wesley was in Scotland, John Barber and Joseph Cownley received ordination at his hands ; and at the ensuing Conference seven

---

[1] Tyerman's Life, vol. iii. p. 418.

others, including Alexander Mather, who was ordained to the office, not only of deacon and elder, but of superintendent. On Ash Wednesday in 1789 Wesley ordained Henry Moore and Thomas Rankin ; and this, we believe, completes the list of those upon whom Wesley laid his hands. All these ordinations were in private, and many of them at four o'clock in the morning. Some of the favoured ones were intended for Scotland ; some for foreign missions ; and a few, as Mather, Moore, and Rankin, were employed in England. In most instances, probably in all, they were ordained deacons on the one day ; and, on the day following, received the ordination of elders, Wesley giving to each letters testimonial.[1]

Wesley thus explains his action for Scotland :—

After Dr Coke's return from America, many of our friends begged I would consider the case of Scotland, where we had been labouring for many years, and had seen so little fruit of our labours. Multitudes, indeed, have set out well, but they were soon turned out of the way ; chiefly by their ministers either disputing against the truth or refusing to admit them to the Lord's Supper, yea, or to baptise their children, unless they would promise to have no fellowship with the Methodists. Many who did so soon lost all they had gained, and became more the children of hell than before. To prevent this I at length consented to take the same step with regard to Scotland which I had done with regard to America. But this is not a separation from the Church at all. Not from the Church of Scotland, for we were never connected therewith any further than we are now ; nor from the

---

[1] Life and Times of Wesley, vol. ii. pp. 441, 442.

Church of England, for this is not concerned in the steps which are taken in Scotland. Whatever then is done in America or Scotland, is no separation from the Church of England. I have no thought of this : I have many objections against it. It is a totally different case. " But for all this, is it not possible there may be such a separation after you are dead ? " Undoubtedly it is. But what I said at our first Conference above forty years ago, I say still : " I dare not omit doing what good I can while I live, for fear of evils that may follow when I am dead." [1]

In ordaining ministers for America and Scotland [says Mr Jackson], Mr Wesley did not think that his only justification arose from the facts of the case. He believed that the act was right in itself, as being in full accordance with the doctrine of Holy Scripture and the practice of the early Christians. It had long been his conviction that, in the apostolic churches, Presbyters and Bishops were of the same order, and therefore had an equal right to ordain.[2]

" When sending these ordained ministers into Scotland," says Mr Smith, the Wesleyan historian, " Wesley advised the societies there to use his abridged form of Common Prayer." [3] It was never popular in Scotland.

Charles Wesley was of the same mind as Lord Mansfield, that " ordination was separation," but John Wesley would not acknowledge it.[4] Among his last utterances was :—

[1] Magazine, 1786, p. 678.
[2] Life of the Rev. Charles Wesley, vol. ii. pp. 384, 385.
[3] History of Wesleyan Methodism, vol. i. p. 526.
[4] Wesley allows that he deviated from Church rules in "preaching abroad," "praying extempore," in forming societies,

Many will be so bold and injudicious as to form a separate party, which will dwindle into a dry, dull, separate sect. In flat opposition to them, I declare once more, that I live and die a member of the Church of England, and that none who regard my judgment will ever separate from it.[1]

## TWENTIETH VISIT, 1786.

Wesley was now eighty-three years of age. He reached Glasgow on May 13, and spent three days there "fully employed." On the 17th and 18th he was at Edinburgh, where he had "much and pleasant work." On the 19th he was at Dundee; and the 20th and 21st at Arbroath, where he "spent the Lord's day in the Lord's work." On the 22nd he left Arbroath at 3.30 A.M., and arrived early at Aberdeen: he spent two days at his work there, and "had an exceeding solemn parting, as I

and employing lay preachers, but he said: "All this is not separating from the Church. So far from it that, whenever I have opportunity, I attend the Church service myself, and advise all our societies so to do. Nevertheless, the generality even of religious people naturally think 'I am inconsistent.' And they cannot but think so, unless they observe my two principles. The one, that I dare not separate from the Church, that I believe it would be a sin so to do; the other, that I believe it would be a sin not to *vary* from it in the points above mentioned. I say, put these two principles together—first, I will not *separate* from the Church; yet, secondly, in cases of necessity, I will *vary* from it—and inconsistency vanishes away. I have been true to my profession from 1730 to this day" (1790).—Tyerman's Life, vol. iii. p. 636.

[1] Overton's Life, p. 212.

reminded them that we could hardly expect to see
each other's face any more till we met in Abraham's
bosom." [1]    The weather was stormy on the return
journey, and he reached Arbroath soon after six on
the 25th, where he addressed a "large and deeply
attentive" congregation.    In crossing the Tay he
encountered heavy weather — "the wind was so
strong that the boat could scarcely keep above
water.    However, our great Pilot brought us safe
to land between one and two in the morning." [2]
On Saturday 27th he pressed through Fife and had
a pleasant passage to Leith.    "After preaching, I
walked to my lovely lodging at Coates and found
rest was sweet."

On Sunday, 28th May, he preached three times
at Edinburgh : morning and evening in his own
chapel, and at noon on the Castlehill.    "I never
saw such a congregation there before.    The chair
was placed just opposite to the sun ; but I soon
forgot it while I expounded these words, 'I saw
the dead, small and great, stand before God.'"    In
the history of missions there is nothing like this:
perhaps some day a gifted painter may yet produce
a suitable memorial of the scene—the venerable
man of eighty-three declaring his message in the
open air to a large multitude on the Castlehill of
Edinburgh.    Genius may yet do it, and the work
would not fail to enlarge and inspire those privi-
leged to see it.

[1] Appendix, p. 306.            [2] Ibid.

N

*Tues. 30.*—I had the happiness of conversing with the Earl of Haddington and his Lady at Dunbar. I could not but observe both the easiness of his behaviour (such as we find in all the Scottish nobility) and the fineness of his appearance, greatly set off by a milk-white head of hair.[1]

On Wednesday 31st May he preached at Berwick-on - Tweed, and thence continued his journey southwards.

Scotland always gave Wesley a respectful reception, and he preached in many of the Scottish parish churches when they were closed to him in England. But goodness and faithfulness to an overmastering ideal like his, and the inestimable impulse he gave to the religion of England and Ireland, disarmed the opposition and brought the due tribute, even in the eighteenth century.

During the last six years of his life [says Mr Overton, the present occupant of his father's pulpit at Epworth], he was universally treated with the utmost reverence. He was no more suspected of being a Jacobite, a Papist, or—worst of all—an enthusiast. He himself was utterly amazed at the change. " I am become," he writes in 1785, " I know not how, an honourable man. The scandal of the cross is ceased ; and all the kingdom, rich and poor, Papists and Protestants, behave with courtesy ; nay, with seeming goodwill." This was written respecting Ireland, but it was just the same in England. He had more invitations to preach in churches than he could possibly accept ; and

---
[1] Appendix, p. 307.

the last pages of his journal are full of notices of churches in which he officiated.[1]

In a letter dated March 12, 1786, from Bristol, Wesley approved of an appeal made for funds to send missionaries to " the Highlands of Scotland," with other places ;[2] but this work was left for Dr Adam Clarke to carry out.

Wesley, we have already said, ordained preachers for Scotland, and in writing one of them, John Pawson, he had addressed him as " Reverend."

Now [1787, says Mr Tyerman] that Pawson was brought back to England, he had to doff his canonicals, and had his letters from Wesley inscribed with " Mr," instead of " Rev." He loudly remonstrated, but got no redress ; and at length, like a good Christian, more anxious to save souls than to wear sacerdotal robes, submitted to obey orders which were strangely inconsistent with Wesley's ordaining acts, and went on his way rejoicing.[3]

## Twenty-first Visit, 1788.

Wesley was now verging on his eighty-sixth year, and life was becoming lonelier to him. In 1785 he had lost by death two of his oldest and dearest friends — Vincent Perronet and John Fletcher, vicars of Shoreham and Madeley. Their counsel and help were always inspirations to him, and Fletcher was Wesley's designated successor.

[1] Life of John Wesley, p. 207.
[2] Tyerman's Life, vol. iii. p. 484.        [3] Ibid., p. 497.

Shortly before leaving the South on his northerly journey, Wesley had received another loss by death. His brother Charles died on March 29, 1788. It is a curious coincidence that Wesley was preaching in Shropshire at the time, and he and his congregation were singing at the very moment of his brother's death Charles's own sweet hymn :—

> " Come let us join our friends above,
>     That have obtained the prize,
> And on the eagle-wings of love
>     To joys celestial rise.
> Let all the saints terrestrial sing,
>     With those to glory gone,
> For all the servants of our King,
>     In earth and heaven, are one.
>
> One family, we dwell in Him,
>     One Church, above, beneath,
> Though now divided by the stream,
>     The narrow stream of death.
> One army of the living God,
>     To His command we bow ;
> Part of His host have crossed the flood,
>     And part are crossing *now*."

A fortnight later, when preaching at Bolton, Wesley attempted to give for praise his brother's hymn, "Come, O Thou Traveller unknown"; but when he came to the lines—

> " My company before is gone,
>     And I am left alone with thee,"

the venerable, sorrow-stricken man broke down,
overcome with emotion; he sat down in the pulpit,
hid his face with his hands, and wept. The tears
of a strong man are impressive, and Wesley, notwithstanding his lonely elevation, had still the
human heart that could be pierced with sorrow.
But the "Traveller unknown" was with him till
travelling days were done on the earth, and Wesley
pressed northwards. On the way he had enormous
congregations, and Mrs Fletcher at Madeley wrote
of him : "I could not but discern a great change
in him. His soul seems far more sunk in God,
and such an unction attends his words that each
sermon was indeed spirit and life." [1]

On May 13, 1788, Wesley arrived at Dumfries,
and preached in the open air. "Rich and poor
attended from every quarter, of whatever denomination, and every one seemed to hear for life.
Surely the Scots are the best hearers in Europe ! " [2]
He paid a noble tribute to his preacher for the
work he had done : this worthy man (Robert
Dall) and his wife had won the respect of all
classes in the town for their attention to the poor
criminals and the sermons in the jail.[3] He was
a man after Wesley's own heart, and his wife had
"both sense and grace." Wesley preached next
morning at five o'clock in the new chapel, and
again in the evening. The clergy of the town

---

[1] Life, p. 251.  [2] Appendix, p. 307.
[3] Tyerman's Life, vol. iii. p. 533.

showed much kindness. He arrived at Glasgow on the 16th, where he preached six times; here he stated the object of his system, and described it as an agency for good which required for admission into it no particular opinions.

There is no other religious society under heaven which requires nothing of men in order to their admission into it, but a desire to save their souls. Look all around you, you cannot be admitted into the Church or society of the Presbyterians, Anabaptists, Quakers, or any others, unless you hold the same opinions with them, and adhere to the same mode of worship.

The Methodists alone do not insist on your holding this or that opinion; but they think, and let think. Neither do they impose any particular mode of worship; but you may continue to worship in your former manner, be it what it may. Now, I do not know any other religious society, either ancient or modern, wherein such liberty of conscience is now allowed, or has been allowed, since the age of the Apostles. Here is our glorying; and a glorying peculiar to us. What society shares it with us.[1]

He reached Edinburgh on the 19th, and spent two days there with much satisfaction: "I still find a frankness and openness in the people of Edinburgh, which I find in few other parts of the kingdom." He likewise preached at Dalkeith and Dunbar.

"As Wesley grew older," says Mr Tyerman, "he took far more interest in visiting scenes of beauty

---

[1] Appendix, p. 309.

and historic buildings than he did in the earlier parts of his illustrious career": this is especially observable in his last Scottish visits.

At the Conference in 1788 an attempt was made to set aside the itinerant plan in Scotland,[1] and this was the occasion of the following letter to Lady Maxwell :—

LONDON, *August* 8, 1788.

MY DEAR LADY,—It is certain many persons, both in Scotland and England, would be well pleased to have the same preachers always. But we cannot forsake the plan of acting which we have followed from the first. For fifty years God has been pleased to bless the itinerant plan ; the last year most of all : it must not be altered till I am removed ; and I hope it will remain till our Lord comes to reign upon earth.

JOHN WESLEY.[2]

Wesley again declined to apply the term "Reverend" to his Scottish ordained preachers when removed to England, neither would he permit them to administer the sacrament in England.[3] A kirk-session had been instituted in Glasgow, and Wesley, being informed, wrote to one of his preachers the following :—

CORK, *May* 10, 1789.

MY DEAR BROTHER,—"Sessions !" "elders !" We Methodists have no such custom, neither any of the churches of God that are under our care. I require

---

[1] Tyerman, vol. iii. p. 561.    [2] Works, vol. xii. p. 328.
[3] See Tyerman, vol. iii. pp. 549, 565, 574.

*you*, Jonathan Crowther, immediately to dissolve that session (so called) at Glasgow. Discharge them from meeting any more. And if they will leave the *society*, let them leave it. We acknowledge only preachers, stewards, and leaders among us, over which the assistant in each circuit presides. You ought to have kept to the Methodist plan from the beginning. Who had my authority to vary from it? If the people of Glasgow, or any other place, are weary of us, we will leave them to themselves. But we are willing to be still their servants, for Christ's sake, according to our own discipline, but no other. JOHN WESLEY.[1]

During this visit to Scotland Wesley felt it necessary to write to his Magazine a letter upon a subject that was occupying much attention at the period. Wesley himself resolved to have as his resting-place the ground connected with City Road Chapel, and he wished his brother to be buried beside him. Charles objected to this, because the ground had not been " consecrated." Shortly before his death he sent for the vicar of his parish and said : " Sir, whatever the world may have thought of me, I have lived, and I die, in the communion of the Church of England, and I will be buried in the yard of my parish church." Wesley loved his brother Charles most affectionately, but he felt it necessary to answer certain opinions that his brother's request had raised. At Dumfries he wrote an article on the consecration of churches and churchyards, in which he states there is no law

[1] Tyerman, vol. iii. pp. 582, 583.

of England, or of the English Church, enjoining
such a practice :—

Neither is it enjoined by the law of God. Where do
we find one word in the New Testament enjoining any
such thing ? Neither do I remember any precedent
of it in the purest ages of the Church. It seems to
have entered, and gradually spread itself, with the
other innovations and superstitions of the Church of
Rome. For this reason I never wished that any bishop
should consecrate any chapel or burial-ground of mine.
Indeed, I should not dare to suffer it, as I am clearly
persuaded the thing is wrong in itself, being not
authorised by any law of God, or by any law of the
land. In consequence of which I conceive that either
the clerk or the sexton may as well consecrate the
church, or the churchyard, as the bishop. . . . I take
the whole of this practice to be a mere relic of Romish
superstition. And I wonder that any sensible Protestant should think it right to countenance it ; much
more that any reasonable man should plead for the
necessity of it ! Surely it is high time now that we
should be guided, not by custom, but by Scripture and
reason.[1]

In connection with Wesley's letter, it is interest-
ing to recall Dean Stanley's reference to City Road
Chapel churchyard, where rests all that is mortal of
John Wesley. In visiting the chapel and cemetery

I asked an old man, who showed me the cemetery,
I asked him perhaps inadvertently, and as an English
Churchman might naturally ask—
" By whom was this cemetery consecrated ?"

---

[1] Magazine, 1788, p. 543.

And he answered : " It was consecrated by the bones of that holy man, that holy servant of God, John Wesley." [1]

Dean Stanley sympathised with the remark, and quoted it with approval.

### TWENTY-SECOND VISIT, 1790.

Wesley was now bordering on eighty-eight years of age, but he was as busy as ever, and did not shrink from the fatigue of another Scottish journey. The words that he used on his eighty-fifth birthday were the inspiration of his closing days :—

> " My remnant of days
> I spend to His praise
> Who died the whole world to redeem ;
> Be they many or few,
> My days are his due,
> And they all are devoted to Him ! " [2]

He proceeded to Scotland on May 10, 1790 ; but of his labours during the next fortnight we know nothing, as the record has perished. He evidently was at Inverness ; he spent an agreeable afternoon with Lady Banff " and her lovely family," and preached in the evening.  On the 25th " we re-turned to Aberdeen ; and I took a solemn farewell of a crowded audience. If I should be permitted to see them again, well ; if not, I have delivered

1 American Addresses and Sermons, p. 38.
2 Diary, vol. iv. p. 410.

my own soul." On the 26th he drove to Brechin,
where he preached in the evening ; "but I was so
faint and ill that I was obliged to shorten my discourse." On the 27th he drove through Forfar
and Cupar to Auchterarder ; on the 28th through
Stirling and Kilsyth to Glasgow. There is sadness
in the words of the good old man—pity his venerable presence and apostolic work did not meet with
a warm welcome : "The congregation was miserably small, verifying what I had often heard before, that the Scots dearly love the Word of the
Lord—on the Lord's day. If I live to come again,
I will take care to spend only the Lord's day at
Glasgow."[1] On Monday, 31st May, he left Glasgow at two in the morning, and arrived in Moffat
about three o'clock in the afternoon. "Taking
fresh horses, we reached Dumfries between six and
seven, and found the congregation waiting ; so after
a few minutes, I preached on Mark iii. 35 : 'Whosoever shall do the will of God, the same is my
brother, and sister, and mother.' " Fortunately a
letter written by one of his preachers gives an account of Wesley's last visit to Dumfries—in fact
his last visit to a Scottish town :—

In the latter end of May Mr Wesley visited us. He
came from Glasgow that day (about seventy miles),
but his strength was almost exhausted, and when he
attempted to preach very few could hear him. His

---

[1] Appendix, p. 311.

sight was likewise much decayed, so that he could neither read the hymn or text. The wheels of life were ready to stand still; but his conversation was agreeably edifying, being mixed with the wisdom and gravity of a parent, and the artless simplicity of a child.[1]

Wesley was evidently not able for the morning service at five o'clock on June 1, but the Diary adds :—

In the day I conversed with many of the people—a candid, humane, well-behaved people; unlike most that I have found in Scotland. In the evening the house was filled; and truly God preached to their hearts. Surely God will have a considerable people here.[2]

Two of Wesley's letters, dated Dumfries, June 1, 1790, give us Wesley's own thoughts; in one he says (referring to the journey from Glasgow) :—

I travelled yesterday nearly eighty miles, and preached in the evening without any pain. The Lord does what pleases Him. Peace be to all your spirits !

In another :—

The dying words of the Prince of Orange are much upon my mind this morning : "Lord, have mercy upon the people !" I never saw so much likelihood of doing good to Scotland as there is now, if only our preachers here would be Methodists indeed ! . . . My sight is much as it was, but I doubt I shall not recover my

---

[1] Magazine, 1795, p. 423.    [2] Appendix, p. 312.

strength till I use that noble medicine, preaching in the morning.[1]

It is pleasant to recall that Lady Maxwell of Pollok, his old friend, was a solace to him in his old age, and pleasant to read in one of his last letters to this noble Scottish lady :—

I really love to write to you, as I love to think of you. And sometimes it may please Him who sends by whom He will send to give you some assistance by me. *And your letters have frequently been an encouragement and a comfort to me. Let them never, my dear friend, be intermitted during the few days I have to stay below.*[2]

Such is the narrative relating to Wesley's Scottish visits; they are but interludes in an almost unbroken apostolic activity of fifty-six years' incessant work. In 1783, when eighty years of age, he enjoyed for the first time—it may be said the only time—"the luxury of a ministerial holiday."[3] His venerable old age was characterised by supreme goodness and happiness :—

His countenance as well as conversation [said Mr Knox] expressed an habitual gaiety of heart which nothing but conscious virtue and innocence could have bestowed. My acquaintance with him has done more to teach me what heaven upon earth is implied in the maturity of Christian piety than all that I have else-

---

[1] Tyerman, vol. iii. p. 609.
[2] Life of D'Arcy, Lady Maxwell of Pollok, p. 99.
[3] Dr Rigg's The Living Wesley, p. 210.

where seen or heard or read, except in the sacred volume.[1]

After leaving Scotland on June 1 he was as busy as ever with his work in England, and wrote on the 28th :—

This day I enter into my eighty-eighth year. For above eighty-six years I found none of the infirmities of old age : my eyes did not wax dim, neither was my natural strength abated ; but last August I found almost a sudden change. My eyes were so dim that no glasses would help me. My strength likewise now quite forsook me ; and probably will not return in this world. But I feel no pain from head to foot ; only it seems nature is exhausted ; and, humanly speaking, will sink more and more till

"The weary springs of life stand still at last."[2]

Although now very weary with years, his spirit was as active as ever, and it is interesting to have it stated on the authority of Mr Moore,[3] and corroborated by Mr Tyerman,[4] that in February 1791 he actually sent his chaise and horses from London to Bristol, and took places for himself and his friends in the Bath coach, intending to start about March 1 for his journey (as was his wont) to North England and Scotland. God had willed it otherwise, and about the time of his contemplated journey to Scotland he was called to his rest and reward in the Church above. He died on March 2, 1791, and his

1 Dr Rigg's The Living Wesley, p. 210.
2 Diary, vol. iv. p. 470.     3 Life, vol. ii. p. 386.
4 Life, vol. iii. p. 647.

death, like his life, exhibited the triumph of his faith. It was indeed "a greeting the Unseen with a cheer": it was the unquenchable faith—

> "I'll see my Pilot face to face,
> When I have crossed the bar."

Wesley's end was a victory: "The best of all is, God is with us"; "I'll praise, I'll praise, I'll praise." His death, like his life, has done more for the triumph of the Christian faith than libraries of apologetic literature. He died the religious guide of 134,549 Methodists,[1] and set up as he was on a height from which the splendour of his Christian character could impress so many connected with him and all beyond his own pale who loved him, the triumph of his life and death has brought thousands then and since to the feet of God. Refuge may still be found in the shadow of his resplendent personality, and it is true to say that Deism and all forms of unbelief have their best answer in Wesley's life and death; that these are the noblest of vindications for the truth and power of the Christian faith. His dying words are the explicit statement of his lifelong faith, and his followers may be said to found their creed upon them. At the centenary services of 1891 the Right Honourable H. H. Fowler, M.P., said:—

If we inherit but the smallest portion of his spirit, we shall claim to be "the friends of all, the enemies of

---

[1] Tyerman, vol. iii. p. 620.

none." His conflict was with vice, with ignorance, with intemperance, and with sin. His motive and his aim was to destroy the works of the devil ; and all who are fighting that battle—no matter what uniform they wear —are the comrades of " the people called Methodists." I would, in closing, in one sentence recall the scene around that death-bed a century ago.

What was his last confession of faith ? What was the creed in which he died ?—

> " I the chief of sinners am,
> But Jesus died for me."

What was his last hymn ?—

> " I'll praise my Maker while I've breath,
> And when my voice is lost in death
> Praise shall employ my nobler powers."

What was his last prayer ?—" Bless the Church and he King. Grant us truth and peace through Jesus Christ our Lord."

And what was his final words of thanksgiving for the past and hope for the future ?—" The best of all is, God is with us ! "

In that confession of faith, in that litany, in that inspiring motto you have an epitome of the Methodism which to-day reverently, thankfully, hopefully gathers around John Wesley's tomb.[1]

Such is the faith which John Wesley has so nobly helped to reawaken in the Churches, and we all praise God for the gift of his great servant. His true proportions are now visible, but they were not so extensively recognised in 1791. As this work specially deals with " Wesley in Scotland," it will

[1] Centenary Sermons and Addresses, pp. 192, 193.

only be appropriate to quote the references that Lady Maxwell, whose letters had frequently been "an encouragement and comfort" to Wesley, made in an Edinburgh newspaper at his death :—

On Wednesday last, at his house in London, died that great and good man the Rev. John Wesley, at a very advanced period, after a life of the most unwearied diligence and unexampled activity in the service of God and the general interests of mankind. His extensive labours were crowned with uncommon success in various parts of different and distant kingdoms. But, as might be expected, his very uncommon abilities and extensive usefulness laid him under that severe tax which all must pay who are so far raised above the common level of mankind. Now that he is no longer the object of envy, it is hoped prejudice will give way to more candid and honourable sentiments, and thereby leave the public at liberty to do justice to one of the greatest characters that has appeared since the apostolic age.[1]

In two other letters there are also to be found the following allusions :—

*March* 14, 1791.

And so that great and good man is gone !—a dispensation big with importance to thousands. I felt keenly, though perfectly satisfied. A year or two more would have reduced him to a state of childhood ; but now he has made an honourable retreat in the possession of all his mental powers : after a long life of unwearied diligence, and unexampled activity, in the

---

[1] Lady Maxwell's Life, p. 99.

O

service of his God and the general interests of mankind, and with most uncommon success attending his
extensive labours. May the Lord still be the Head of
the large body of Christians he has left behind! O
that one soul may animate the whole! . . . I trace
him worshipping before the throne, and by faith hold
fellowship with his spirit.[1]

*March* 19, 1791.

I do not know that I ever heard of a life so crowned
with action ; so unweariedly filled up with and for
God. Not one vacant moment in the twenty-four
hours. Many sons have done well ; but, if I do not
view him through a too flattering medium, he excels
them all.[2]

It is the glory of this Scottish lady that she
recognised Wesley's spiritual genius from the very
first, and felt the mighty religious impulse which
his work brought to the country. The following
are her testimonies to Wesley's Scottish societies
and the people he gathered around him :—

The class that meets in my house is become quite a
Penuel. Deity is so present that all within each heart
confesses a present God. . . . The chapel "was not
only the house of God, but the gate of heaven."[3]

The Methodists are a highly favoured body of Christians, both ministers and people. I meet with none
who enjoy so much of the comforts of religion, of
communion and fellowship with the Father and the
Son, as they do ; nor with any that have such clear
views of the new and everlasting covenant.[4]

---

1 Life, p. 360.      2 Ibid., p. 361.
3 Ibid., p. 456.     4 Ibid., p. 490.

Surely these Scottish disciples were worthy of their great spiritual leader : they continued Wesley's spirit, which has never ceased to live in them, their present successors, and all the Churches.

We lost the true notion of human culture [says Dr James Martineau] when we threw away the "lives of the saints." . . . The soul grows Godlike, not by its downward gaze at inferior nature, but by its uplifted look at thought and goodness greater than its own.[1]

And Protestantism has its saints as well as Catholicism—men and women who not only sighed after the New Jerusalem, but did much to bring it nearer. Prominent among such is John Wesley. The weary ages will turn to him for impulse and inspiration, for he was one of God's greatest gifts to the world. As an undaunted preacher of the eternal love and righteousness ; as one who set aside comfort, ease, and worldly preferment that he might convince the country that it had a soul to be filled with the life of God ; as a prophet, reformer, inspirer, who dared all things for his Master, and faced the perils of land and sea, as well as undeserved calumny, that he might be true to the heavenly vision ; as, withal, a great leader and ruler of men, yet possessed with the gentleness and docility of a little child ; as a spiritual splendour, who brought heaven near this earth,—Wesley is unique, and his spirit speaks to thousands beyond his own communion, who thank God for him, and

[1] Faith and Self-Surrender, pp. 18, 19.

feel strengthened by the Godlike force that spoke
through him, and radiates from his memory still.
No Church can be what it was before, no indi-
vidual can remain as he was, after knowing what
John Wesley, strengthened by the grace of God,
was able to achieve. A spark of heaven's fire
enters the soul and leads life onwards to nobler
issues. His secret was best expressed in the hymn
of Tersteegen, which he translated :—

> " Thou hidden Love of God, whose height,
>     Whose depth unfathomed, no man knows,
> I see from far Thy beauteous light,
>     I inly sigh for Thy repose :
> My heart is pained, nor can it be
> At rest till it finds rest in Thee.
>     .    .    .    .    .    .
> Is there a thing beneath the sun
>     That strives with Thee my heart to share ?
> Ah ! tear it thence, and reign alone,
>     The Lord of every motion there :
> Then shall my heart from earth be free,
> When it has found repose in Thee."

A somewhat similar movement to that headed
by Wesley and Whitefield is to be found in the
thirteenth century—that founded by St Francis of
Assisi and St Dominic. Unquestionably the differences were great, and the movements took different expressions in accordance with their different
respective centuries. When the great Benedictine
abbeys were growing luxurious in their wealth, and
forgetting the spiritual functions for which they

existed ; when the secular clergy were no less faith-
less,—the spiritual life of the thirteenth century
found expression and inspiration in two great orders
—the one founded by Dominic and the other by
Francis of Assisi.  Both condemned the unfaithful-
ness of the Church, and were prophets who sought
to reform it.  St Dominic founded the order of
Preaching Friars and asserted the necessity of prophesying in the Christian Church ; St Francis of
Assisi founded the order of the Brothers Minor,—
and both in doing so saved religion.  "The thirteenth century, with juvenile ardour, overtook this
revolution, which has not yet reached its end.  In
the north of Europe it became incarnate in cathedrals, in the south in saints. . . . The thirteenth
century saints were true prophets."[1]  The life-
purpose of both St Dominic and St Francis was
the awakening of the Church, the quickening and
organisation of its spiritual life ; they both sought
to attain this by working within the Church itself,
and, after the manner of the thirteenth century, by
the creation of orders.  Whitefield and Wesley
were workers inspired by the same spirit, but they
belonged to the eighteenth century and worked in
accordance with its conditions.  Whitefield may be
compared to St Dominic, and those who became
inspired by his aims were many of the clergy
within the Churches ; Wesley may be compared to
St Francis of Assisi—and his societies, intended to

[1] Life of St Francis of Assisi, by Paul Sabatier, pp. xiii, xv.

quicken the spiritual life of the Church, were anal-
ogous to the fraternities of St Francis which spread
themselves over Europe. Wesley and St Francis
were brothers in spirit. When Wesley wrote—

> " No foot of land do I possess,
>    No cottage in this wilderness :
>        A poor, wayfaring man,
>    I lodge awhile in tents below ;
>    Or gladly wander to and fro,
>        Till I my Canaan gain.
>
> Nothing on earth I call my own,
> A stranger, to the world unknown,
>     I all their goods despise ;
> I trample on their whole delight,
> And seek a country out of sight,
>     A country in the skies ; "

he was uttering in verse the same life-purpose that
inspired St Francis when he said, " Deus meus,
mea omnia "—" My God is my all." Both were
" pilgrims of eternity " in time, and both were
workers for that city which endureth throughout
all generations ; both saved religion by the impulse
they gave the Church through their societies.

The rulers of the medieval Church recognised the
work of St Dominic and St Francis by giving official
imprimatur to two new orders, and by so doing
Popes Innocent III. and Honorius III. preserved
the unity of their Church, and kept within its pale
a great outburst of spiritual life that preserved
its unity for three centuries longer. Now Wesley

did the same work ; and although he bore a lifelong testimony to the fact that he was still a member of the Church of England, and desired his followers not to separate, the Church of the eighteenth century gave him no official recognition, and thus allowed the greatest of spiritual movements to become separated from it.   Dean Stanley held that the National Church possessed capabilities which have never yet been fully developed,[1] and if ever there was an occasion for developing them, it was at the period when John Wesley trod British roads, doing the work that the Church had failed to do, and preaching the Father-God to Calvinistic Scotland.   Wesley always attended church during his itinerancy, and never intended to separate from it; if he did so in fact—if, like a man in the boat, " he looked one way but moved in another " [2]—it was on account of the indifference with which he was met.   The Church of the eighteenth century needed flexibility and inventiveness to rise to the great occasion ; had it done so, Wesley's ideal would have been realised in the manner that he fondly desired it.

Wesley [says Dean Farrar] ought to have been made the General of a great Christian order within the Church of England, or a bishop *in partibus infidelium* for the evangelisation of the waste places, so to speak, —then the Methodist separation would never have taken place.[3]

---

[1] Life, vol. ii. p. 262.
[2] Rev. Price Hughes' Presidential Address, July 19, 1898.
[3] Wesley Centenary Volume, p. 179.

To take it according to its etymology [says Mrs
Oliphant], it (the term "Methodist") might as well
have been applied to the followers of Benedict or
Francis as those of John Wesley; and, in fact, this
movement, of which no one foresaw the importance,
was at its beginning much more like the foundation of
a monastic order than anything else. Had Wesley (we
repeat) been a Roman Catholic, from his hermitage he
would have come forth like Benedict to the formation
of a great community. His country, his race and
birth were, however, too many for him. . . . Had he
been in the Church of Rome (and there can be no
doubt that there was his fittest sphere), Wesley would
have been splendidly utilised, would have taken his
place with Dominic and Francis — founder of a vast
community. The Church of England, less wise, let the
man and his followers slip through her fingers. . . .
Wesley died as he lived, no schismatic, but a true son
of the Church, which was too sleepy even to eject him
for his innovations. But her sleep ended with the
generation which laughed horse-laughs at the Methodists, and shut their pulpits against their leader. The
work of Wesley lived after him, like every great work.
Long as his life was, it was not long enough to see the
full effect of his influence. And there can be no
doubt that, had he lived to see it, the awakening of
the Church of England would have been to him a more
joyful event than even the increase of the great society
which for nearly a hundred years has borne his name.[1]

Yet the Wesleyan movement affected the Scottish Church no less potently, and both Wesley
and they who bear his honoured name in Scotland

[1] Blackwood's Magazine: Historical Sketches of the Reign of
George II., pp. 437, 438, 456.

have wielded a quiet, unobtrusive, but earnest testimony for personal religion and piety in Scotland. They have been witnesses against a religion of opinion, and for a deep, spiritual Christianity; they have influenced Scottish religion for over a century by being centres of spiritual light and life—by existing for the advancement of purely spiritual aims and purposes. If the Wesley of Scottish history did not apparently achieve much by founding an extensive Church organisation on Scottish soil, the Wesley *within* Scottish religion has achieved very much. He has helped most efficiently in pervading the Churches with a more spiritual atmosphere, with greater endeavours towards a personal religion—towards a belief in God as a living Spirit, acting directly upon the soul, as the Redeemer of the human will, as giving in Christ a present redemption from the power of sin. The theological atmosphere of the eighteenth century was against Wesley, and called him Arminian, or, as that term was then understood, Socinian; but the living Wesley has entered all the Churches through the lovely hymns he and his brother wrote — through the lovely hymns which his movement inspired far and wide. If theology shut the door against him, Scottish piety opened its door to him; and every time Scottish congregations sing his hymns, they are admitting the Wesleyan influence, and are finding (perhaps unconsciously) an impulse and a warmth given to aspiration toward God. Those who could not say "Amen" to his theology have glowed with his piety, and the Wesleys have received thereby a new reign, which is broadening and not lessening. The outburst of sacred song that accompanied the Wesleyan revival has been assimilated into the hymnology of the Scottish Churches, and has acquired an influence of the most potent kind in moulding Scottish religion. Methodism has entered the Scottish Church as a great swelling praise and aspiration ; its hearty joyousness has swayed modern religious life.

Dean Stanley claimed Wesley as the "father of the Broad Church," and the "Broad Church" of which he was the pioneer in Scotland was that which afterwards found its typical names in M'Leod Campbell of Row, Thomas Erskine of Linlathen, and Bishop Ewing. His teaching was founded more on the Fatherhood than the Sovereignty of God; more on the paternal than the mere governmental relation of God to all men. He was, in the days of "particular election" and "limited atonement" and "unalterable decrees," an apostle of the Fatherhood, a preacher of God's love to all men, and of Christ's death as an atonement for all men ; of life as an education and not a trial. The Fatherhood of God was the ground of Wesley's teaching and the strength of Wesley's life, and it was to him "no mere amiability, but an equivalent for righteousness." Last century he was as "a voice

crying in the wilderness," but his voice was the
prophecy of the larger love and wider catholicity that
characterise the religious teaching of to-day. In
this sense Wesley was again a pioneer in Scotland.

As to the practical work of the Church, his
influence was no less profound. It is his glory
that he went to the English waste-places and had
a message of hope and comfort to the lost: his
work was from beginning to end a great Home
Mission work expanding into a great Foreign
Mission work, for the two cannot be separated.
It awakened the Church of England, but spiritual
momentum cannot be limited, and it told no less
potently upon the work of the Church of Scotland.
Begun at the close of last century, the movement
led to the awakening of the Church to its duty as
a National Church; it found afterwards its most
eloquent exponent in Chalmers and his great
scheme for Church Extension; it led to the
quickening of spiritual life over the country. The
movement has been nobly sustained by great and
earnest workers in all the Scottish Churches; it
has risen from zero to blood-heat; but who can
measure John Wesley's initial impulse? or the
spiritual influence he has wielded in moulding
those who have moulded others, and in organising
a great communion which has deeply affected the
religious tone of the English-speaking people?
The powers within the region of man's spirit cannot be tabulated, still it is historically true to

say that John Wesley's influence within the Church in inspiring the Home Mission and Foreign Mission movements cannot be gainsaid. The development of Guilds, connected with all the Churches, and within the Churches, is an acceptance of John Wesley's original idea of his societies. It is the derided ideal of one century becoming the accepted one for the next, and the great Guild system connected with the Scottish Church is the assimilation of John Wesley's ideal in forming his societies for the purpose of organising and stimulating the work of the Church. John Wesley anticipated by nearly a century Church expansion in Scotland as well as England, and development has been on his lines.

To a certain degree [said Dean Stanley] the Church of England has profited by his warnings ; and the services and sermons which have now been set on foot in almost every cathedral town of England—varying the stationary teaching by the constant introduction of new preachers, coming again and again, so as to infuse new life into these old congregations and a new spirit into these old grooves—are examples of the manner by which John Wesley's principles may be ingrafted into Churches seeming at first to be very far removed from Wesleyan institutions.[1]

It has been not less so in the Scottish Churches, and the Guild and Home Mission expansion are

[1] American Addresses, pp. 44, 45.

virtually the acceptance of the principles for which Wesley testified in the eighteenth century.

It is no exaggeration [says Mr Lecky] to say that Wesley has had a wider constructive influence in the sphere of practical religion than any other man who has appeared since the sixteenth century.[1]

I consider Wesley [said Mr Southey] as the most influential mind of the last century—the man who will have produced the greatest effects, centuries or perhaps millenniums hence, if the present race of men should continue so long.[2]

If the John Wesley of Scottish history founded no extensive organisation on Scottish soil, the John Wesley *in* Scottish religion has been an influence of the deepest and most pervading kind. In Scotland, assuredly, Wesley's work has been a victory; the spirit of his movement within the Church has been an expansive force.

But Scotland not only was influenced by Methodism, it also influenced Methodism. It produced some of its ablest preachers and exponents. "Scotland has been to Methodism at large what Britain was to the Roman Empire and what the Indian Empire has been to Britain—the training-ground of her ablest soldiers."[3] Scotland gave Wesley many able coadjutors, among whom may be mentioned Thomas Rankin, a native of Dunbar, who was appointed by Wesley in 1772 to the head of all

---

[1] History of the Eighteenth Century, vol. ii. p. 632.
[2] Letter to Wilberforce.      [3] Scotsman, March 2, 1891.

the Methodist ministry in America;[1] Alexander
Mather, born at Brechin in 1733, who came under
Wesley's influence in 1754, became one of his
preachers, and was always regarded as a confidential
adviser.   He was the second President of the Conference, after Wesley's death,[2] and thus attained the
highest position in the communion.   But supreme
among them all for ability and learning was Dr
Adam Clarke (1762-1832), who, although born in
Ireland, was of Scottish extraction.   He resembled
Wesley in his vast learning and attainments in
languages.   His first work was a Bibliographical
Dictionary (8 volumes); his greatest, an edition of
the Holy Scriptures with a Commentary.   His mis-
cellaneous works were published in 13 volumes, and
in vol. xiii. will be found an interesting diary of his
work in the Shetland Islands.   At the time when the
great Church Extension Scheme was going on in the
larger centres, Shetland had been overlooked ; there
were but twelve ministers there for a widely-scattered
population of 26,000 souls,[3] and Dr Clarke organised
in the islands Wesleyan mission stations in 1822 and
subsequent years.   Dr Clarke and the preachers
were everywhere kindly received, and did noble
work in Ultima Thule.   The diaries of the preachers
and the records of his own visits amid the perils of
the deep form a fascinating chapter in biography.

[1] Daniels' History, p. 219; and Jackson's Early Methodist
Preachers, vol. v. p. 136.
[2] Wesley and his Successors, pp. 27, 28.     [3] Vol. xiii. p. 128.

He was most earnest in pleading the interests of Shetlanders, and succeeded in raising £3000 in England for the purpose of providing churches in the islands.[1] Earnest Wesleyan, he was still an upholder of the Establishment, and in connection with the building of a new parish church at Lerwick wrote as follows to the building committee :—

Gentlemen,—While I consider the public ministry of the Word of God to be of infinite importance to mankind, I am also convinced that an established national religion in which all the essential doctrines of the Lord Jesus Christ are distinctly recognised and faithfully preached is one of the greatest blessings : under this conviction, I feel it my duty, not only to wish well to all such establishments, but to pray for their prosperity. As a proof of my sincerity in this profession, and of my respect for the inhabitants of Lerwick, have the goodness to receive the accompanying ten guineas as my donation towards the erection of your church in this town. — I have the honour to be, &c., ADAM CLARKE.

Church extension, inspired by such a spirit, was not sectarian rivalry but Christian service, and Dr Clarke's memory ought to be treasured by the Shetland people for his constant striving to serve their highest interests. It was said of him : "Christum pectore, Christum ore, Christum opere spirabat." [2] His advice to his preachers was : "Go on believingly. Read much. Pray much. Believe much." [3] His

---

[1] Vol. xiii. p. 458.    [2] Etheridge's Life of Dr Clarke, p. 163.
[3] Ibid., p. 429.

encouragement was : "I believe the infant work
in Shetland to be worth the whole kingdom." [1]
Almost his last public utterance was the following
noble testimony at Frome in 1831 :—

Fifty years have now passed since I first came to
this place, preaching the unsearchable riches of Christ.
Then, your preacher was a boy in years, unskilled in
experience, untaught in knowledge, but not wholly un-
learned in that truth which maketh wise the simple.
Since that time I have been always learning. I have
studied my own heart, and there is work there to be
done. I have been observing the ways, and striving
to know the love of God, in which is, indeed, a height
to attain, a depth to penetrate, a breadth to understand, which increases in magnitude as we draw nearer
to the fountain of light and glory. And now, my
brethren, I come again before you. My hairs are now
grey ; yet I acknowledge it as my proudest boast, that
Adam Clarke is still a learner at the feet of his
Master. [2]

Scotland, in giving workers such as these, gave
back a tribute to Wesley for his great work : it gave
as well as received. Scotland again influenced the
Church government of Methodism. Says Professor
Cowan of Aberdeen :—

While in many respects the Church of the Wesleys
differs from Presbyterianism both in doctrine and
in discipline, there can be no doubt, in the trans-
formation of Methodism towards the close of the

[1] Dunn's Life of Dr Clarke, p. 149.
[2] Life and Labours of Dr Adam Clarke, pp. 359, 360.

eighteenth century from a society within the Church
of England into an organisation outside of it, the
neighbourhood of a national Presbyterian Church in
Scotland exercised an appreciable influence both as
an incentive and as a model. "As soon as I am
dead," said Wesley, "the Methodists will be a regular
Presbyterian Church." His own maternal grandfather
and great-grandfather had been notable Presbyterians :
his father had been educated as a Presbyterian student,
and he himself in his system adopted the compromise
between Episcopacy and Presbytery which in the Scottish Reformed Church had been originally instituted,
but afterwards discarded—the office of the superintendent, above the ordinary pastors as individuals,
but subject to their jurisdiction as a body. In 1792
the Wesleyan leader Samuel Bradburn—the Methodist
Demosthenes as he has been called—frankly declared
in a controversial tract : "Our quarterly meetings answer to those Church meetings in Scotland called the
Presbytery ; our district meetings agree exactly with
the Synod ; and the Conference with the National or
General Assembly." "Whatever we may choose to
call ourselves, we must be Presbyterians." A few
years later, in 1796, a movement originated among the
Methodists in favour of an equal proportion of pastors
and laymen in the General Conference, after the model
of the Scottish Church courts ; and it is significant
that the leader of this new departure, Alexander Kilham, had laboured for three years as a superintendent
in Scotland.[1] The movement, although defeated, was
strong enough to result in the secession of 3000 members, who formed the New Connexion, now numbering 30,000 ; and within recent years the main body of

---

[1] Smith's Wesleyan Methodism, vol. ii. pp. 35-144.

P

Methodists have substantially adopted the views of the seceders by the establishment of a Representative Conference (auxiliary of the Conference proper), which takes place prior to that of pastors and superintendents, and in which ministers and lay deputies sit together. The approach of Methodism to Presbyterianism has thus become another stage closer than before.[1]

Another prominent man in this movement besides Alexander Kilham was the Rev. W. Thom, who was born at Aberdeen in 1741, and was included by Wesley in the "Legal Hundred." He was President of the first New Connexion Conference in 1797, as well as of five subsequent ones. So that along with the Rev. A. Kilham, who was born at Epworth, the Scottish minister, Mr Thom, not only gained the esteem of all who knew him, but had no small influence in moulding the polity of the Wesleyan Church.[2]

If Dean Stanley's hope be ever realised, that in the United Church of the future the Methodists will prove the link of unity between the Church of England and English Dissent, this connection just indicated between Presbytery and Methodism may yet prove a meeting-point for a greater unity still. Far-reaching results have been brought about by causes that have often seemed trivial : who knows

[1] The Scottish Church in Christendom. Baird Lectures for 1895. Pp. 82-84.

[2] See The Centenary of the Methodist New Connexion, pp. 85, 86.

what the future has in store, and what forces working in the present may bring it about?

This sketch must now be closed by mentioning
another celebration in connection with John Wesley
in Scotland. The centenary of Wesley's death on
March 2, 1891, was observed by a service in St
Giles' Cathedral, Edinburgh, in which prominent
clergymen of all Churches took part, and at
which representatives were officially present from
the Senate of the University of Edinburgh and the
Municipality of Edinburgh. The great Cathedral
was crowded to overflowing, and all classes did
honour to the memory of the great and good man.
The preacher described Wesley "as the greatest
religious reformer of modern times, and the dis-
coverer of the art of preaching." The 'Scotsman'
in commenting, both prospectively and retrospec-
tively, on the service, said :—

It is not always that the modern passion for cen-
tennial celebrations has such ample justification as it
has to-day. . . . Nowhere, however, can it have a
more striking celebration than is to be accorded to it
in the Scottish capital. The memorial service is in
itself a significant proof of the importance of the work
which John Wesley accomplished. Had the observance been confined to the handful of his disciples this
side the Border, it might have been indulgently passed
over. The world is never too severe when well-meant
endeavour is exaggerated by those whom it has en-
riched—when the memory of a personal benefactor is
tinged by a grateful idolatry. But the commemoration

in the Edinburgh cathedral means more than this. The presence of university and municipal representatives, along with ministers from other than Methodist Churches, is an independent testimony from minds well able to judge to the value of great religious movements, of which Wesley was the great propelling force.[1]

In Wesley, Britain acknowledges one of the greatest of her sons, and Christianity one of the most devoted of its modern disciples.[2]

The Scotland of the eighteenth century always gave John Wesley a courteous and respectful reception ; the Scotland of the nineteenth honoured him by the presence of her distinguished sons in her great Cathedral, and by prominent representatives of all the Churches presiding at what may be called the National Thanksgiving for his beautiful life and his unique work. In doing so, Scotland duly and worthily recognised the venerable apostle, who walked with God, and now rests in the rest of God.

[1] Scotsman, March 2, 1891.   [2] Ibid., March 3, 1891.

# APPENDIX.

First Visit of the Rev. Rev. John Wesley to
Scotland, 1751.

*Wed., 24 [April 1751].*—Mr Hopper and I took horse
between three and four (from Berwick-upon-Tweed)
and about seven came to Old Camus. Whether the
country was good or bad we could not see, having a
thick mist all the way. The Scotch towns are like
none which I ever saw, either in England, Wales, or
Ireland : there is such an air of antiquity in them all,
and such a peculiar oddness in their manner of building. But we were most surprized at the entertainment we met with in every place, so far different from
common report. We had all things good, cheap, in
great abundance, and remarkably well-dressed. In
the afternoon we rode by Preston-Field, and saw the
place of battle, and Colonel Gardiner's house. The
Scotch here affirm that he fought on foot after he was
dismounted, and refused to take quarter. ˙Be it as
it may, he is now " where the wicked cease from
troubling, and where the weary are at rest."
  We reached Musselborough between four and five.
I had no intention to preach in Scotland, nor did I
imagine there were any that desired I should. But I
was mistaken. Curiosity (if nothing else) brought
abundance of people together in the evening. And
whereas in the kirk (Mrs G—— informed me) there
used to be laughing and talking, and all the marks of
the grossest inattention ; but it was far otherwise

here : they remained as statues from the beginning of the sermon to the end.

*Thur.*, *25.*—We rode to Edinburgh, one of the dirtiest cities I had ever seen, not excepting Cölen in Germany.

We returned to Musselborough to dinner, whither we were followed in the afternoon by a little party of gentlemen from Edinburgh. I know not why any 'should complain of the shyness of the Scots towards strangers. All I spoke with were as free and open with me as the people of Newcastle or Bristol ; nor did any person move any dispute of any kind, or ask me any question concerning my opinion.

I preached again at six, on. " Seek ye the Lord while He may be found." I used great plainness of speech toward them ; and they all received it in love : so that the prejudice which the Devil had been several years planting, was torn up by the roots in one hour. After preaching, one of the Bailies of the town, with one of the Elders of the Kirk, came to me, and begged " I would stay with them awhile, if it were but two or three days, and they would fit up a far larger place than the school, and prepare seats for the congregation." Had not my time been fixed, I should gladly have complied. All I could now do was, to give them a promise that Mr Hopper would come back the next week and spend a few days with them.

*Fri.*, *26.*—I rode back to Berwick.[1]

## SECOND VISIT, 1753.

*Sun.*, *15* [*April 1753*].—I preached in the afternoon at Cockermouth, to wellnigh all the inhabitants of the town. Intending to go from thence into Scotland, I inquired concerning the road, and was informed I could not pass the arm of the sea which parts the two Kingdoms, unless I was at Bonas, about thirty miles from Cockermouth, soon after five in the morn-

[1] The Journal of the Rev. John Wesley, A.M., vol. ii. pp. 184, 185.

ing. At first I thought of taking an hour or two's sleep, and setting out at eleven or twelve ; but, upon farther consideration, we chose to take our journey first, and rest afterward. So we took horse about seven, and having a calm, moonshiny night, reached Bonas before one. After two or three hours' sleep, we set out again, without any faintness or drowsiness.

Our landlord, as he was guiding us over the Frith, very innocently asked, " How much a year we got by preaching thus ?" This gave me an opportunity of explaining to him that kind of gain which he seemed utterly a stranger to. He appeared to be quite amazed, and spake not one word, good or bad, till he took his leave. Presently after he went, my mare stuck fast in a quagmire, which was in the midst of the high road. But we could well excuse this : for the road all along for near fifty miles after, was such as I never saw any natural road, either in England or Ireland : nay, far better, notwithstanding the continued rain, than the turnpike road between London and Canterbury.

We dined at Dumfries, a clean, well-built town, having two of the most elegant churches (one at each end of the town) that I have seen. We reached Thorny - Hill in the evening. What miserable accounts pass current in England of the inns in Scotland ! Yet here, as well as wherever we called in our whole journey, we had not only everything we wanted, but everything readily, and in good order, and as clean as I ever desire.

*Tues.*, *17*.—We set out about four, and rode over several high, but extremely pleasant mountains, to Lead-Hill, a village of miners, resembling Placey, near Newcastle. We dined at a village called Lesmahaggy, and about eight in the evening reached Glasgow. A gentleman who had overtaken us on the road, sent one with us to Mr Gillies's house.

*Wed.*, *18*.—I walked over the city, which I take to be as large as Newcastle-on-Tyne. The University (like that of Dublin) is only one College, consisting of two small squares : I think not larger, nor at all handsomer, than those of Lincoln College in

Oxford. The habit of the Students gave me surprise. They wear scarlet gowns, reaching only to
their knees. Most I saw were very dirty, some
very ragged, and all of very coarse cloth. The high
church is a fine building : the outside is equal to that
of most cathedrals in England ; but it is miserably
defaced within, having no form, beauty, or symmetry
left.

At seven in the evening Mr G. began the service at
his own (the College) church. It was so full before
I came, that I could not get in without a good deal of
difficulty. After singing and prayer, he explained a
part of the Catechism, which he strongly and affectionately applied. After sermon he prayed and sung
again, and concluded with the blessing.

He then gave out, one after another, four hymns,
which about a dozen young men sung. He had before
desired those who were so minded, to go away : but
scarce any stirred till all was ended.

*Thur., 19.*—At seven I preached about a quarter of
a mile from the town. But it was an extremely rough
and blustering morning. And few people came either
at the time or place of my preaching : the natural consequence of which was, that I had but a small congregation. About four in the afternoon, a tent, as they
term it, was prepared, a kind of moving pulpit, covered
with canvas at the top, behind, and on the sides. In
this I preached, near the place where I was in the
morning, to near six times as many people as before.
And I am persuaded what was spoken came to some
of their hearts, not in word only, but in power.

*Fri., 20.*—I had designed to preach at the same
place ; but the rain made it impracticable. So Mr G.
desired me to preach in his church, where I began
between seven and eight. Surely with God nothing
is impossible ! Who would have believed, five and
twenty years ago, either that the Minister would have
desired it, or that I should have consented to preach
in a Scotch kirk ?

We had a far larger congregation at four in the
afternoon than the church could have contained. At

seven Mr G. preached another plain, homely, affectionate sermon. Has not God still a favour for this city? It was long eminent for serious religion. And He is able to repair what is now decayed, and to build up the waste places.

*Sat., 21.*—I had designed to ride to Edinburgh, but, at the desire of many, I deferred my journey till Monday. Here was now an open and effectual door; and not many adversaries: I could hear of none but a poor Seceder, who went up and down, and took much pains. But he did not see much fruit of his labour: the people would come and hear for themselves: both in the morning, when I explained (without touching the controversy) "Who shall lay anything to the charge of God's elect?" And in the afternoon, when I enforced, "Seek ye the Lord while He may be found."

*Sun., 22.*—It rained much. Nevertheless, upwards (I suppose) of a thousand people stayed with all willingness, while I explained and applied, "This is life eternal, to know Thee, the only true God, and Jesus Christ whom Thou hast sent." I was desired to preach afterwards at the prison, which I did about nine o'clock. All the felons, as well as debtors, behaved with such reverence as I never saw at any prison in England. It may be some, even of these sinners, will occasion joy in heaven.

The behaviour of the people at church, both morning and afternoon, was beyond any thing I ever saw, but in our congregations. None bowed or curtsied to each other, either before or after the service: from the beginning to the end of which none talked, or looked at any but the Minister. Surely much of the power of godliness was here, when there is so much of the form still.

The meadow, where I stood in the afternoon, was filled from side to side. I spoke as closely as ever in my life. Many of the students, and many of the soldiers, were there: and I bear them witness, they could bear sound doctrine.

*Mon., 23.*—I had a great desire to go round by Kilsythe, in order to see that venerable man, Mr Robe, who was every day expecting (what his soul longed for) "to depart and be with Christ." But the continual rains had made it impracticable for us to add so many miles to our day's journey. So we rode on, straight by the Kirk of Shots : reached Edinburgh by five in the afternoon : lodged at Tranent, and on Tuesday, 24, came to Berwick in good time, where I preached on the Bowling-Green at six.[1]

## THIRD VISIT, 1757.

*Mon., 30 [May 1757].*—I rode to Wigton : a neat, well-built town, on the edge of Cumberland. . . . Between four and five we crossed Solway Firth, and before seven reached an ill-looking house, called The Brow, which we came to by mistake, having passed the house we were directed to. I believe God directed us better than man. Two young women, we found, kept the house, who had lost both their parents : their mother very lately. I had great liberty in praying with them and for them. Who knows but God will fasten something upon them, which they will not easily shake off ?

*Tues., 31.*—I breakfasted at Dumfries, and spent an hour with a poor backslider of London, who had been for some years settled there. We then rode through an uncommonly pleasant country (so widely distant is common report from truth) to Thorny-Hill, two or three miles from the Duke of Queensborough's seat : an ancient and noble pile of building, delightfully situated, on the side of a pleasant and fruitful hill : but it gives no pleasure to its owner, for he does not even behold it with his eyes. Surely this is a sore evil under the sun : a man has all things, and enjoys nothing.

We rode afterward partly over, and partly between some of the finest mountains, I believe, in Europe,

---

[1] Journal, vol. ii. pp. 239-242.

higher than most, if not than any in England, and
clothed with grass to the very top. Soon after four
we came to Lead-hill, a little town at the foot of the
mountains, wholly inhabited by miners.

*Wednesday, June 1.*—We rode on to Glasgow : a
mile short of which we met Mr Gillies, riding out to
meet us.

In the evening the tent (so they call a covered
pulpit) was placed in the yard of the poorhouse, a
very large and commodious place. Fronting the pulpit was the infirmary, with most of the patients at
or near the windows. Adjoining to this was the hospital for lunatics : several of them gave deep attention.
And cannot God give them also the spirit of a sound
mind? After sermon they brought four children
to baptize. I was at the kirk in the morning,
while the Minister baptized several, immediately
after sermon : so I was not at a loss as to their
manner of baptizing. I believe this removed much
prejudice.

*Fri., 3 [June].*—At seven the congregation was increased, and earnest attention sat on every face. In
the afternoon we walked to the college, and saw the
new library, with the collection of pictures. Many of
them are by Raphael, Rubens, Vandyke, and other
eminent hands : but they have not room to place them
to advantage, their whole building being very small.

*Sat., 4.*—I walked through all parts of the old cathedral, a very large and once beautiful structure ; I
think more lofty than that at Canterbury, and nearly
the same length and breadth : we then went up the
main steeple, which gave us a fine prospect, both of
the city and the adjacent country. A more fruitful
and better cultivated plain is scarce to be seen in
England. Indeed nothing is wanting but more trade
(which would naturally bring more people) to make a
great part of Scotland no way inferior to the best
counties in England.

I was much pleased with the seriousness of the
people in the evening ; but still I prefer the English
congregation. I cannot be reconciled to men sitting at

prayer, or covering their heads while they are singing praise to God.

*Sun.,* *5.* — At seven the congregation was just as large as my voice could reach ; and I did not spare them at all ; so if any will deceive himself, I am clear of his blood. In the afternoon it was judged two thousand, at least, went away, not being able to hear ; but several thousands heard very distinctly, the evening being calm and still. After preaching I met as many as desired it, of the members of the praying societies. I earnestly advised them to meet Mr Gillies every week ; and at their other meetings not to talk loosely, and in general, (as their manner had been,) on some head of religion, but to examine each other's hearts and lives.

*Mon.,* *6.*—We took horse early, and in three hours reached the Kirk of Shots, where the landlord seemed to be unusually affected by a few minutes' conversation ; as did also the woman of the house where we dined. We came to Musselborough at five. I went to an inn, and sent for Mr Bailiff Lindsey, whom I had seen several years ago. He came immediately, and desired me to make his house my home. At seven I preached in the poor-house, to a large, and deeply attentive congregation. But the number of people making the room extremely hot, I preached in the morning before the door. Speaking afterwards to the members of the society, I was agreeably surprised to find more than two-thirds knew in whom they had believed ; and the tree was known by its fruits. The national shyness and stubbornness were gone, and they were as open and teachable as little children. At seven five or six and forty of the fifty dragoons, and multitudes of the town's-people attended. Is the time come, that even these wise Scots shall become fools for Christ's sake ?

*Wed.,* *8.*—I rode to Dunbar. Here also I found a little society, most of them rejoicing in God their Saviour. At eleven I went out into the main street, and began speaking to a congregation of two men and two women. These were soon joined by above twenty

little children, and not long after by a large number of
young and old. On a sudden the sun broke out and
shone full in my face ; but in a few moments I felt it
not. In the afternoon I rode to Berwick-upon-Tweed.
They did not expect me till the next day ; however, a
congregation quickly assembled, and one as large, if
not larger, at five in the morning.

*Thur.*, *9.*—To-day, ' Douglas,' the play which has
made so much noise, was put into my hands. I was
astonished to find it is one of the finest tragedies I
ever read. What pity that a few lines were not left
out ! and that it was ever acted at Edinburgh !

*Fri.*, *10.*—I found myself much out of order, till the
flux stopped at once, without any medicine ; but being
still weak, and the sun shining extremely hot, I was
afraid I should not be able to go round by Kelso. Vain
fear ! God took care for this also. The wind which
had been full east for several days, turned this morning
full west, and blew just in our face ; and about ten the
clouds rose, and kept us cool till we came to Kelso.

At six William Coward and I went to the Market-
house. We stayed some time, and neither man,
woman, nor child came near us. At length I began
singing a Scotch psalm, and fifteen or twenty people
came within hearing, but with great circumspection,
keeping their distance, as though they knew not what
might follow. But while I prayed, their number
increased, so that in a few minutes there was a pretty
large congregation. I suppose the chief men of the
town were there, and I spared neither rich nor poor.
I almost wondered at myself, it not being usual with
me to use so keen and cutting expressions ; and I
believe many felt that, for all their form, they were
but heathens still.

*Sat.*, *11.*—Near as many were present at five, to
whom I spoke full as plain as before. Many looked
as if they would look us through ; but the shyness
peculiar to this nation, prevented their saying anything
to me, good or bad, while I walked through them to
our inn.[1]

[1] Diary, vol. ii. pp. 357-360.

FOURTH VISIT, 1759.

*Mon.*, *21* [*May 1759*].—I preached at ten, in the
Market-place at Wigton, and came to Solway Frith,
just as the water was fordable.  At some times it is so,
three hours in twelve ; at other times barely one.

After making a short bait at Rothwell, we came to
Dumfries before six o'clock.  Having time to spare, we
took a walk in the church-yard, one of the pleasantest
places I ever saw.  A single tomb I observed there,
which was about an hundred and thirty years old.
But the inscription was very hardly legible : "Quando-
quidem remanent ipsis quoque fata sepulchris !"  So
soon do even our sepulchres die !  Strange, that men
should be so careful about them !  But are not many
self - condemned therein ?  They see the folly, while
they run into it.  So poor Mr Prior, speaking of his
own tomb, has those melancholy words : " For this
last piece of human vanity I bequeath five hundred
pounds."

*Tues.*, *22.*—We rode through a pleasant country, to
Thorny-Hill ; near which is the grand seat of the
Duke of Queensborough.  How little did the late
Duke imagine, that his son would plough up his
park, and let his house run to ruin !  But let it go !
In a little time the earth itself, and all the works
of it, shall be burned up.

Hence we rode through and over huge mountains,
green to the very top, to Lead-hills, a village containing five hundred families who have had no Minister
for these four years.  So in Scotland the poor have not
the Gospel preached !  Who shall answer for the blood
of these men ?

Early in the evening we came to Lesmahagow, a
village not so large as Lead-hills.  It has, however,
two Ministers.  Here also we walked down to the
churchyard, by the side of which a little clear river
runs, near the foot of a high and steep mountain.  The
wood which covers this makes the walks that run on

its sides pleasant beyond imagination. But what taste have the good people of the town for this? As much as the animals that graze on the river bank.

*Wed.*, *23.*—We took horse soon after four, and did not stop before we came to Glasgow ; having hardly seen a cloud in the sky since we set out from Whitehaven.

I preached at seven, in the Poorhouse ; and at seven in the morning, Thursday, 24th. But in the evening we were obliged to be abroad, and I used great plainness of speech. All suffered the word of exhortation ; some seemed to be a little affected.

*Sat.*, *26.*—I found the little Society which I had joined here two years since had soon split in pieces. In the afternoon I met several of the Members of the praying societies, and showed them what Christian fellowship was, and what need they had of it. About forty of them met me on Sunday 27, in Mr Gillies's kirk, immediately after evening service. I left them determined to meet Mr Gillies weekly, at the same time and place. If this be done, I shall try to see Glasgow again ; if not, I can employ my time better.

At seven in the morning we had a numerous congregation, though small compared to that in the evening. Yet my voice was so strengthened that I believe all could hear. I spoke very plain on, "Ye must be born again." Now I am clear of the blood of this people. I have delivered my own soul.

*Mon.*, *28.*—I rode through Edinburgh to Musselburgh, and preached in the evening to a deeply attentive congregation.

*Wed.*, *30.*—I rode on to Dunbar, and at six in the evening preached in a large, open place (as also the next day). Both poor and rich quickly attended, though most of them shivering with cold ; for the weather was so changed within a few days, that it seemed more like December than May.

Lodging with a sensible man, I inquired particularly into the present discipline of the Scotch parishes. In one parish, it seems, there are twelve ruling Elders ; in another there are fourteen. And what are these?

Men of great sense and deep experience? Neither one nor the other. But they are the richest men in the parish. And are the richest of course the best and the wisest men? Does the Bible teach this? I fear not. What manner of governors then will these be? Why, they are generally just as capable of governing a parish as of commanding an army.[1]

## FIFTH VISIT, 1761.

*Mon.*, *27* [*April 1761*].—Before noon we came to Solway Frith. The guide told us it was not passable, but I resolved to try, and got over well. Having lost ourselves but twice or thrice in one of the most difficult roads I ever saw, we came to Moffat in the evening.

*Tues.*, *28.*—We rode partly over the mountains, partly with mountains on either hand, between which was a clear, winding river, and about four in the afternoon reached Edinburgh.

Here I met Mr Hopper, who had promised to preach in the evening, in a large room, lately an episcopal meeting-house.

*Wed.*, *29.*—It being extremely cold, I preached in the same room at seven. Some of the reputable hearers cried out in amaze, "Why, this is sound doctrine! Is this he of whom Mr Wh. used to talk so?" Talk as he will, I shall not retaliate.

I preached again in the evening, and the next day rode round by the Queen's-Ferry to Dundee; but the wind being high, the boatmen could not, at least would not, pass. Nor could we pass the next day till between nine and ten. We then rode on through Montrose to Stonehaven. Here Mr Memis met us, and on Saturday morning brought us to his house at Aberdeen.

In the afternoon, I sent to the Principal and Regent to desire leave to preach in the College-Close. This

---

[1] Diary, vol. ii. pp. 427-429.

was readily granted; but as it began to rain, I was desired to go into the hall. I suppose this is full a hundred feet long, and seated all round. The congregation was large, notwithstanding the rain, and full as large at five in the morning.

*Sunday, May 3d.*—I heard two useful sermons at the Kirk, one preached by the Principal of the College, the other by the Divinity Professor. A huge multitude afterwards gathered together in the College-Close; and all that could hear seemed to receive the truth in love. I then added about twenty to the little Society. Fair blossoms! But how many of these will bring forth fruit?

*Mon., 4.*—We had another large congregation at five. Before noon, twenty more came to me, desiring to cast in their lot with us, and appearing to be cut to the heart.

About noon, I took a walk to the King's College, in Old Aberdeen. It has three sides of a square handsomely built, not unlike Queen's College in Oxford. Going up to see the Hall, we found a large company of ladies, with several gentlemen. They looked and spoke to one another, after which one of the gentlemen took courage and came to me. He said, "We came last night to the College-Close, but could not hear, and should be extremely obliged if you would give us a short discourse here." I knew not what God might have to do, and so began without delay, on, "God was in Christ, reconciling the world unto Himself." I believe the word was not lost. It fell as dew on the tender grass.

In the afternoon, I was walking in the Library of the Marischal College, when the Principal, and the Divinity Professor, came to me, and the latter invited me to his lodgings, where I spent an hour very agreeably. In the evening, the eagerness of the people made them ready to trample each other under foot. It was some time before they were still enough to hear; but then they devoured every word. After preaching, Sir Archibald Grant (whom business had called to town) sent and desired to speak to me. I could not then, but promised to wait upon him, with God's leave, on my return to Edinburgh.

*Tues., 5.*—I accepted the Principal's invitation, and spent an hour with him at his house. I observed no stiffness at all, but the easy good breeding of a man of sense and learning. I suppose both he and all the Professors, with some of the Magistrates, attended in the evening. I set all the windows open, but the hall, notwithstanding, was as hot as a bagnio. But this did not hinder either the attention of the people, or the blessing of God.

*Wed., 6.*—We dined at Mr Ogilvey's, one of the Ministers, between whom the city is divided. A more open-hearted, friendly man, I know not that I ever saw. And indeed I have scarce seen such a set of Ministers in any town of Great Britain or Ireland. At half an hour after six, I stood in the College-Close, and proclaimed Christ crucified. My voice was so strengthened that all could hear : all were earnestly attentive. I have now cast my bread upon the waters : may I find it again after many days !

*Thur., 7.*—Leaving near ninety members in the Society, I rode over to Sir A. Grant's, near Monymusk, about twenty miles north-west from Aberdeen. It lies in a fruitful and pleasant valley, much of which is owing to Sir Archibald's improvements, who has ploughed up abundance of waste ground, and planted some millions of trees. His stately old house is surrounded by gardens, and rows of trees, with a clear river on one side : and about a mile from his house, he has laid out a small valley into walks and gardens, on one side of which the river runs. On each side rises a steep mountain ; one rocky and bare, the other covered with trees, row above row, to the very top.

About six, we went to the church. It was pretty well filled with such persons as we did not look for, so near the Highlands. But if we were surprised at their appearance, we were much more so at their singing. Thirty or forty sang an anthem after sermon, with such voices as well as judgment, that I doubt whether they could have been excelled at any cathedral in England.

*Fri., 8.*—We rode to Glammis, about sixty-four measured miles ; and on Saturday, 9th, about sixty-six more to Edinburgh. I was tired : however, I would not disappoint the congregation : and God gave me strength according to my day.

*Sun., 10.*—I had designed to preach near the Infirmary ; but some of the managers would not suffer it. So I preached in our Room, morning and evening, even to the rich and honourable. And I bear them witness, they will endure plain dealing, whether they profit by it or not.

*Mon., 11.*—I took my leave of Edinburgh for the present. The situation of the city, on a hill shelving down on both sides, as well as to the east, with the stately castle upon a craggy rock on the west, is inexpressibly fine ; and the main street so broad and finely paved, with the lofty houses on either hand (many of them seven or eight stories high), is far beyond any in Great Britain. But how can it be suffered, that all manner of filth should still be thrown even into this street continually ? Where are the magistrates, the gentry, the nobility of this land ? Have they no concern for the honour of their nation ? How long shall the capital city of Scotland, yea, and the chief street of it, stink worse than a common sewer ? Will no lover of his country, or of decency and common sense, find a remedy for this ?

Holyrood House, at the entrance of Edinburgh, the ancient palace of the Scottish kings, is a noble structure ; it was rebuilt and furnished by King Charles the Second. One side of it is a picture gallery, wherein are pictures of all the Scottish kings ; and an original one of the celebrated Queen Mary. It is scarce possible for any who looks at this, to think her such a monster as some have painted her : nor indeed for any who considers the circumstances of her death, equal to that of an ancient martyr.

I preached in the evening at Musselborough, and at five in the morning. Then we rode on to Haddington, where (the rain driving me in) I preached, between nine and ten, in Provost Dickson's parlour. About one I preached at North Berwick, a pretty large town, close to the sea-shore ; and at seven in the evening, (the rain continuing) in the house at Dunbar.

*Wed., 13.*—It being a fair, mild evening, I preached near the Quay, to most of the inhabitants of the town, and spoke full as plain as the evening before. Every one seemed to receive it in love : probably if there was regular preaching here, much good might be done.

*Thur., 14.*—I set out early, and preached, at noon, on the Bowling-Green at Berwick-upon-Tweed. In the evening I preached at Alnwick.[1]

## SIXTH VISIT, 1763.

*Mon., May 16 [1763].*—Setting out a month later than usual, I judged it needful to make the more haste ; so I took postchaises, and, by that means, easily reached Newcastle on Wednesday, 18th. Thence I went on at leisure, and came to Edinburgh on Saturday, 21st. The next day I had the satisfaction of spending a little time with Mr Whitefield. Humanly speaking, he is worn out : but we have to do with Him who hath all power in heaven and earth.

*Mon., 23.*—I rode to Forfar, and on Tuesday, the 24th, rode on to Aberdeen.

*Wed., 25.*—I inquired into the state of things here. Surely never was there a more open door. The four Ministers of Aberdeen, the Minister of the adjoining town, and the three Ministers of Old Aberdeen, hitherto seem to have no dislike, but rather to "wish us good luck in the name of the Lord." Most of the town's people as yet seem to wish us well, so that there is no opposition of any kind. O what spirit ought a Preacher to be of, that he may be able to bear all this sunshine !

---

[1] Diary, vol. iii. pp. 50-53.

About noon I went to Gordon's Hospital, built near the town for poor children. It is an exceeding handsome building, and (what is not common) kept exceeding clean. The gardens are pleasant, well laid out, and in extremely good order. But the old bachelor who founded it, has expressly provided, That no woman should ever be there.

At seven, the evening being fair and mild, I preached to a multitude of people in the College-Close, on, "Stand in the ways and see, and ask for the old paths." But the next evening, the weather being raw and cold, I preached in the College-hall. What an amazing willingness to hear runs through this whole Kingdom! There want only a few zealous, active labourers, who desire nothing but God, and they might soon carry the Gospel through all this country, even as high as the Orkneys.

*Fri., 27.*—I set out for Edinburgh again. About one, I preached at Brechin. All were deeply attentive. Perhaps a few may not be forgetful hearers. Afterwards we rode on to Broughty Castle, two or three miles below Dundee. We were in hopes of passing the river here, though we could not at the town : but we found our horses could not pass till eleven or twelve at night. So we judged it would be best to go over ourselves, and leave them behind. In a little time we procured a kind of a boat, about half as long as a London wherry, and three or four feet broad. Soon after we had put off, I perceived it leaked on all sides, nor had we anything to lade out the water. When we came toward the middle of the river, which was three miles over, the wind being high, and the water rough, our boatmen seemed a little surprised. But we encouraged them to pull away, and, in less than half an hour, we landed safe. Our horses were brought after us, and the next day we rode on to Kinghorn Ferry, and had a pleasant passage to Leith.

*Sun., 29.*—I preached at seven, in the High School-yard at Edinburgh. It being the time of the General Assembly, which drew together not the Ministers only, but abundance of the nobility and gentry, many of both sorts were present : but abundantly more at five in the afternoon. I spoke as plain as ever I did in my life : but I never knew any in Scotland offended at plain-dealing. In this respect, the North Britons are a pattern to all mankind.

*Mon., 30.*—I rode to Dunbar. In the evening it was very cold, and the wind was exceeding high. Nevertheless I would not pen myself up in the room, but resolved to preach in the open air. We saw the fruit : many attended, notwithstanding the cold, who never set foot in the room ; and I am still persuaded much good will be done here, if we have zeal and patience.[1]

SEVENTH VISIT, 1764.

The next evening [*May 24*] I preached at Dunbar : and on Friday, 25th, about ten, at Haddington, in Provost D——'s yard, to a very elegant congregation. But I expect little good will be done here : for we begin at the wrong end. Religion must not go " from the greatest to the least," or the power "would appear to be of men." In the evening I preached at Musselborough, and the next, on the Calton Hill at Edinburgh. It being the time of the General Assembly, many of the Ministers were there. The wind was high and sharp, and blew away a few delicate ones : but most of the congregation did not stir till I had concluded.

*Sun., 27.*—At seven I preached in the High School-yard, on the other side of the city. The morning was extremely cold. In the evening it blew a storm. However, having appointed to be on the Calton Hill, I began there, to a huge congregation. At first, the wind was a little troublesome, but I soon forgot it : and so did the people, for an hour and a half, in which I fully delivered my own soul.

*Mon., 28.* — I spent some hours at the General

<hr>

[1] Diary, vol. iii. pp. 129, 130.

Assembly, composed of about a hundred and fifty Ministers. I was surprised to observe, 1. That any one was admitted, even lads twelve or fourteen years old : 2. That the chief speakers were lawyers, six or seven on one side only : 3. That a single question took up the whole time, which, when I went away, seemed to be as far from a conclusion as ever, namely, "Shall Mr Lindsay be removed to Kilmarnock parish or not ?" The argument for it was, "He has a large family, and this living is twice as good as his own." The argument against it was, "The people are re-solved not to hear him, and will leave the kirk if he comes." If then the real point in view had been, as their law directs, "Majus bonum Ecclesiae," instead of taking up five hours, the debate might have been determined in five minutes.

On Monday and Tuesday I spoke to the members of the society severally.

*Thur., 31.*—I rode to Dundee, and, about an hour after six, preached on the side of a meadow near the town. Poor and rich attended. Indeed there is seldom fear of wanting a congregation in Scotland. But the misfortune is they know everything : so they learn nothing.

*Friday, June 1.*—I rode to Brechin, where Mr Blair received me in the most friendly manner. In the afternoon, I preached on the side of a hill near the town, where we soon forgot the cold. I trust there will be not only a knowing, but a loving people in this place. About seven, Mr B. was occasionally mentioning what had lately occurred in the next parish. I thought it worth a farther inquiry, and therefore ordered our horses to be brought immediately. Mr B. guided us to Mr Ogilvie's house, the Minister of the parish, who informed us, "That a strange disorder had appeared in his parish between thirty and forty years ago : but that nothing of the kind had been known there since, till some time in September last. A boy was then taken ill, and so continues still. In the end of January or beginning of February, many other children were taken, chiefly girls, and a few

grown persons. They begin with an involuntary
shaking of their hands and feet. Then their lips are
convulsed : next their tongue, which seems to cleave
to the roof of their mouth : then the eyes are staring
terribly, and the whole face variously distorted :
presently they start up, and jump ten, fifteen, or
twenty times together straight upwards, two, three,
or more feet from the ground. Then they start
forward and run with amazing swiftness, two, three
or five hundred yards. Frequently they run up like
a cat to the top of a house, and jump on the ridge of
it, as on the ground : but wherever they are, they
never fall or miss their footing at all. After they
have run and jumped for some time, they drop down
as dead. When they come to themselves, they usually
tell when and where they shall be taken again :
frequently, how often and where they shall jump,
and to what places they shall run."

I asked, "Are any of them near ?" He said, "Yes,
at those houses." We walked thither without delay.
One of them was four years and a half old, the other
about eighteen. The child, we found, had had three
or four fits that day, running and jumping like the
rest, and in particular leaping many times from a
high table to the ground without the least hurt. The
young woman was the only person of them all, who
used to keep her senses during the fit. In answer to
many questions, she said, "I first feel a pain in my
left foot, then in my head : then my hands and feet
shake, and I cannot speak : and quickly I begin to
jump or run." While we were talking, she cried out,
"O ! I have a pain in my foot : it is in my hand : it
is here at the bending of my arm. O ! my head, my
head, my head." Immediately her arms were stretched
out, and were as an iron bar : I could not bend one
of her fingers : and her body was bent backward :
the lower part remaining quite erect, while her back
formed exactly half a circle, her head swinging
even with her hips. I was going to catch her, but
one said, "Sir you may let her alone, for they never
fall." But I defy all mankind to account for her

not falling, when the trunk of her body hung in that manner.

In many circumstances this case goes far beyond the famous one mentioned by Boerhaave, particularly in that—their telling before, when and how they should be taken again. Whoever can account for this on natural principles, has my free leave : I cannot. I therefore believe, if this be in part a natural distemper, there is something preternatural too. Yet supposing this, I can easily conceive, Satan will so disguise his part therein, that we cannot precisely determine which part of the disorder is natural, and which preternatural.

*Sat. 2.*—I rode to Aberdeen ; and preached in the evening in the College Hall, and at seven in the morning, Sunday, the 3rd. At four in the afternoon, I preached to a crowded audience in the College Kirk, at Old Aberdeen. At seven I preached in the College-Close, at New Aberdeen : but the congregation was so exceeding large that many were not able to hear : however, many did hear, and I think feel, the application of "Thou art not far from the kingdom of God."

We want nothing here but a larger house : and the foundation of one is laid already. It is true we have little money, and the Society is poor : but we know in whom we have believed.

*Thur., 7.*—I rode over to Sir Archibald Grant's, twelve computed miles from Aberdeen. It is surprising to see how the country between is improved, even within these three years. On every side the wild, dreary moors are ploughed up, and covered with rising corn. All the ground near Sir Archibald's in particular, is as well cultivated as most in England. About seven I preached : the Kirk was pretty well filled, though upon short notice. Certainly this is a nation "swift to hear, and slow to speak," though not "slow to wrath."

Mr Grant, a gentleman from the county of Murray, came in soon after us : and understanding we were going north, desired we would call at the Grange Green in our way.

*Fri., 8.*—In the morning I rode to Old-Meldrum, and preached in the Market-place at noon, to a large and serious congregation, among whom were the Minister and his wife : but I was more surprised to see a company of our friends from Aberdeen, several of whom had come on foot, twelve old Scotch miles, and intended to walk back thither the same day. In the afternoon we rode on to Banff. I had designed to preach, but the stormy weather would not permit. We set out early on Saturday morning, and reached Nairn in the evening.

*Sun., 10.*—About eight we reached Inverness. I could not preach abroad, because of the rain, nor could I hear of any convenient room, so that I was afraid my coming hither would be in vain, all ways seeming to be blocked up. At ten I went to the Kirk. After service Mr Fraser, one of the Ministers, invited us to dinner, and then to drink tea. As we were drinking tea, he asked, "At what hour I would please to preach." I said, "At half an hour past five." The high kirk was filled in a very short time : and I have seldom found greater liberty of spirit. The other Minister came afterwards to our inn, and showed the most cordial affection. Were it only for this day, I should not have regretted the riding a hundred miles.

*Mon., 11.*—A gentleman, who lives three miles from the town, invited me to his house, assuring me, the Minister of his parish would be glad if I would make use of his kirk ; but time would not permit as I had appointed to be at Aberdeen on Wednesday. All I could do was to preach once more at Inverness. I think the church was fuller now than before : and I could not but observe the remarkable behaviour of the whole congregation after service. Neither man, woman, nor child spake one word all the way down the main street : indeed the seriousness of the people is the less surprising, when it is considered that for at least a hundred years this town has had such a succession of pious ministers as very few in Great Britain have known.

After Edinburgh, Glasgow, and Aberdeen, I think

Inverness is the largest town I have seen in Scotland. The main streets are broad and straight, the houses mostly old, but not very bad nor very good. It stands in a pleasant and fruitful country, and has all things needful for life and godliness. The people, in general, speak remarkably good English, and are of a friendly, courteous behaviour.

About eleven we took horse. While we were dining at Nairn, the innkeeper said, "Sir, the gentlemen of the town have read the little book you gave me on Saturday, and would be glad if you would please to give them a sermon." Upon my consenting, the bell was immediately rung, and the congregation was quickly in the kirk. O what a difference is there between South and North Britain ! Every one here at least loves to hear the word of God : and none takes it into his head to speak one uncivil word to any, for endeavouring to save their souls.

Doubting whether Mr Grant was come home, Mr Kershaw called at the Grange Green, near Forres, while I rode forward : but Mr Grant soon called me back. I have seldom seen a more agreeable place. The house is an old castle, which stands on a little hill, with a delightful prospect all four ways : and the hospitable master left nothing undone to make it still more agreeable. He showed us all his improvements, which are very considerable, in every branch of husbandry. In his gardens many things were more forward than at Aberdeen, yea, or Newcastle. And how is it that none but one Highland gentleman has discovered that we have a tree in Britain, as easily raised as an ash, the wood of which is of full as fine a red as mahogany, namely, the Laburnum? I defy any mahogany to exceed the chairs which he has lately made of this.

*Thur.*, *12.*—We rode through the pleasant and fertile county of Murray to Elgin. I never suspected before that there was any such country as this near a hundred and fifty miles beyond Edinburgh ; a county which is supposed to have generally six weeks more sunshine in a year than any part of Great Britain.

At Elgin are the ruins of a noble cathedral, the largest that I remember to have seen in the kingdom. We rode thence to the Spey, the most rapid river, next the Rhine, that I ever saw. Though the water was not breast high to our horses, they could very hardly keep their feet. We dined at Keith, and rode on to Strathbogie, much improved by the linen manufacture. All the country from Fochabers to Strathbogie has little houses scattered up and down : and not only the valleys but the mountains themselves are improved with the utmost care ; there want only more trees to make them more pleasant than most of the mountains in England. The whole family at our inn, eleven or twelve in number, gladly joined with us in prayer at night : indeed so they did at every inn where we lodged : for among all the sins they have imported from the English, the Scots have not yet learned, at least not the common people, to scoff at sacred things.

*Wed., 13.*—We reached Aberdeen about one. Between six and seven, both this evening and the next, I preached in the shell of the new house, and found it a time of much consolation.

*Fri., 15.*—We set out early, and came to Dundee just as the boat was going off. We designed to lodge at the house on the other side, but could not get meat, drink, or good words ; so we were constrained to ride on to Cupar. After travelling near ninety miles, I found no weariness at all ; neither were our horses hurt. Thou, O Lord, dost save both man and beast !

*Sat., 16.*—We had a ready passage at Kinghorn, and in the evening I preached on the Calton Hill, to a very large congregation ; but a still larger assembled at seven on Sunday morning, in the High Schoolyard. Being afterwards informed that the Lord's Supper was to be administered in the West Kirk, I knew not what to do, but at length I judged it best to embrace the opportunity, though I did not admire the manner of administration. After the usual morning service, the Minister enumerated several sorts of sinners, whom he forbade to approach. Two long tables were set on the sides of one aisle, covered with tablecloths. On each side of them a bench was placed for the people. Each table held four- or five-and-thirty. Three Ministers sat at the top, behind a cross-table ; one of whom made a long exhortation, closed with the words of our Lord ; and then breaking the bread, gave it to him who sat on each side him. A piece of bread was then given to him who sat first on each of the four benches. He broke off a little piece, and gave the bread to the next ; so it went on, the Deacons[1] giving more when wanted. A cup was then given to the first person on each bench, and so by one to another. The Minister continued his exhortation all the time they were receiving. Then four verses of the twenty-second Psalm were sung, while new persons sat down at the tables. A second Minister then prayed, consecrated, and exhorted. I was informed the service usually lasted till five in the evening. How much more simple, as well as more solemn, is the service of the Church of England ?

The evening congregation on the hill was far the largest I have seen in the kingdom, and the most deeply affected ; many were in tears, more seemed cut to the heart. Surely this time will not soon be forgotten. Will it not appear in the annals of eternity ?

*Mon.*, *18.*—I set out early, and reached Wooler about four in the afternoon.[2]

EIGHTH VISIT, 1765.

*Tues.*, *23* [*April 1765*].—I preached at Dunbar about noon, and in the evening at Edinburgh. My coming was quite seasonable (though unexpected), as those bad letters, published in the name of Mr Hervey, and reprinted here by Mr John Erskine, had made a great deal of noise.

---

[1] Elders !        [2] Diary, vol. iii. pp. 171-177.

*Wed.*, *24.*—I preached, at four in the afternoon, on the ground where we had laid the foundation of our house.

*Fri.*, *26.*—About noon I preached at Musselborough, where are a few living souls still. In the evening we had another blessed opportunity at Edinburgh, and I took a solemn leave of the people. Yet how I should be able to ride I knew not. At Newcastle I had observed a small swelling less than a pea; but in six days it was as large as a pullet's egg and exceeding hard. On Thursday it broke. I feared riding would not agree with this, especially a hard trotting horse. However, trusting God, I set out early on Saturday morning ; before I reached Glasgow it was much decreased, and in two or three days more it was quite gone. If it was a boil, it was such an one as I never heard of; for it was never sore first to last, nor ever gave me any pain.

This evening I preached in the hall of the hospital ; the next day, morning and afternoon, in the yard. So much of the form of religion is here still as is scarce to be found in any town in England. There was once the power too. And shall it not be again? Surely the time is at hand.

*Mon.*, *29.*—I rode with James Kershaw, through a fruitful country to Kilmarnock and thence to Ayr. After a short bait at Maybole in the afternoon, we went on to Girvane, a little town on the sea-shore.

*Tues.*, *30.*—We rode over high and steep mountains, between Ballintrae and Strangrawer, where we met with as good entertainment of every kind as if we had been in the heart of England.

We reached Portpatrick about three o'clock, and were immediately surrounded with men offering to carry us over the water ; but the wind was full in our teeth. I determined to wait till morning, and then go forward or backward, as God should please.

*Wed.*, *May 1.*—The wind was quite fair, so as soon as the tide served, I went on board. It seemed strange to cross the sea in an open boat, especially when the waves ran high. I was a little sick, till I fell asleep. In five hours and a half we reached Donaghadee, but my mare could not land till five hours after ; so that 1 did not reach Newtown till past eight.[1]

## NINTH VISIT, 1766.

*Fri.*, *23* [*May 1766*].—I had designed to preach abroad at Dunbar in the evening ; but the rain drove us into the house. It was for good. I now had a full stroke at their hearts, and I think some felt themselves sinners.

*Sat.*, *24.* — In the afternoon, notice having been given a week before, I went to the room at Preston-Pans. And I had it all to myself ; neither man, woman, nor child, offered to look me in the face. So I ordered a chair to be placed in the street. Then forty or fifty crept together ; but they were mere stocks and stones, no more concerned than if I had talked Greek. In the evening I preached in the new room, at Edinburgh, a large and commodious building.

*Mon.*, *26.*—I spent some hours at the meeting of the National Assembly. I am very far from being of Mr Whitefield's mind, who greatly commends the solemnity of this meeting. I have seen few less solemn ; I was extremely shocked at the behaviour of many of the members. Had any Preacher behaved so at our Conference, he would have had no more place among us.

*Wed.*, *28.*—I preached at Leith, and spoke exceeding plain. A few received the truth in the love thereof.

*Sun.*, *June 1.*—Many of the Ministers were present at seven, with a large and serious congregation. In the afternoon I heard a thundering sermon in the new kirk, occasioned by Mr Jardin, a Minister, dropping down dead in the Assembly a day or two before. I preached in the evening, on, "The Spirit and the Bride say, Come !" A few, I trust, closed with the invitation.

[1] Diary, vol. iii. pp. 201, 202.

*Mon.*, 2.—I came to Dundee, wet enough. But it cleared up in the evening, so that I preached abroad to a large congregation, many of whom attended in the morning.

*Tues.*, 3.—The congregation was still larger in the evening, but on Wednesday the rain kept us in the house.

*Thur.*, 5.—It being fair, we had a more numerous congregation than ever; to whom, after preaching, I took occasion to repeat most of the plausible objections which had been made to us in Scotland. I then showed our reasons for the things which had been objected to us, and all seemed to be thoroughly satisfied.

The sum of what I spoke was this :—

I love plain dealing. Do not you? I will use it now. Bear with me.

I hang out no false colours, but show you all I am, all I intend, all I do.

I am a member of the Church of England ; but I love good men of every Church.

My ground is the Bible. Yea, I am a Bible-bigot. I follow it in all things, both great and small.

Therefore, 1. I always use a short, private prayer, when I attend the public service of God. Do not you? Why do you not? Is not this according to the Bible?

2. I stand whenever I sing the praise of God in public. Does not the Bible give you plain precedents for this?

3. I always kneel before the Lord my Maker, when I pray in public.

4. I generally in public use the Lord's Prayer, because Christ has taught me when I pray to say——

I advise every Preacher connected with me, whether in England or Scotland, herein to tread in my steps.

*Fri.*, 6.—We went on to Aberdeen, about seventy measured miles. The congregation in the evening was larger than the usual one at Edinburgh. And the number of those who attended in the morning showed they were not all curious hearers.

*Sun., 8.*—Knowing no reason why we should make God's day the shortest of the seven, I desired Joseph Thomson to preach at five. At eight I preached myself. In the afternoon I heard a strong, close sermon, at Old Aberdeen ; and afterward preached in the College - Kirk, to a very genteel, and yet serious congregation. I then opened and enforced the way of holiness, at New Aberdeen, on a numerous congregation.

*Mon., 9.*—I kept a watch-night, and explained to abundance of genteel people, "One thing is needful ;" a great number of whom would not go away, till after the noon of night.

*Tues., 10.*—I rode over to Sir Archibald Grant's. The church was pretty well filled, and I spoke exceeding plain : yet the hearers did not appear to be any more affected than the stone walls.

*Wed., 11.*—I returned to Aberdeen, where many of the people were much alive to God. With these our labour has not been in vain ; and they are worth all the pains we have taken in Scotland.

*Fri., 13.*—We reached Brechin a little before twelve. Quickly after, I began preaching in the flesh-market, on the "one thing needful." It being the fair-day, the town was full of strangers, and perhaps some of them were found of Him they sought not. I preached, in the evening, at Dundee, with greater liberty than before.

*Sat., 14.*—It rained from the moment we set out till (about one) we came to Kinghorn. Finding the boat was not to move till four o'clock, I purposed to hire a pinnace ; but the wind springing up fair, I went into the large boat. Quickly it fell calm again, so that we did not get over till past seven.

*Sun., 15.*—Our room was very warm in the afternoon, through the multitude of people, a great number of whom were people of fashion, with many Ministers. I spoke to them with the utmost plainness, and I believe not in vain ; for we had such a congregation at five in the morning, as I never saw at Edinburgh before. It is scarce possible to speak too plain in

England ; but it is scarce possible to speak plain
enough in Scotland. And if you do not, you lose
all your labour, you plough upon the sand.

*Mon.*, *16.*—I took a view of one of the greatest
natural curiosities in the kingdom ; what is called
Arthur's Seat, a small rocky eminence, six or seven
yards across, on the top of an exceeding high mountain, not far from Edinburgh. The prospect from
the top of the castle is large, but it is nothing in
comparison of this. In the evening we had another
Sunday's congregation, who seemed more affected than
the day before.

*Tues.*, *17.*—It rained much, yet abundance of people
came, and again God made bare His arm. I can
now leave Edinburgh with comfort, for I have fully
delivered my own soul.

*Wed.*, *18.*—I set out for Glasgow. In the afternoon
the rain poured down, so that we were glad to take
shelter in a little house, where I soon began to talk
with our host's daughter, eighteen or nineteen years
old ; but, to my surprise, I found her as ignorant of
the nature of religion as a Hottentot. And many
such I have found in Scotland ; able to read, nay,
and repeat the Catechism, but wholly unacquainted
with all true religion, yea, and all genuine morality.
This evening we were in the house ; but the next
I preached abroad, to many more than the house
could contain. On Friday the number was greatly
increased ; but much more on Saturday. I then
enlarged upon communion with God, as the only real,
scriptural religion. And I believe many felt, that
with all their orthodoxy, they had no religion still.

What a difference there is between the society here
and that at Dundee ! There are about sixty members
there, and scarce more than six scriptural believers ;
here are seventy - four members, and near thirty
among them lively, zealous believers : one of whom
was justified thirty years ago, and another of them
two - and - forty ; and several of them had been for
many years rejoicing in God their Saviour.

*Sun.*, *22.*—At seven I was obliged to preach abroad,

and the word sunk deep into the hearers. I almost wondered at myself for speaking so plain, and wondered how they could bear it. It is the Lord's doing! In the afternoon Mr Gillies was unusually close and convincing. At five I preached on, "O that thou hadst known, at least in this thy day, the things that make for thy peace." I almost despaired of making the whole congregation hear ; but by their behaviour it seemed they did. In the close I enlarged upon their prejudices, and explained myself with regard to most of them. Shame, concern, and a mixture of various passions were painted on most faces. And I perceived the Scots, if you touch but the right key, receive as lively impressions as the English.

*Mon.*, *23*.—We rode in a mild, cool day to Thorny-Hill, about sixty measured miles from Glasgow. Here I met with Mr Knox's 'History of the Church of Scotland' ; and could any man wonder, if the members of it were more fierce, sour, and bitter of spirit than some of them are ? for what a pattern have they before them ! I know it is commonly said, "The work to be done needed such a spirit." Not so : the work of God does not, cannot need the work of the devil to forward it. And a calm even spirit goes through rough work far better than a furious one. Although, therefore, God did use, at the time of the Reformation, some sour, overbearing, passionate men, yet He did not use them because they were such, but notwithstanding they were so : and there is no doubt He would have used them much more, had they been of a humbler and milder spirit.

*Tues.*, *24*.—Before eight we reached Dumfries, and after a short bait we pushed on, in hopes of reaching Solway Frith before the sea was come in. Designing to call at an inn by the Frith side, we inquired the way, and were directed to leave the main road, and go straight to the house, which we saw before us. In ten minutes Duncan Wright was embogged. However, the horse plunged on, and got through. I was inclined to turn back ; but Duncan telling me I needed only go a little to the left, I did so, and sunk at once to my horse's shoulders. He sprung up twice, and twice sunk again, each time deeper than before. At the third plunge he threw me on one side, and we both made shift to scramble out. I was covered with fine, soft mud, from my feet to the crown of my head; yet, blessed be God, not hurt at all. But we could not cross till between seven and eight o'clock. An honest man crossed with us, who went two miles out of his way to guide us over the sands to Skilborneze, where we found a little clean house, and passed a comfortable night.[1]

## TENTH VISIT, 1767.

*Wed., 29 [July 1767].*— . . . It was so late when we landed (from Donaghadee), after a passage of five hours, that we could only reach Stranrawer that night.

*Thur., 30.*—We rode through a country swiftly improving to Ayr, and passed a quiet and comfortable night.

*Fri., 31.*—Before two we reached Glasgow. In the evening I preached and again at five in the morning.

*Saturday, August the 1st.*—As both my horse and myself were a little tired, I took the stage-coach to Edinburgh.

Before I left Glasgow I heard so strange an account, that I desired to hear it from the person himself. He was a sexton, and yet for many years had little troubled himself about religion. I set down his words, and leave every man to form his own judgment upon them : " Sixteen weeks ago, I was walking an hour before sunset behind the high Kirk, and looking on one side I saw one close to me, who looked me in my face, and asked me how I did ? I answered, ' Pretty well.' He said, ' You have had many troubles. But how have you improved them ?' He then told me all that ever I did, and the thoughts that had been in my heart, adding, ' Be ready for my second coming ' :

---

[1] Journal, vol. ii. pp. 243-247.

and he was gone I knew not how. I trembled all over, and had no strength in me, but sunk down to the ground. From that time I groaned continually under the load of sin, till at the Lord's Supper it was all taken away."

*Sun.*, *2.*—I was sorry to find both the society and the congregations smaller than when I was here last. I impute this chiefly to the manner of preaching which has been generally used. The people have been told frequently and strongly of their coldness, deadness, heaviness, and littleness of faith, but very rarely of anything that would move thankfulness. Hereby many were driven away, and those that remained were kept cold and dead.

I encouraged them strongly at eight in the morning, and about noon preached upon the Castle-Hill on, "There is joy in heaven over one sinner that repenteth." The sun shone exceeding hot upon my head, but all was well; for God was in the midst of it. In the evening, I preached on Luke xx. 34, &c., and many were comforted; especially while I was enlarging on those deep words, "Neither can they die any more, but are equal to the angels, and are the children of God, being the children of the resurrection."

*Mon.*, *3.*—I visited as many as I could, sick and well, and endeavoured to confirm them. In the evening I preached at seven, and again at nine : we concluded about twelve. One then came to me with an unexpected message. A gentleman in Scotland was a serious, sensible man, but violently attached both to the doctrine and discipline of the Kirk. His eldest daughter dreamed some months since, that she was poisoned, and must die in an hour. She waked in the utmost consternation, which issued in a deep conviction of sin. Soon after she had an earnest desire to see me, though not perceiving any possibility of it. But business calling Mr H—— to Edinburgh, he brought her with him three days before I came. On Sunday morning he heard the preaching for the first time, and afterwards omitted no opportunity.

He now sent his daughter to beg I would come, if possible,-to the west, and to desire that I, or any of our Preachers, would make his house our home.

*Tues.*, *4.*—I rode to Dunbar, and endeavoured, if possible, to rouse some of the sleepers, by strongly, yea, roughly enforcing those words, "Lord, are there few that be saved?" And this I must say for the Scots in general, I know no men like them for bearing plain dealing. On Thursday I reached Newcastle.[1]

## ELEVENTH VISIT, 1768.

*Mon.*, *18* [*April 1768*].—Taking horse at four, I reached Solway Frith before eight, and finding a guide ready, crossed without delay, dined at Dumfries, and then went on to Drumlanrig.

*Tues.*, *19.*—I rode through heavy rain to Glasgow. On Thursday and Friday I spoke to most of the members of the society. I doubt we have few societies in Scotland like this : the greater part of those I saw, not only have found peace with God, but continue to walk in the light of His countenance. Indeed that wise and good man, Mr G——, has been of great service to them ; encouraging them, by all possible means, to abide in the grace of God.

*Sat.*, *23.*—I rode over the mountains to Perth. I had received magnificent accounts of the work of God in this place ; so that I expected to find a numerous and lively society. Instead of this I found not above two believers, and scarce five awakened persons in it. Finding I had all to begin, I spoke exceeding plain in the evening, to about a hundred persons, at the Room ; but, knowing this was doing nothing, on Sunday, the 24th, I preached about noon, at the end of Watergate. A multitude of people were soon assembled, to whom I cried aloud, "Seek ye the Lord, while He may be found : call upon Him while He is near." All were deeply attentive, and I had a little hope that some were profited.

At the Old Kirk we had useful sermons, both in the morning, and at five in the afternoon. Immediately after service, I preached on "God forbid that I should glory, save in the cross of our Lord Jesus Christ." The congregation was so exceeding large, that I doubt many could not hear. After preaching, I explained the nature of a Methodist society ; adding, that I should not look on any persons in Perth as such, unless they spoke to me before I left the city. Four men and four women did speak to me, two of whom I think were believers : and one or two more seemed just awakening, and darkly feeling after God. In truth, the Kingdom of God, among these, is as yet but as a grain of mustard-seed.

*Mon., 25.*—Mr Fr——, Minister of a neighbouring parish, desired us to breakfast with him. I found him a serious, benevolent, sensible man, not bigoted to any opinions. I did not reach Brechin till it was too late to preach.

*Tues., 26.*—I came to Aberdeen. Here I found a society truly alive, knit together in peace and love. The congregations were large both morning and evening, and, as usual, deeply attentive. But a company of strolling players, who have at length found place here also, stole away the gay part of the hearers. Poor Scotland ! poor Aberdeen ! this only was wanting to make them as completely irreligious as England.

*Fri., 29.*—I read over an extremely sensible book, but one that surprised me much. It is 'An Inquiry into the Proofs of the Charges commonly advanced against Mary Queen of Scotland.' By means of original papers, he has made it more clear than one would imagine it possible at this distance — 1. That she was altogether innocent of the murder of Lord Darnley, and no way privy to it : 2. That she married Lord Bothwell (then near seventy years old, herself but four-and-twenty) from the pressing instance of the nobility in a body, who at the same time assured her, he was innocent of the King's murder : 3. That

Murray, Morton, and Lethington themselves, con-
trived that murder, in order to charge it. upon her,
as well as forged those vile letters and sonnets, which
they palmed upon the world for hers.

"But how then can we account for the quite contrary story, which has been almost universally received ?" Most easily ; it was penned and published
in French, English, and Latin (by Queen Elizabeth's
order) by George Buchanan, who was Secretary to
Lord Murray, and in Queen Elizabeth's pay. So he
was sure to throw dirt enough : nor was she at liberty
to answer for herself. But what then was Queen
Elizabeth ? as just and merciful as Nero, and as good
a Christian as Mahomet.

*Sun., May the 1st.*—I preached at seven in the New
Room ; in the afternoon at the College-Kirk in Old
Aberdeen. At six, knowing our house could not contain the congregation, I preached in the Castle-Gate on
the paved stones. A large number of people were all
attention ; but there were many rude, stupid creatures
round about them, who knew as little of reason as of
religion. I never saw such brutes in Scotland before.
One of them threw a potato, which fell on my arm.
I turned to them and some were ashamed.

*Mon., 2.*—I set out early from Aberdeen, and about
noon preached in Brechin. After sermon, the Provost
desired to see me, and said, "Sir, my son had epileptic
fits from his infancy. Dr Ogylvie prescribed for him
many times, and at length told me he could do no
more. I desired Mr Blair last Monday to speak to
you. On Tuesday morning my son said to his mother,
he had just been dreaming that his fits were gone, and
he was perfectly well. Soon after I gave him the
drops you advised. He is perfectly well, and has not
had one fit since." In the evening I preached to a
large congregation at Dundee. They heard atten-
tively, but seemed to feel nothing. The next evening
I spoke more strongly, and to their hearts, rather
than their understanding ; and I believe a few felt
the word of God sharp as a two-edged sword.

*Thur., 5.*—We rode through the pleasant and fruitful Carse of Gowry, a plain fifteen or sixteen miles long, between the river Tay and the mountains, very thick inhabited, to Perth. In the afternoon we walked over to the royal palace at Scone. It is a large old house, delightfully situated, but swiftly running to ruin. Yet there [are] a few good pictures, and some fine tapestry left, in what they call the Queen's and the King's chambers. And what is far more curious, there is a bed and a set of hangings, in the once-royal apartment, which was wrought by poor Queen Mary, while she was imprisoned in the castle at Lochlevin. It is some of the finest needle-work I ever saw, and plainly shows both her exquisite taste and unwearied industry.

*Saturday, May the 14th, 1768.*—I walked once more through Holyrood-House, a noble pile of building ; but the greatest part of it left to itself, and so (like the palace at Scone) swiftly running to ruin. The tapestry is dirty and quite faded ; the fine ceilings dropping down, and many of the pictures in the gallery torn or cut through. This was the work of good General Hawley's soldiers (like General, like men !) who, after running away from the Scots at Falkirk, revenged themselves on the harmless canvas !

*Sun., 15.*—At eight I preached in the High-School yard ; and I believe not a few of the hearers were cut to the heart. Between twelve and one a far larger congregation assembled on the Castle - Hill ; and I believe my voice commanded them all, while I opened and enforced those awful words, " I saw the dead, small and great, stand before God." In the evening our house was sufficiently crowded, even with the rich and honourable. " Who hath warned these to flee from the wrath to come ?" O may they at length " awake, and arise from the dead ! "

*Mon., 16.*—I preached in the evening at Dunbar, near the shore, to an unusually large congregation.

*Tues., 17.*—I looked over Dr Shaw's Travels : great part of them is very dull and unentertaining ; but some remarks are extremely curious. I was a little surprised at one of them ; namely, that the celebrated

Mount Atlas is not higher than many of our English mountains, and nothing near so high as the Alps. But it was much farther from Rome. So travellers might make it as high as the moon, and few in England could contradict them.

*Wed., 18.*—I came to poor dead Berwick. However, I found a few living souls even here. At seven, I preached in the Townhall to an exceeding serious, though not numerous, congregation. The next evening I preached in the Market-place at Alnwick.[1]

## TWELFTH VISIT, 1770.

*April, 15 [1770].*— . . . Afterwards we took horse, and before eight reached an admirable inn at Dumfries.

*Mon. 16.*—We had a fair morning till we began to climb up Enterkine, one of the highest mountains in the west of Scotland. We then got into a Scotch mist, and were dropping wet, before we came to the Lead Hills. In the evening we reached Lesmahagow, and Glasgow on Tuesday, where I spent two days with much satisfaction. I had designed to go straight from hence to Perth ; but being desired to take Edinburgh in my way, I rode thither on Friday, and endeavoured to confirm those whom many had strove to turn out of the way. What pity is it that the children of God should so zealously do the Devil's work ! How is it that they are still ignorant of Satan's devices ? Lord, what is man ?

*Sat. 21.*—Pushing through violent wind and rain, we came to Perth in the afternoon. This evening the Tolbooth contained the congregation, and at eight in the morning. The stormy wind would not suffer me to preach abroad in the evening ; so we retired into the Court-house, as many as could, and had a solemn and comfortable hour.

*Mon., 23.*—I walked over to Scone, and took another

---

[1] Journal, vol. ii. pp. 307-315.

view of that palace of ancient men of renown, long
since mouldered into common dust. The buildings
too are now decaying apace. So passes the dream of
human greatness!

*Tues., 24.*—I spent a few agreeable hours with Dr
O——, an upright, friendly, sensible man. Such,
likewise, I found Mr Black, the senior Minister at
Perth, who soon after went to Abraham's bosom.

*Wed., 25.*—Taking horse at five, we rode to Dunkeld,
the first considerable town in the Highlands. We
were agreeably surprised: a pleasanter situation cannot be easily imagined. Afterwards we went some
miles on a smooth, delightful road, hanging over the
river Tay, and then went on, winding through the
mountains, to the Castle at Blair. The mountains, for
the next twenty miles, were much higher and covered
with snow. In the evening we came to Dalwhinny,
the dearest inn I have met with in North Britain.
In the morning we were informed so much snow had
fallen in the night, that we could get no farther. And
indeed three young women, attempting to cross the
mountain to Blair, were swallowed up in the snow.
However, we resolved, with God's help, to go as far as
we could. But about noon we were at a full stop;
the snow, driving together on the top of the mountain,
had quite blocked up the road. We dismounted, and
striking out of the road warily, sometimes to the left,
with many stumbles, but no hurt, we got on to Dalma-
garry, and before sunset, to Inverness.

Benjamin and William Chappel, who had been here
three months, were waiting for a vessel to return to
London. They had met a few people every night, to
sing and pray together; and their behaviour, suitable
to their profession, had removed much prejudice.

*Fri., 27.*—I breakfasted with the senior Minister,
Mr M'Kenzie, a pious and friendly man. At six in
the evening I began preaching in the church, and with
very uncommon liberty of spirit. At seven in the
morning I preached in the library, a large commodious
room; but it would not contain the congregation:
many were constrained to go away. Afterwards I

rode over to Fort George, a very regular fortification,
capable of containing four thousand men. As I was
just taking horse, the commanding officer sent word,
" I was welcome to preach." But it was a little too
late ; I had then but just time to ride back to
Inverness.

*Sun., 29.*—At seven, the benches being removed, the
library contained us tolerably well ; and I am persuaded God shook the hearts of many outside Christians. I preached in the church at five in the afternoon.
Mr Helton designed to preach abroad at seven, but
the Minister desired he would preach in the church,
which he did, to a large and attentive congregation.
Many followed us from the church to our lodgings,
with whom I spent some time in prayer, and then
advised them, as many as could, to meet together, and
spend an hour every evening in prayer and useful
conversation.

*Mon., 30.*—We set out in a fine morning. A little
before we reached Nairn, we were met by a messenger
from the Minister, Mr Dunbar, who desired I would
breakfast with him, and give them a sermon in his
church. Afterwards we hastened to Elgin, through a
pleasant and well-cultivated country. When we set
out from hence, the rain began, and poured down till
we came to the Spey, the most impetuous river I ever
saw. Finding the large boat was in no haste to move,
I stepped into a small one just going off. It whirled
us over the stream almost in a minute. I waited at
the inn at Fochabers (dark and dirty enough in all
reason) till our friends overtook me with the horses.
The outside of the inn at Keith was of the same hue,
and promised no great things ; but we were agreeably
disappointed. We found plenty of everything, and so
dried ourselves at leisure.

*Tuesday, May the 1st.*—I rode on to Aberdeen, and
spent the rest of the week there. It fell out well, for
the weather was uncommon, we had storms of snow or
rain every day ; and it seems the weather was the same
as far as London. So general a storm has scarce been
in the memory of man.

*Sun., 6.*—I preached in the College - Kirk at Old Aberdeen, to a very serious (though mostly genteel) congregation. In the evening I preached at our own room, and early in the morning took my leave of this loving people. We came to Montrose about noon. I had designed to preach there, but found no notice had been given. However, I went down to the Green, and sung a hymn. People presently flocked from all parts; and God gave me great freedom of speech, so that I hope we did not meet in vain.

At seven in the evening I preached at Arbroath (properly Aberbrothwick). The whole town seems moved ; the congregation was the largest I have seen since we left Inverness ; and the society, though but of nine months' standing, is the largest in the kingdom, next to that of Aberdeen.

*Tues., 8.*—I took a view of the small remains of the Abbey. I know nothing like it in all North Britain. I paced it, and found it a hundred yards long ; the breadth is proportionable. Part of the west end, which is still standing, shows it was full as high as Westminster Abbey. The south end of the cross aisle likewise is standing, near the top of which is a large circular window. The zealous Reformers, they told us, burnt this down : God deliver us from reforming mobs !

I have seen no town in Scotland which increases so fast, or which is built with so much common sense as this. Two entire new streets, and part of a third, have been built within these two years. They run parallel with each other, and have a row of gardens between them ; so that every house has a garden ; and thus both health and convenience are consulted.

*Wed., 9.*—I rode on to Dundee. The Ministers here, particularly Mr Small, are bitter enough : notwithstanding which, the society is well established, and the congregations exceeding large. I dealt very plainly with them at six, and still more so the next evening, yet none appeared to be offended.

*Fri., 11.*—I went forward to Edinburgh.

*Sat., 12.*—I received but a melancholy account of

the state of things here. The congregations were nearly as usual ; but the society, which, when I was here before, consisted of above one hundred and sixty members, was now shrunk to about fifty. Such is the fruit of a single Preacher's staying a whole year in one place ! together with the labours of good Mr Townshend.

*Sun., 13.*—At seven I preached in the chapel taken by Lady Glenorchy, which stands at a great distance from ours, in the most honourable part of the city. Between twelve and one I preached in the High-School yard, it being too stormy to preach on the Castle-Hill. A little before six I preached in our chapel, crowded above and below ; but, I doubt, with little effect ; exceeding few seemed to feel what they heard.

*Mon., 14.*—After ten years' inquiry, I have learned what are the Highlands of Scotland. Some told me, " The Highlands begin when you cross the Tay ; " others, " when you cross the North Esk ; " and others, " when you cross the river Spey." But all of them missed the mark ; for the truth of the matter is, the Highlands are bounded by no river at all, but by Cairns, or heaps of stones laid in a row, south-west and north-east, from sea to sea. These formerly divided the kingdom of the Picts from that of the Caledonians, which included all the country north of the Cairns, several whereof are still remaining. It takes in Argyleshire, most of Perthshire, Murrayshire, with all the north-west counties. This is called the Highlands, because a considerable part of it (though not the whole) is mountainous. But it is not more moun-tainous than North Wales, nor than many parts of England and Ireland ; nor do I believe it has any mountain higher than Snowdon Hill or the Skiddaw in Cumberland. Talking Erse, therefore, is not the thing that distinguishes these from the Lowlands. Neither is this or that river, both the Tay, the Esk, and the Spey, running through the Highlands, not south of them.

*Thurs., 17.*—At five in the morning I took a solemn

leave of our friends at Edinburgh. About eight I preached at Musselburgh, and found some hope, there will be a blessing in the remnant. In the evening I preached in the new house at Dunbar, the cheerfullest in the kingdom.

*Fri., 18.*—We rode over to the Earl of Haddington's seat, finely situated between two woods. The house is exceeding large and pleasant, commanding a wide prospect both ways ; and the Earl is cutting walks through the woods, smoothing the ground, and much enlarging and beautifying his garden. Yet he is to die ! In the evening, I trust God broke through some of the stony hearts of Dunbar. A little increase here is in the society likewise : and all the members walk unblamably.[1]

## THIRTEENTH VISIT, 1772.

*Tues., 14 [April 1772].* — Afterwards [at Carlisle] inquiring for the Glasgow road, I found it was not much round to go by Edinburgh. So I chose that road, and went five miles forward this evening to our friends' houses. Here we had a hearty welcome *sub lare parvulo*, with sweet and quiet rest.

*Wed., 15.*—Though it was a lone house, we had a large congregation at five in the morning. Afterwards we rode, for upwards of twenty miles, through a most delightful country, the fruitful mountains rising on either hand, and the clear stream running beneath. In the afternoon we had a furious storm of rain and snow : however we reached Selkirk safe. Here 1 observed a little piece of stateliness which was quite new to me. The maid came in and said, "Sir, the lord of the stable waits to know if he should feed your horses." We call him ostler in England. After supper, all the family seemed glad to join with us in prayer.

---

[1] Journal, vol. iii. pp. 384-388.

*Thur.*, *16.*—We went on through the mountains, covered with snow, to Edinburgh.

*April 17.*—Being Good-Friday, I went to the Episcopal Chapel, and was agreeably surprised : not only the prayers were read well, seriously and distinctly, but the sermon, upon the sufferings of Christ, was sound and unexceptionable. Above all, the behaviour of the whole congregation, rich and poor, was solemn and serious.

*Sat.*, *18.*—I set out for Glasgow. One would rather have imagined it was the middle of January, than the middle of April. The snow covered the mountains on either hand, and the frost was exceeding sharp ; so I preached within, both this evening and on Sunday morning. But in the evening the multitude constrained me to stand in the street. My text was, "What God hath cleansed, that call not thou common." Here I took occasion to fall upon their miserable bigotry for opinions and modes of worship. Many seemed to be not a little convinced ; but how long will the impression continue ?

*Mon.*, *20.*—I went on to Greenock, a sea-port town, twenty miles west of Glasgow. It is built very much like Plymouth Dock, and has a safe and spacious harbour. The trade and inhabitants, and consequently the houses, are increasing swiftly ; and so is cursing, swearing, drunkenness, and all manner of wickedness. Our room is about thrice as large as that at Glasgow, but it would not near contain the congregation. I spoke exceeding plain, and not without hope that we may see some fruit, even among this hard-hearted generation.

*Tues.*, *21.*—The house was very full in the morning. And they showed an excellent spirit ; for after I had spoke a few words on the head, every one stood up at the singing. In the afternoon, I preached at Port-Glasgow, a large town, two miles east of Greenock. Many gay people were there, careless enough, but the greater part seemed to hear with understanding. In the evening I preached at Greenock : and God gave them a loud call, whether they will hear, or whether they will forbear.

*Wed.*, *22.*—About eight, I preached once more in the Masons' Lodge at Port-Glasgow. The house was crowded greatly : and I suppose all the gentry of the town were a part of the congregation. Resolving not to shoot over their heads, as I had done the day before, I spoke strongly of death and judgment, heaven and hell. And there was no more laughing among them, or talking with each other, but all were quietly and deeply attentive.

In the evening, when I began at Glasgow, the congregation being but small, I chose a subject fit for experienced Christians ; but soon after, a heap of fine gay people came in. Yet I could not decently break off what I was about, though they gaped and stared abundantly. I could only give a short exhortation in the close, more suited to their capacity.

*Thursday*, *23d*, was the fast before the Lord's Supper. It was kept as a Sunday ; no shops open or business done. Three Ministers came to assist Mr Gillies, with whom I had much conversation. They all seemed to be pious as well as sensible men. As it rained in the evening, I preached in the Grammar School, a large, commodious room. I know not that ever I spoke more plain, nor perhaps with more effect.

*Fri.*, *24.*—We had a large congregation at five, and many of the rich and gay among them. I was aware of them now, and they seemed to comprehend perfectly well, what it is, to be "ashamed of the Gospel of Christ." I set out at seven ; in the evening I preached at Edinburgh, on, "My son, give me thy heart," and after preaching in the morning, on Saturday, 25th, set out for the North.

I reached Perth in the evening, and sent to the Provost to desire the use of the Guildhall ; in which I preached, Sunday, 26th, in the morning, and (it being very cold) in the evening. Afterwards I accepted of the Provost's invitation, to lodge at his house ; and spent an agreeable evening with him and three Ministers, concluded with solemn prayer.

*Mon.*, *27.*—I spent three or four hours in conversation with Dr Oswald and Mr Fraser, two as pious and

S

sensible Ministers as any I know in Scotland. From
Methven we went on to Dunkeld, once the capital of
the Caledonian kingdom ; now a small town, standing
on the bank of the Tay, and at the foot of several
rough, high mountains. The air was sharp ; yet the
multitude of people constrained me to preach abroad ;
and I trust not in vain ; for great was the power of
God in the midst of them.

*Tues.*, *28.*—We walked through the Duke of Athol's
gardens, in which was one thing I never saw before, a
summer-house in the middle of a green-house, by means
of which one might, in the depth of winter, enjoy the
warmth of May, and sit surrounded with greens and
flowers on every side.

In the evening I preached once more in Perth, to a
large and serious congregation. Afterwards they did
me an honour I never thought of, presented me with
the freedom of the city. The diploma ran thus :—

"Magistratuum illustris ordo et honorandus senatorum coetus inclytae civitatis Perthensis, in debiti
amoris et affectus tesseram erga Johannem W——y,
immunitatibus praefatae civitatis, societatis etiam et
fraternitatis aedilitiae privilegiis donarunt.

"*Aprilis die* 28° *anno Sal.* 1772°."

I question whether any diploma from the city of London be more pompous, or expressed in better Latin.

In my way to Perth, I read over the first volume of
Dr Robertson's 'History of Charles V.' I know not
when I have been so disappointed. It might as well
be called the History of Alexander the Great. Here
is a quarto volume of eight or ten shillings' price,
containing dry, verbose dissertations on feudal government ! The substance of all which might be comprised
in half a sheet of paper. But Charles the Fifth ; where
is Charles the Fifth ?

"Leave off thy reflections and give us thy tale ! "

*Wed.*, *29.*—I went on to Brechin, and preached in the
Town-hall to a congregation of all sorts, Seceders,

Glassites, Nonjurors, and what not! O what excuse have Ministers in Scotland for not declaring the whole counsel of God, where the bulk of the people not only endure, but love plain dealing?

*Friday and Saturday.*—I rested at Aberdeen.

*Sunday, May 3.*—I went in the morning to the English Church. Here, likewise, I could not but admire the exemplary decency of the congregation. This was the more remarkable, because so miserable a reader I never heard before. Listening with all attention, I understood but one single word, *Balak*, in the First Lesson ; and one more, *begat*, was all I could possibly distinguish in the Second. Is there no man of spirit belonging to this congregation ? Why is such a burlesque upon public worship suffered ? Would it not be far better to pay this gentleman for doing nothing, than for doing mischief ? For bringing a scandal upon religion ?

About three I preached at the College Kirk in the Old Town, to a large congregation, rich and poor ; at six, in our own house, on "the narrow way." I spoke exceeding plain, both this evening and the next ; yet none were offended. What encouragement has every Preacher in this country, "by manifestation of the truth" to "commend himself to every man's conscience in the sight of God !"

*Tues., 5.*—I read over, in my journey, Dr Beattie's ingenious 'Enquiry after Truth.' He is a writer quite equal to his subject, and far above the match of all the minute philosophers, David Hume in particular, the most insolent despiser of truth and virtue that ever appeared in the world. And yet, it seems, some complain of this Doctor's using him with too great severity ! I cannot understand how that can be, unless he treated him with rudeness (which he does not), since he is an avowed enemy to God and man, and to all that is sacred and valuable upon earth.

In the evening I preached in the new-house at Arbroath (properly Aberbrotheck). In this town there is a change indeed ! It was wicked to a proverb ; remarkable for Sabbath-breaking, cursing, swearing, drunkenness, and a general contempt of religion. - But it is not so now : no drunkenness seen in the streets : and many have not only ceased from evil and learned to do well, but are witnesses of the inward Kingdom of God, "righteousness, peace, and joy in the Holy Ghost."

*Wed., 6.*—The Magistrates here also did me the honour of presenting me with the freedom of their corporation. I valued it as a token of their respect, though I shall hardly make any further use of it.

*Thur., 7.*—I took Thomas Cherry away with me ; but it was too late. He will hardly recover. Let all observe, (that no more Preachers may murder them-selves,) here is another martyr to screaming !

We had a huge congregation in the evening at Dundee, it being the fast-day, before the Sacrament. Never in my life did I speak more plain or close : let God apply it as it pleaseth Him.

*Fri., 8.*—I laboured to reconcile those, who (accord-ing to the custom of the place) were vehemently con-tending about nothing.

*Sat., 9.*—I went to Edinburgh.

*Sun., 10.*—I attended the Church of England service in the morning, and that of the Kirk in the afternoon. Truly "no man having drunk old wine, straightway desireth new." How dull and dry did the latter appear to me, who had been accustomed to the former. In the evening I endeavoured to reach the hearts of a large congregation, by applying part of the Sermon on the Mount. And I am persuaded God applied it with power to many consciences.

*Mon., 11.*—I spoke severally to the members of the society as closely as I could. Out of ninety (now united) I scarce found ten of the original society ; so indefatigable have the good Ministers been to root out the seed God had sown in their hearts.

*Thur., 12.*—I preached at Ormiston, ten miles south of Edinburgh, to a large and deeply serious congrega-tion. I dined at the Minister's, a sensible man, who heartily bid us God speed. But he soon changed his mind : Lord H——n informed him that he had received a letter from Lady H——, assuring him, that we were "dreadful heretics, to whom no countenance should be given." It is pity ! Should not the children of God leave the Devil to do his own work ?

*Wed., 13.*—I preached at Leith in the most horrid, dreary room I have seen in the kingdom. But the next day I found another kind of room, airy, cheerful and lightsome, which Mr Parker undertook to fit up for the purpose, without any delay.

*Sun., 17.*—I had appointed to preach at noon in the Lady's Walk, at Leith ; but being offered the use of the Episcopal chapel, I willingly accepted it, and both read prayers and preached. Here also the behaviour of our congregation did honour to our Church.

*Mon., 18.*—Dr Hamilton brought with him Dr Monro and Dr Gregory. They satisfied me what my disorder was ; and told me there was but one method of cure. Perhaps but one natural one ; but I think God has more than one method of healing either the soul or the body.

In the evening (the weather being still severe) I preached in the new house at Leith, to a lovely audience, on, " Narrow is the way that leadeth unto life." Many were present again at five in the morning. How long have we toiled here almost in vain ! Yet I cannot but hope, God will at length have a people even in this place.

*Wed., 20.*—I took my leave of Edinburgh in the morning, by strongly enforcing the Apostle's exhortation, " Be careful for nothing, but in every thing make your requests known unto God with thanksgiving."

I had designed to preach (as usual) at Provost Dixon's, in Haddington, in the way to Dunbar. But the Provost too had received light from the " circular letter," and durst not receive those heretics. So we went round by the Marquis of Tweedale's seat, completely finished within and without. But he that took so much delight in it, is gone to his long home, and has left it to one who has no taste or regard for it. So rolls the world away !

In the evening I preached at Dunbar.

*Thur.*, *21.*—I went to the Bass, seven miles from it, which in the horrid reign of Charles the Second, was the prison of those venerable men who suffered all things for a good conscience. It is a high rock, surrounded by the sea, two or three miles in circumference, and about two miles from the shore. The strong east winds made the water so rough, that the boat could hardly live. And when we came to the only landing place (the other sides being quite perpendicular), it was with much difficulty that we got up, climbing on our hands and knees. The castle, as one may judge from what remains, was utterly inaccessible. The walls of the chapel, and of the Governor's house, are tolerably entire. The garden walls are still seen near the top of the rock, with the well in the midst of it ; and round the walls there are spots of grass that feed eighteen or twenty sheep. But the proper natives of the island are solan-geese, a bird about the size of a Muscovy duck, which breeds by thousands, from generation to generation, on the sides of the rock. It is peculiar to these, that they lay but one egg, which they do not sit upon at all, but keep it under one foot (as we saw with our own eyes) till it is hatched. How many prayers did the holy men confined here offer up in that holy day ! And how many thanksgivings should we return, for all the liberty, civil and religious, which we enjoy !

At our return, we walked over the ruins of Tantallon Castle, once the seat of the great Earls of Douglas. The front walls (it was four square) are still standing, and, by their vast height and huge thickness, give us a little idea of what it once was. Such is human greatness !

*Fri.*, *22.*—We took a view of the famous Roman camp, lying on a mountain, two or three miles from the town. It is encompassed with two broad and deep ditches, and is not easy of approach on any side. Here lay General Lesley with his army, while Cromwell was starving below. He had no way to escape ; but the enthusiastic fury of the Scots delivered him.

When they marched into the valley to swallow him up, he mowed them down like grass.

*Sat., 23.*—I went to Alnwick, and preached in the Town-hall. What a difference between an English and a Scotch congregation! These judge themselves rather than the Preacher, and their aim is, not only to know, but to love and obey.[1]

FOURTEENTH VISIT, 1774.

*Mon., 9 [May 1774].*—I set out for Scotland. At eight I preached in the Castle-yard at Cockermouth, to abundance of careless people, on, "Where their worm dieth not, and the fire is not quenched." In the evening I preached at Carlisle. On Tuesday I went on to Selkirk, and on Wednesday to Edinburgh, which is distant from Carlisle ninety-five miles, and no more.

*Thurs., 12.*—I went in the stage-coach to Glasgow; and on Friday and Saturday preached on the Old-Green, to a people, the greatest part of whom hear much, know everything, and feel nothing.

*Sun., 15.*—My spirit was moved within me at the sermons I heard, both morning and afternoon. They contained much truth, but were no more likely to awaken one soul, than an Italian opera. In the evening a multitude of people assembled on the Green, to whom I earnestly applied these words, "Though I have all knowledge, though I have all faith, though I give all my goods to feed the poor," &c., "and have not love, I am nothing."

*Mon., 16.*—In the afternoon, as also at seven in the morning, I preached in the kirk at Port-Glasgow. My subjects were death and judgment, and I spoke as home as I possibly could. The evening congregation at Greenock was exceeding large. I opened and enforced those awful words, "Strait is the gate, and narrow is the way that leadeth unto life." I know not that ever I spoke more strongly. And some fruit of it quickly appeared; for the house, twice as large as that at Glasgow, was thoroughly filled at five in the morning. In the evening, Tuesday, the 17th, I preached on the Green at Glasgow once more, although the north wind was piercing cold. At five in the morning I commended our friends to God.

How is it that there is no increase in this society? It is exceeding easy to answer. One Preacher stays here two or three months at a time, preaching on Sunday morning, and three or four evenings in a week. Can a Methodist Preacher preserve bodily health, or spiritual life, with this exercise? And if he is but half alive, what will the people be. Just so it is at Greenock too.

*Wed., 18.*—I went to Edinburgh, and on Thursday to Perth. Here likewise the morning preaching had been given up; consequently the people were few, dead, and cold. These things must be remedied, or we must quit the ground. In the way to Perth, I read that ingenious tract, Dr Gregory's 'Advice to his Daughters.' Although I cannot agree with him in all things (particularly as to dancing, decent pride, and both a reserve and a delicacy, which I think are quite unnatural), yet I allow there are many fine strokes therein, and abundance of common-sense. And if a young woman followed this plan in little things, in such things as daily occur, and in great things copied after Miranda, she would form an accomplished character.

*Fri., 20.*—I rode over to Mr Fraser's at Moneydie, whose mother-in-law was to be buried that day. O what a difference is there between the English and the Scotch method of burial! The English does honour to human nature; and even to the poor remains, that were once a temple of the Holy Ghost! But when I see in Scotland a coffin put into the earth, and covered up without a word spoken, it reminds me of what was spoken concerning Jehoiakim, "He shall be buried with the burial of an ass."

*Sat., 21.*—I returned to Perth and preached in the evening to a large congregation ; but I could not find the way to their hearts. The generality of the people here are so wise, that they need no more knowledge ; and so good, that they need no more religion ! Who can warn them that are brim-full of wisdom and goodness to flee from the wrath to come ?

*Sun., 22.*—I endeavoured to stir up this drowsy people, by speaking as strongly as I could, at five, on, "Awake, thou that sleepest !" at seven, on, "Where their worm dieth not ;" and in the evening, on, "I saw the dead, small and great, stand before God." In the afternoon a young gentleman in the West Kirk preached such a close, practical sermon, on, "Enoch walked with God," as I have not heard since I came into the kingdom.

*Mon., 23.*—About ten, I preached to a considerable number of plain, serious, country-people, at Rait, a little town in the middle of that lovely valley, called the Carse of Gowry. In riding on to Dundee, I was utterly amazed at reading and considering a tract put into my hands, which gave a fuller account than I had ever seen, of the famous Gowry Conspiracy in 1600. And I was thoroughly convinced — 1. From the utter improbability, if one should not rather say, absurdity, of the King's account (the greater part of which rests entirely on his own single word) ; 2. From the many contradictions in the depositions which were made to confirm some parts of it ; and, 3. From the various collateral circumstances, related by contemporary writers, that the whole was a piece of king-craft, the clumsy invention of a covetous and bloodthirsty tyrant, to destroy two innocent men, that he might kill and also take possession of their large fortunes.

In the evening I preached at Dundee, and on Tuesday, the 24th, went on to Arbroath. In the way I read Lord K——'s plausible 'Essays on Morality and Natural Religion.' Did ever man take so much pains to so little purpose, as he does in his 'Essay on Liberty and Necessity' ? *Cui bono?* What good

would it do to mankind, if he could convince them,
that they are a mere piece of clock-work? that they
have no more share in directing their own actions,
than in directing the sea or the north wind? He
owns that "if men saw themselves in this light, all
sense of moral obligation, of right and wrong, of good
or ill desert, would immediately cease." Well, my
Lord sees himself in this light; consequently if his
own doctrine is true, he has "no sense of moral
obligation, of right and wrong, of good or ill desert."
Is he not then excellently well qualified for a Judge?
Will he condemn a man for not "holding the wind in
his fist"?

The high and piercing wind made it impracticable
to preach abroad in the evening. But the house contained the people tolerably well, as plain and simple
as those at Rait. I set out early in the morning;
but not being able to ford the North Esk, swollen
with the late rains, was obliged to go round some
miles. However I reached Aberdeen, in the evening.

Here I met with another curious book, 'Sketches
of the History of Man.' Undoubtedly, the author is
a man of strong understanding, lively imagination,
and considerable learning; and his book contains
some useful truths. Yet some things in it gave me
pain: 1. His affirming things that are not true; as
that all negro children turn black the ninth or tenth
day from their birth. No; most of them turn partly
black on the second day, entirely so on the third.
That all the Americans are a copper colour. Not so;
some of them are as fair as we are. Many more such
assertions I observed, which I impute not to design,
but to credulity. 2. His flatly contradicting himself;
many times within a page or two. 3. His asserting,
and labouring to prove, that man is a mere piece of
clock-work; and, lastly, his losing no opportunity of
vilifying the Bible, to which he appears to bear a
most cordial hatred. I marvel, if any but his brother
infidels, will give two guineas for such a work as this!

*Sun., 29.*—At seven the congregation was large. In
the evening the people were ready to tread upon each

other. I scarce ever saw people so squeezed together. And they seemed to be all ear, while I exhorted them, with strong and pointed words, not to "receive the grace of God in vain."

*Mon., 30.* — I set out early from Aberdeen, and preached at Arbroath in the evening. I know no people in England who are more loving, and more simple of heart, than these.

*Tues., 31.*—I preached at Easthaven, a small town inhabited by fishermen. I suppose all the inhabitants were present ; and all were ready to devour the word. In the evening I preached at Dundee, and had great hope that brotherly love would continue.

In my way hither I read Dr Reid's ingenious Essay. With the former part of it I was greatly delighted ; but afterwards I was much disappointed. I doubt whether the sentiments are just ; but I am sure his language is so obscure, that to most readers it must be mere Arabic. But I have a greater objection than this ; namely, his exquisite want of judgment, in so admiring that prodigy of self-conceit, Rousseau ; a shallow, yet supercilious infidel, two degrees below Voltaire ! Is it possible, that a man who admires him can admire the Bible ?

*Wednesday, June 1.*—I went to Edinburgh, and the next day examined the society one by one. I was agreeably surprised. They have fairly profited since I was here last. Such a number of persons having sound Christian experience I never found in this society before. I preached in the evening to a very elegant congregation, and yet with great enlargement of heart.

*Sat., 4.*—I found uncommon liberty at Edinburgh, in applying Ezekiel's vision of the dry bones. As I was walking home, two men followed me, one of whom said, "Sir, you are my prisoner. I have a warrant from the Sheriff to carry you to the Tolbooth." At first I thought he jested ; but finding the thing was serious, I desired one or two of our friends to go up with me. When we were safe lodged in a house adjoining to the Tolbooth, I desired the officer to let

me see his warrant. I found the prosecutor was one
George Sutherland, once a member of the society. He
had deposed, "That Hugh Saunderson, one of John
Wesley's Preachers, had taken from his wife one
hundred pounds in money, and upwards of thirty
pounds in goods; and had, besides that, terrified
her into madness, so that through the want of her
help, and the loss of business, he was damaged five
hundred pounds."

Before the Sheriff, Archibald Cockburn, Esq., he had
deposed, "That the said John Wesley and Hugh Saunderson, to evade her pursuit, were preparing to fly
the country, and therefore he desired this warrant to
search for, seize, and incarcerate them in the Tolbooth,
till they should find security for their appearance."
To this request the Sheriff had assented, and given
his warrant for that purpose.

But why does he incarcerate John Wesley? Nothing
is laid against him, less or more. Hugh Saunderson
preaches in connection with him. What then? Was
not the Sheriff strangely overseen?

Mr Sutherland furiously insisted that the officer
should carry us to the Tolbooth without delay. However, he waited till two or three of our friends came,
and gave a bond for our appearance on the 24th inst.
Mr S—— did appear, the cause was heard, and the
prosecutor fined one thousand pounds!

*Sun., 5.* — About eight I preached at Ormiston,
twelve miles from Edinburgh. The house being
small, I stood in the street and proclamed "the grace
of our Lord Jesus Christ." The congregation behaved
with the utmost decency; so did that on the Castle-
Hill in Edinburgh, at noon; though I strongly insisted,
that God "now commandeth all men everywhere to
repent." In the evening the house was thoroughly
filled; and many seemed deeply affected. I do not
wonder that Satan, had it been in his power, would
have had me otherwise employed this day.

*Wed., 8.*—I took my leave of our affectionate friends,
and in the evening preached at Dunbar.[1]

[1] Journal, vol. iv. pp. 13-17.

Fifteenth Visit, 1776.

*Tues.*, *May 7.*—I went on to Selkirk [from Carlisle]. The family came to prayer in the evening ; after which the mistress of it said, "Sir, my daughter Jenny would be very fond of having a little talk with you. She is a strange lass ; she will not come down on the Lord's day but to public worship, and spends all the rest of the day in her own chamber." I desired she would come up, and found one that earnestly longed to be altogether a Christian. I satisfied her mother that she was not mad, and spent a little time in advice, exhortation, and prayer.

*Wed.*, *8.*—We set out early, but found the air so keen, that before noon our hands bled as if cut with a knife. In the evening I preached at Edinburgh, and the next evening, near the river-side in Glasgow.

*Fri.*, *10.*—I went to Greenock ; it being their Fast-day before the Sacrament (ridiculously so called, for they do not fast at all, but take their three meals, just as on other days), the congregation was larger than when I was there before, and remarkably attentive. The next day I returned to Glasgow, and on Sunday, 12th, went in the morning to the High Kirk (to show I was no bigot), and in the afternoon to the Church of England Chapel. The decency of behaviour here surprises me more and more. I know nothing like it in these kingdoms, except among the Methodists. In the evening the congregation by the river-side was exceeding numerous, to whom I declared the whole counsel of God.

*Mon.*, *13.*—I returned to Edinburgh, and the next day went to Perth, where (it being supposed no house would contain the congregation) I preached at six on the South Inch, though the wind was cold and boisterous. Many are the stumbling-blocks which have been laid in the way of this poor people ; they are removed, but the effects of them still continue.

*Wed., 15.*—I preached at Dundee, to nearly as large a congregation as that at Port-Glasgow.

*Thurs., 16.*—I attended an ordination at Arbroath. The service lasted about four hours; but it did not strike me. It was doubtless very grave; but I thought it was very dull.

*Fri., 17.*—I reached Aberdeen in good time.

*Sat., 18.*—I read over Dr Johnson's 'Tour to the Western Isles.' It is a very curious book, wrote with admirable sense, and, I think, great fidelity; although, in some respects, he is thought to bear hard on the nation, which I am satisfied he never intended.

*Sun., 19.*—I attended the morning service at the kirk, full as formal as any in England, and no way calculated either to awaken sinners or to stir up the gift of God in believers. In the afternoon I heard a useful sermon at the English Chapel, and was again delighted with the exquisite decency, both of the Minister and the whole congregation. The Methodist congregations come the nearest to this. But even these do not come up to it. Our house was sufficiently crowded in the evening; but some of the hearers did not behave like those at the chapel.

*Mon., 20.*—I preached, about eleven, at Old Meldrum, but could not reach Banff till near seven in the evening. I went directly to the parade, and proclaimed to a listening multitude, "The grace of our Lord Jesus Christ." All behaved well but a few gentry, whom I rebuked openly; and they stood corrected.

After preaching, Mrs Gordon, the Admiral's widow, invited me to supper. There I found five or six as agreeable women as I have seen in the kingdom, and I know not when I have spent two or three hours with greater satisfaction. In the morning I was going to preach in the Assembly Room, when the Episcopal Minister sent and offered me the use of his chapel. It was quickly filled. After reading prayers, I preached on those words in the Second Lesson, "What lack I yet?" and strongly applied them to those in particular who supposed themselves to be rich, and increased in goods, and lacked nothing. I then set out for Keith.

Banff is one of the neatest and most elegant towns that I have seen in Scotland. It is pleasantly situated on the side of a hill, sloping from the sea, though close to it, so that it is sufficiently sheltered from the sharpest winds. The streets are straight and broad. I believe it may be esteemed the fifth if not the fourth town in the kingdom. The county, quite from Banff to Keith, is the best peopled of any I have seen in Scotland. This is chiefly, if not entirely, owing to the late Earl of Findlater. He was indefatigable in doing good, took pains to procure industrious men from all parts, and to provide such little settlements for them as enabled them to live with comfort.

About noon I preached at the New-Mills, nine miles from Banff, to a large congregation of plain simple people. As we rode in the afternoon, the heat overcame me, so that I was weary and faint before we came to Keith. But I no sooner stood up in the marketplace than I forgot my weariness; such were the seriousness and attention of the whole congregation, though as numerous as that at Banff. Mr Gordon, the Minister of the parish, invited me to supper, and told me his kirk was at my service. A little society is formed here already, and is in a fair way of increasing. But they were just now in danger of losing their preaching-house, the owner being determined to sell it. I saw but one way to secure it for them, which was to buy it myself. So (who would have thought it?) I bought an estate, consisting of two houses, a yard, a garden, with three acres of good land. But he told me flat, "Sir, I will take no less for it than sixteen pounds ten shillings, to be paid, part now, part at Michaelmas, and the residue next May."

Here Mr Gordon showed me a great curiosity. Near the top of the opposite hill a new town is built, containing, I suppose, a hundred houses, which is a town of beggars. This, he informed me, was the professed, regular occupation of all the inhabitants. Early in spring they all go out, and spread themselves over the kingdom; and in autumn they return, and do what is requisite for their wives and children.

*Wed., 22.*—The wind turning north, we stepped at once from June to January. About one I preached at Inverury, to a plain, earnest, loving people, and before five came to Aberdeen.

*Thurs., 23.*—I read over Mr Pennant's 'Journey through Scotland,' a lively as well as judicious writer. Judicious, I mean, in most respects ; but I cannot give up to all the Deists in Great Britain the existence of witchcraft, till I give up the credit of all history, sacred and profane. And at the present time I have not only as strong, but stronger proofs of this, from eye and ear witnesses, than I have of murder ; so that I cannot rationally doubt of one any more than the other.

*Fri., 24.*—I returned to Arbroath, and lodged at Provost Grey's. So, for a time, we are in honour ! I have hardly seen such another place in the three kingdoms as this is at present. Hitherto there is no opposer at all, but every one seems to bid us God-speed !

*Sat., 25.*—I preached at Westhaven (a town of fishermen) about noon, and at Dundee in the evening.

*Sun., 26.*—I went to the New Church, cheerful, lightsome, and admirably well finished. A young gentleman preached such a sermon, both for sense and language, as I never heard in North Britain before ; and I was informed his life is as his preaching. At five we had an exceeding large congregation ; and the people of Dundee in general behave better at public worship than any in the kingdom, except the Methodists, and those at the Episcopal chapels. In all other kirks the bulk of the people are bustling to and fro, before the Minister has ended his prayer. In Dundee all are quiet, and none stir at all till he has pronounced the blessing.

*Mon., 27.*—I paid a visit to St Andrews, once the largest city in the kingdom. It was eight times as large as it is now, and a place of very great trade. But the sea rushing from the north - east, gradually destroyed the harbour and the trade together ; in consequence of which whole streets (that were) are now meadows and gardens. Three broad, straight, handsome streets remain, all pointing at the old cathedral, which by the ruins appears to have been above three hundred feet long, and proportionably broad and high; so that it seems to have exceeded York Minster, and to have at least equalled any cathedral in England. Another church, afterwards used in its stead, bears date 1124. A steeple standing near the cathedral is thought to have stood thirteen hundred years.

What is left of St Leonard's College is only a heap of ruins. Two colleges remain. One of them has a tolerable square; but all the windows are broke, like those of a brothel. We were informed, "The students do this before they leave the college." Where are their blessed governors in the mean time? Are they all fast asleep? The other college is a mean building, but has a handsome library newly erected. In the two colleges, we learned, were about seventy students, near the same number as at Old Aberdeen. Those at New Aberdeen are not more numerous; neither those at Glasgow. In Edinburgh, I suppose, there are a hundred. So four Universities contain three hundred and ten students! These all come to their several colleges in November, and return home in May! So they may study five months in the year, and lounge all the rest! O where was the common-sense of those who instituted such colleges? In the English colleges every one may reside all the year, as all my pupils did; and I should have thought myself little better than a highwayman if I had not lectured them every day in the year but Sundays.

We were so long detained at the passage, that I only reached Edinburgh time enough to give notice of my preaching the next day. After preaching at Dunbar, Alnwick, and Morpeth, on Saturday, June 1, I reached Newcastle.[1]

SIXTEENTH VISIT, 1779.

*Wed., May 26, 1779.*—We had such a congregation at Dunbar as I have not seen there for many years.

[1] Journal, vol. iv. pp. 71-75.

*Thurs., 27.*—I went on to Edinburgh. I was agreeably surprised at the singing in the evening : I have not heard such female voices, so strong and clear, anywhere in England !

*Fri., 28.*—I went to Glasgow, and preached in the house, but the next evening by the river-side.

*Sun., 30.*—At seven I spoke exceeding strong words in applying the parable of the Sower. In the afternoon I went to the English Chapel ; but how was I surprised ! Such decency have I seldom seen even at West-Street, or the New Room in Bristol. 1. All, both men and women, were dressed plain : I did not see one high head. 2. No one took notice of any one at coming in, but after a short ejaculation sat quite still. 3. None spoke to any one during the service, nor looked either on one side or the other. 4. All stood, every man, woman, and child, while the Psalms were sung. 5. Instead of an unmeaning voluntary, was an anthem, and one of the simplest and sweetest I ever heard. 6. The prayers, preceding a sound, useful sermon, were seriously and devoutly read. 7. After service, none bowed, or curtsied, or spoke, but went quietly and silently away.

After church I preached again by the river-side, to a huge multitude of serious people ; I believe full as many more as we had the Sunday before at Newcastle. Surely we shall not lose all our labour here !

*Mon., 31.*—I returned to Edinburgh, and, June 1, set out on my northern journey. In the evening I preached at Dundee. The congregation was, as usual, very large and deeply attentive ; but that was all. I did not perceive that any one was affected at all. I admire this people ! so decent ! so serious ! and so perfectly unconcerned !

*Wed., June 2.*—We went on to Arbroath, where was near as large a congregation as at Dundee, but nothing so serious ; the poor Glassites here, pleading for a merely notional faith, greatly hinder either the beginning or the progress of any real work of God.

*Thurs., 3.*—I preached at Aberdeen, to a people that can feel as well as hear.

*Fri., 4.*—I set out for Inverness, and about eight preached at Inverury, to a considerable number of plain, country-people, just like those we see in Yorkshire. My spirit was much refreshed among them, observing several of them in tears. Before we came to Strathbogie (now new-named Huntly), Mr Brackenbury was much fatigued ; so I desired him to go into the chaise, and rode forward to Keith.

Mr Gordon, the Minister, invited us to drink tea at his house. In the evening I went to the market-place. Four children, after they had stood a while to consider, ventured to come near me, then a few men and women crept forward, till we had upwards of a hundred. At nine, on Sunday, 6, I suppose they were doubled, and some of them seemed a little affected. I dined at Mr Gordon's, who behaved in the most courteous, yea, and affectionate manner. At three I preached in the kirk, one of the largest I have seen in the kingdom, but very ruinous. It was thoroughly filled, and God was there in an uncommon manner. He sent forth His voice, yea, and that a mighty voice ; so that I believe many of the stout-hearted trembled. In the evening I preached once more in the market-place, on those awful words, "Where their worm dieth not, and the fire is not quenched."

*Mon., 7.*—I came to Grange - Green, near Fores, [Forres ?] about twelve o'clock. But I found the house had changed its master since I was here before, nine years ago. Mr Grant (who then lived in his brother's house) was now Sir Lodowick Grant, having succeeded to the title and estate of Sir Alexander, dying without issue. But his mind was not changed with his fortune : he received me with cordial affection, and insisted on my sending for Mrs Smith and her little girl, whom I had left at Fores. We were all here as at home, in one of the most healthy and most pleasant situations in the kingdom ; and I had the satisfaction to observe my daughter sensibly recovering her strength, almost every hour. In the evening all the family were called in to prayers, to whom I first expounded a portion of Scripture. Thus ended this comfortable day ! So has God provided for us in a strange land.

*Tues., 8.*—I found another hearty welcome from Mr Dunbar, the Minister of Nairn. A little after ten I preached in his kirk, which was full from end to end. I have seldom seen a Scotch congregation so sensibly affected ; indeed it seemed that God smote rocks, and brake the hearts of stone in pieces.

In the afternoon I reached Inverness, but found a new face of things there. Good Mr Mackenzie had been for some years removed to Abraham's bosom. Mr Fraser, his colleague, a pious man of the old stamp, was likewise gone to rest. The three present Ministers are of another kind ; so that I have no more place in the kirk, and the wind and rain would not permit me to preach on the Green : however, our house was large, though gloomy enough. Being now informed (which I did not suspect before), that the town was uncommonly given to drunkenness, I used the utmost plainness of speech, and I believe not without effect. I then spent some time with the society, increased from twelve to between fifty and sixty. Many of these knew in whom they had believed, and many were going on to perfection ; so that all the pains which have been taken to stop the work of God here have hitherto been in vain.

*Wed., 9.*—We had another rainy day, so that I was again driven into the house ; and again I delivered my own soul to a larger congregation than before. In the morning we had an affectionate parting, perhaps to meet no more. I am glad, however, that I have made three journeys to Inverness ; it has not been lost labour.

Between ten and eleven I began preaching at Nairn. The house was pretty well filled again ; and many more of the gentry were there than were present on Tuesday. It pleased God to give me again liberty of speech, in opening and applying those words, " God is a Spirit, and they that worship Him, must worship Him in spirit and in truth."

About two we reached Sir Lodowick Grant's. In

the evening we had a very serious congregation; afterwards I spent an hour very agreeably with the family, and two or three neighbouring gentlemen.

*Fri., 11.*—We did not stop at Keith, but went on to Strathbogie. Here we were in a clean, convenient house, and had everything we wanted. All the family very willingly joined us in prayer. We then slept in peace.

*Sat., 12.*—About one, I preached at Inverury, to a larger congregation than before, and was again refreshed with the simplicity and earnestness of the plain country-people. In the evening I preached at Aberdeen.

*Sun., 13.*—I spoke as closely as I could, both morning and evening, and made a pointed application to the hearts of all that were present. I am convinced this is the only way whereby we can do any good in Scotland. This very day I heard many excellent truths delivered in the kirk; but as there was no application, it was likely to do as much good as the singing of a lark. I wonder the pious Ministers in Scotland are not sensible of this; they cannot but see that no sinners are convinced of sin, none converted to God, by this way of preaching. How strange it is then, that neither reason nor experience teaches them to take a better way!

*Mon., 14.*—I preached again at Arbroath.

*Tues., 15.*—At Dundee; and Wed., 16, at Edinburgh.

*Thurs., 17.*—I examined the society. In five years I found five members had been gained! Ninety-nine being increased to a hundred and four. What then have our Preachers been doing all this time? 1. They have preached four evenings in the week, and on Sunday morning; the other mornings they have fairly given up. 2. They have taken great care not to speak too plain, lest they should give offence. 3. When Mr Brackenbury preached the old Methodist doctrine, one of them said, "You must not preach such doctrine here; the doctrine of Perfection is not calculated for the meridian of Edinburgh." Waiving then all other hindrances, is it any wonder that the work of God has not prospered here ?

On Friday and Saturday I preached with all possible plainness, and some appeared to be much stirred up.

On Sunday, 20, I preached at eight, and at half an hour past twelve, and God gave us a parting blessing.

I was in hopes of preaching abroad at Dunbar in the evening, but the rain would not permit.[1]

SEVENTEENTH VISIT, 1780.

*Mon.*, *15* [*May 1780*].—I set out for Scotland, and Tuesday, 16, came to Berwick-upon-Tweed. Such a congregation I have not seen there for many years. Perhaps the seed which has so long seemed to be sown in vain may at length produce a good harvest.

*Wed.*, *17.*—I went on to Dunbar. I have seldom seen such a congregation here before ; indeed some of them seemed at first disposed to mirth, but they were soon serious as death. And truly the power of the Lord was present to heal those that were willing to come to the throne of grace.

*Thurs.*, *18.*—I read with great expectation Dr Watts' 'Essay on Liberty,' but I was much disappointed. It is abstruse and metaphysical. Surely he wrote it either when he was very young or very old. In the evening I endeavoured to preach to the hearts of a large congregation at Edinburgh. We have cast much bread upon the waters here ; shall we not find it again, at least, after many days ?

*Fri.*, *19.* — I preached at Joppa, a settlement of colliers, three miles from Edinburgh. Some months ago, as some of them were cursing and swearing, one of our Local Preachers going by, reproved them. One of them followed after him, and begged he would give them a sermon ; he did so several times. Afterwards the Travelling Preachers went, and a few quickly agreed to meet together. Some of these now know in

[1] Journal, vol. iv. pp. 147-150.

whom they have believed, and walk worthy of their profession.

*Sat., 20.*—I took one more walk through Holyrood House, the mansion of ancient Kings. But how melancholy an appearance does it make now! The stately rooms are dirty as stables ; the colours of the tapestry are quite faded ; several of the pictures are cut and defaced ; the roof of the royal chapel is fallen in, and the bones of James the Fifth, and the once beautiful Lord Darnley, are scattered about like those of sheep or oxen. Such is human greatness! Is not a "living dog better than a dead lion"?

*Sun., 21.*—The rain hindered me from preaching at noon upon the Castle-Hill. In the evening the house was well filled, and I was enabled to speak strong words. But I am not a Preacher for the people of Edinburgh. Hugh Saunderson and Michael Fenwick are more to their taste.

*Tues., 23.*—A gentleman took me to see Roslyn Castle, eight miles from Edinburgh. It is now all in ruins, only a small dwelling-house is built on one part of it. The situation of it is exceeding fine, on the side of a steep mountain, hanging over a river, from which another mountain rises, equally steep and clothed with wood. At a little distance is the chapel, which is in perfect preservation, both within and without. I should never have thought that it had belonged to any one less than a sovereign prince! The inside being far more elegantly wrought with variety of Scripture-histories in stone-work, than I believe can be found again in Scotland, perhaps not in England.

Hence we went to Dunbar.

*Wednesday, 24.*—In the afternoon I went through the lovely garden of a gentleman in the town, who has laid out walks hanging over the sea, and winding among the rocks ; one of them leads to the castle, wherein that poor injured woman, Mary Queen of Scots, was confined. But time has wellnigh devoured it, only a few ruinous walls are now standing.

*Thurs., 25.*—We went on to Berwick.[1]

[1] Journal, vol. iv. pp. 176, 177.

EIGHTEENTH VISIT, 1782.

*Mon.*, *27* [*May 1782*].—I set out for Scotland, and Wednesday, 29th, reached Dunbar. The weather was exceeding rough and stormy ; yet we had a large and serious congregation.

*Thurs.*, *20.*—Finding the grounds were so flooded, that the common roads were not passable, we provided a guide to lead us a few miles round, by which means we came safe to Edinburgh.

*Fri.*, *31.*—As I lodged with Lady Maxwell at Saughton-Hall (a good old mansion-house three miles from Edinburgh), she desired me to give a short discourse to a few of her poor neighbours. I did so, at four in the afternoon, on the story of Dives and Lazarus. About seven I preached in our house at Edinburgh, and fully delivered my own soul.

*Sat.*, *June 1.*—I spent a little time with forty poor children whom Lady Maxwell keeps at school. They are swiftly brought forward in reading and writing, and learn the principles of religion. But I observe in them all the *ambitiosa paupertas.* Be they ever so poor, they must have a scrap of finery. Many of them have not a shoe to their foot, but a girl in rags is not without her ruffles.

*Sun.*, *2.*—Mr Collins intended to have preached on the Castle-hill at twelve o'clock ; but the dull Minister kept us in the kirk till past one. At six the house was well filled, and I did not shun to declare the whole counsel of God. I almost wonder at myself. I seldom speak anywhere so roughly as in Scotland ; and yet most of the people hear and hear, and are just as they were before.

*Mon.*, *3.*—I went on to Dundee. The congregation was large and attentive, as usual ; but I found no increase, either of the society, or of the work of God.

*Tues.*, *4.*—The house at Arbroath was well filled with serious and attentive hearers. Only one or two pretty flutterers seemed inclined to laugh, if any would have encouraged them.

*Wed., 5.*—We set out early, but did not reach Aberdeen till between five and six in the evening. The congregations were large both morning and evening, and many of them much alive to God.

*Fri., 7.*—We received a pleasing account of the work of God in the north. The flame begins to kindle even at poor dull Keith ; but much more at a little town near Fraserburgh ; and most of all at Newburgh, a small fishing town fifteen miles from Aberdeen, where the society swiftly increases ; and not only men and women, but a considerable number of children, are either rejoicing in God, or panting after him.

*Sat., 8.*—I walked with a friend to Mr Lesley's seat, less than a mile from the city. It is one of the pleasantest places of the kind I ever saw, either in Britain or Ireland. He has laid his gardens out on the side of a hill, which gives a fine prospect both of sea and land ; and the variety is beyond what could be expected within so small a compass ; but still

> " Valeat possessor oportet,
> Si comportatis rebus benè cogitat uti."

Unless a man have peace within, he can enjoy none of the things that are round about him.

*Sun., 9.*—We had a lovely congregation in the morning, many of whom were athirst for full salvation. In the evening God sent forth his voice, yea, and that a mighty voice. I think few of the congregation were unmoved ; and we never had a more solemn parting.

*Mon., 10.*—We went to Arbroath ; Tuesday, 11th, to Dundee ; and Wednesday, 12th, to Edinburgh. We had such congregations, both that evening and the next, as had not been on a week-day for many years. Some fruit of our labours here we have had already ; perhaps this is a token that we shall have more.

*Fri., 14.*—We travelled through a pleasant country to Kelso, where we were cordially received by Dr. Douglas. I spoke strong words in the evening, concerning judgment to come : and some seemed to awake out of sleep. But how shall they keep awake, unless they "that fear the Lord, speak often together"?

*Sat., 15.*—As I was coming down-stairs, the carpet slipped from under my feet, which, I know not how, turned me round, and pitched me back with my head foremost for six or seven stairs. It was impossible to recover myself till I came to the bottom. My head rebounded once or twice from the edge of the stone stairs ; but it felt to me exactly as if I had fallen on a cushion or a pillow. Dr. Douglas ran out sufficiently affrighted ; but he needed not, for I rose as well as ever, having received no damage, but the loss of a little skin from one or two of my fingers. Doth not God "give his angels charge over us, to keep us in all our ways"?[1]

### NINETEENTH VISIT, 1784.

*Friday, 23 [April 1784].*—The road from hence [Longtown] to Langholm is delightfully pleasant, running mostly by the side of a clear river ; but it was past seven before we reached Selkirk.

*Sat., 24.*—We had frost in the morning, snow before seven, piercing winds all day long, and in the afternoon vehement hail ; so that I did not wonder we had a small congregation at Edinburgh in the evening.

*Sun., 25.*—I attended the Tolbooth Kirk at eleven. The sermon was very sensible ; but having no application, was no way likely to awaken drowsy hearers. About four I preached at Lady Maxwell's, two or three miles from Edinburgh, and at six in our own house. For once it was thoroughly filled. I preached on "God is a Spirit ; and they that worship him, must worship him in spirit and in truth." I am amazed at this people. Use the most cutting words, and apply them in the most pointed manner ; still they hear, but feel no more than the seats they sit upon !

*Mon., 26.*—I went to Glasgow, and preached in the

[1] Journal, vol. iv. pp. 222-224.

evening to a very different congregation. Many attended in the morning, although the morning preaching had been long discontinued both here and at Edinburgh. In the evening, many were obliged to go away, the house not being able to contain them.

*Wed., 28.*—We found the same inconvenience, but those who could get in found a remarkable blessing.

*Thurs., 29.*—The house was thoroughly filled at four, and the hearts of the people were as melting wax. Afterwards I returned to Edinburgh, and in the evening the house was well filled; so that we must not say, "The people of Edinburgh love the Word of God only on the Lord's day."

*Fri., 30.*—We went to Perth, now but the shadow of what it was, though it begins to lift up its head. It is certainly the sweetest place in all North Britain, unless perhaps Dundee. I preached in the Tolbooth, to a large and well-behaved congregation. Many of them were present again at five in the morning, May 1. I then went to Dundee, through the Carse of Gowry, the fruitfullest valley in the kingdom: and I observe a spirit of improvement prevails in Dundee, and all the country round about it. Handsome houses spring up on every side, trees are planted in abundance, wastes and commons are continually turned into meadows and fruitful fields. There wants only a proportionable improvement in religion, and this will be one of the happiest countries in Europe.

In the evening I preached in our own ground to a numerous congregation: but the next afternoon to one far more numerous; on whom I earnestly enforced, "How long halt ye between two opinions?" Many of them seemed almost persuaded to halt no longer: but God only knows the heart.

*Mon., May 3.*—I was agreeably surprised at the improvement of the land between Dundee and Arbroath. Our preaching-house at Arbroath was completely filled. I spoke exceeding plain, on the difference of building upon the sand, and building upon the rock. Truly these "approve the things that are excellent," whether they practice them or not.

I found this to be a genuine Methodist society : they are all thoroughly united to each other. They love and keep our rules. They long and expect to be perfected in love : if they continue so to do, they will and must increase in number as well as in grace.

*Tues., 4.*—I reached Aberdeen between four and five in the afternoon.

*Wed., 5.*—I found the morning preaching had been long discontinued ; yet the bands and the select society were kept up. But many were faint and weak for want of morning preaching and prayer-meetings, of which I found scarce any trace in Scotland.

In the evening I talked largely with the Preachers, and showed them the hurt it did both them and the people for any one Preacher to stay six or eight weeks together in one place. Neither can he find matter for preaching every morning and evening, nor will the people come to hear him. Hence he grows cold by lying in bed, and so do the people. Whereas, if he never stays more than a fortnight together in one place, he may find matter enough, and the people will gladly hear him. They immediately drew up such a plan for their circuit, which they determined to pursue.

*Thurs., 6.*—We had the largest congregation at five which I have seen since I came into the kingdom. We set out immediately after preaching, and reached Old Meldrum about ten. A servant of Lady Banff's was waiting for us there, who desired I would take post-horses to Fort-Glen. In two hours we reached an inn, which the servant told us was four little miles from her house. So we made the best of our way, and got thither in exactly three hours. All the family received us with the most cordial affection. At seven I preached to a small congregation, all of whom were seriously attentive, and some, I believe deeply affected.

*Fri., 7.*—I took a walk round about the town. I know not when I have seen so pleasant a place. One part of the house is an ancient castle, situated on the top of a little hill. At a small distance runs a clear river, with a beautiful wood on its banks. Close to it is a shady walk to the right, and another on the left hand. On two sides up the house there is abundance of wood ; on the other, a wide prospect over fields and meadows. About ten I preached again, and with much liberty of spirit, on, "Love never faileth." About two I left this charming place, and made for Keith. But I know not how we could have got thither had not Lady Banff sent me forward through that miserable road with four stout horses.

I preached about seven to the poor of this world (not a silk coat was seen among them) ; and to the greatest part of them at five in the morning. And I did not at all regret my labour.

*Sat., 8.*—We reached the banks of the Spey. I suppose there are few such rivers in Europe. The rapidity of it exceeds even that of the Rhine ; and it was now much swelled with melting snow. However, we made shift to get over before ten ; and about twelve reached Elgin. Here I was received by a daughter of good Mr Plenderleith, late of Edinburgh, with whom, having spent an agreeable hour, I hastened towards Fores [Forres] : but we were soon at a full stop again ; the river Findhorn also was so swollen, that we were afraid the ford was not passable. However, having a good guide, we passed it without much difficulty. I found Sir Lodowick Grant almost worn out. Never was a visit more seasonable. By free and friendly conversation his spirits were so raised, that I am in hopes it will lengthen his life.

*Sun., 9.*—I preached to a small company at noon, on, " His commandments are not grievous." As I was concluding, Colonel Grant and his lady came in ; for whose sake I began again, and lectured, as they call it, on the former part of the fifteenth chapter of St Luke. We had a larger company in the afternoon, to whom I preached on "judgment to come." And this subject seemed to affect them most.

*Mon., 10.*—I set out for Inverness. I had sent Mr M'Allum before on George Whitfield's horse, to give notice of my coming. Hereby I was obliged to take

both George and Mrs M'Allum with me in my chaise.
To ease the horses, we walked forward from Nairn,
ordering Richard to follow us, as soon as they were
fed ; he did so, but there were two roads.  So we took
one, and he took the other, we walked about twelve
miles and a half of the way through heavy rain.  We
then found Richard waiting for us at a little ale-
house, and drove on to Inverness.  But, blessed be
God, I was no more tired than when I set out from
Nairn.  I preached at seven to a far larger congregation than I had seen here since I had preached in
the kirk.  And surely the labour was not in vain ; for
God sent a message to many hearts.

*Tues.*, *11.*—Notwithstanding the long discontinuance
of morning preaching, we had a large congregation at
five.  I breakfasted at the first house I was invited to
at Inverness, where good Mr M'Kenzie then lived.  His
three daughters live in it now ; one of whom inherits
all the spirit of her father.  In the afternoon we took
a walk over the bridge, into one of the pleasantest
countries I have seen.  It runs along by the side of
the clear river, and is well cultivated and well wooded.
And here first we heard abundance of birds, wel-
coming the return of spring.  The congregation was
larger this evening than the last, and great part of
them attended in the morning.  We had then a
solemn parting, as we could hardly expect to meet
again in the present world.

*Wed.*, *12.*—I dined once more at Sir Lodowick
Grant's, whom likewise I scarce expect to see any
more.  His lady is lately gone to rest, and he seems
to be simply following her.  A church being offered
me at Elgin, in the evening I had a multitude of
hearers, whom I strongly exhorted to " Seek the
Lord while he may be found."

*Thurs.*, *13.*—We took a view of the poor remains of
the once magnificent cathedral.  By what ruins are
left, the workmanship appears to have been exquisitely
fine.  What barbarians must they have been who
hastened the destruction of this beautiful pile by
taking the lead off the roof !

The church was again well filled in the evening by those who seemed to feel much more than the night before. In consequence, the morning congregation was more than doubled, and deep attention sat on every face. I do not despair of good being done, even here, provided the Preachers be "sons of thunder."

*Fri.*, *14.*—We saw at a distance the Duke of Gordon's new house, six hundred and fifty feet in front! Well might the Indian ask, "Are you white men no bigger than we red men? Then why do you build such lofty houses?" The country between this and Banff is well cultivated, and extremely pleasant. About two I read prayers and preached in the Episcopal Chapel at Banff, one of the neatest towns in the kingdom. About ten I preached in Lady Banff's dining-room at Fort-glen, to a very serious, though genteel congregation; and afterwards spent a most agreeable evening with the lovely family.

*Sat.*, *15.*—We set out early, and dined at Aberdeen. On the road I read Ewen Cameron's translation of Fingal. I think he has proved the authenticity of it beyond all reasonable contradiction. But what a poet was Ossian! Little inferior to either Homer or Virgil; in some respects superior to both. And what a hero was Fingal! Far more humane than Hector himself, whom we cannot excuse for murdering one that lay upon the ground; and with whom Achilles, or even pious Æneas, is not worthy to be named. But who is this excellent translator, Ewen Cameron? Is not his other name Hugh Blair?

*Sun.*, *16.*—I went to Newburgh, a small fishing town, fifteen miles north of Aberdeen. Here is at present, according to its bigness, the liveliest society in the kingdom. I preached in a kind of Square to a multitude of people, and the whole congregation appeared to be moved, and ready prepared for the Lord.

At two in the afternoon Mr Black read prayers, and I preached, in Trinity Chapel. It was crowded with people of all denominations. I preached from 1 Cor. xiii., 1-3, in utter defiance of their common saying, "He is a good man, though he has bad tempers."

Nay, if he has bad tempers, he is no more a good man than the devil is a good angel.   At five I preached in our own chapel, exceedingly crowded, on, "The form and the power of godliness."   I am now clear of these people, and can cheerfully commend them to God.

*Mon., 17.*—I reached Arbroath, and inquired into that odd event which occurred there in the latter end of the last war.   The famous Captain Fell came one afternoon to the side of the town, and sent three men on shore, threatening to lay the town in ashes unless they sent him thirty thousand pounds.   That not being done, he began firing on the town the next day, and continued it till night.   But perceiving the country was alarmed, he sailed away the next day, having left some hundred cannon-balls behind him ; but not having hurt man, woman, or child, or anything else, save one old barn door.

*Tues., 18.*—I preached at Dundee.

*Wed., 19.*—I crossed over the pleasant and fertile county of Fife, to Melval-House, the grand and beautiful seat of Lord Leven.   He was not at home, being gone to Edinburgh as the King's Commissioner ; but the Countess was, with two of her daughters and both her sons-in-law.   At their desire I preached in the evening on, "It is appointed unto men once to die," &c.   I believe God made the application.

*Thurs., 10.*—It blew a storm.   Nevertheless, with some difficulty, we crossed the Queen's Ferry.

*Fri., 21.*—I examined the society, and found about sixty members left.   Many of these were truly alive to God ; so our labour here is not quite in vain.

*Sat., 22.*—I had some close conversation with L. M., who appeared to be clearly saved from sin, although exceedingly depressed by the tottering tenement of clay.   About noon I spent an hour with her poor scholars, forty of whom she has provided with a serious master, who takes pains to instruct them in the principles of religion, as well as in reading and writing.   A famous actress just come down from London, which, for the honour of Scotland, just during the sitting of the Assembly, stole away a great part of our congregation to-night. How much wiser are these Scots than their forefathers !

*Sun., 23.*—I went in the morning to the Tolbooth Kirk ; in the afternoon to the old Episcopal chapel ; but they have lost their glorying ; they talked the moment service was done, as if they had been in London. In the evening the Octagon was well filled, and I applied with all possible plainness, "God is a Spirit ; and they that worship him must worship him in spirit and in truth."

*Mon., 24.*—I preached at Dunbar.

*Tues., 25.*—I spent an hour with Mr and Mrs F., a woman every way accomplished. Neither of them had ever yet heard a sermon out of the kirk ; but they ventured that evening, and I am in hope they did not hear in vain.

*Wed., 26.*—We went on to Berwick-upon-Tweed. The congregation in the Town-hall was very numerous. So it was likewise at five in the morning.

*Thurs., 27.* — We travelled through a delightful country to Kelso. Here the two Seceding Ministers have taken true pains to frighten the people from hearing us, by retailing all the ribaldry of Mr Cudworth, Toplady, and Rowland Hill ; but God has called one of them to his account already, and in a fearful manner. As no house could contain the congregation, I preached in the churchyard ; and a more decent behaviour I have scarce ever seen. Afterwards we walked to the Duke of Roxburgh's seat, about half a mile from the town, finely situated on a rising ground, near the ruins of Roxburgh Castle. It has a noble castle ; the front and the offices round, make it look like a little town. Most of the apartments within are finished in an elegant, but not in a costly manner. I doubt whether two of Mr Lascelles's rooms at Harewood House did not cost more in furnishing than twenty of these. But the Duke's house is far larger, containing no less than forty bed-chambers ; but it is not near finished yet, nor probably will be, till the owner is no more seen.[1]

[1] Journal, vol. iv. pp. 265-271.

## TWENTIETH VISIT, 1786.

*Fri., 12 [May 1786].*—I preached at Carlisle ; and Saturday, the 13th, after a long day's journey, at Glasgow. After spending three days here fully employed, on Wednesday, the 17th, we went on to Edinburgh. Here, likewise, I had much and pleasant work. On Friday, the 19th, I went forward to Dundee ; and on Saturday, the 20th, to Arbroath, where I spent the Lord's day in the Lord's work.

*Mon., 22.*—Having a long day's journey before us, we set out at half-past three. So we came early to Aberdeen.

*Wed., 24.*—We had an exceeding solemn parting ; as I reminded them that we could hardly expect to see each other's face any more, till we met in Abraham's bosom.

*Thur., 25.*—We set out early ; but when we came to Bervey the inn was full ; there was no room for man or beast. So we were constrained to go a double stage to Montrose. But the storm was so high, we could not pass for several hours ; however, we reached Arbroath soon after six. And a large congregation was deeply attentive, while I applied, "To him that hath shall be given ; but from him that hath not shall be taken away even what he assuredly hath."

The storm was still so high, that unless we set out at night, we could not pass till nine in the morning. So we went on board at eleven ; the wind was then so strong, that the boat could scarce keep above water. However, our Great Pilot brought us safe to land, between one and two in the morning.

*Sat., 27.*—About three we came to the New Inn, and rested till between six and seven ; thence going gently on to Kinghorn, we had a pleasant passage to Leith. After preaching, I walked to my lovely lodging at Coates, and found rest was sweet.

*Sun., 28.*—I preached first at our own house, and

at noon on the Castle-Hill. I never saw such a congregation there before. The chair was placed just opposite to the sun. But I soon forgot it, while I expounded those words, "I saw the dead, small and great, stand before God." In the evening the whole audience seemed to feel, "Without holiness no man shall see the Lord."

*Tues., 30.*—I had the happiness of conversing with the Earl of H—— and his Lady, at Dunbar. I could not but observe both the easiness of his behaviour (such as we find in all the Scottish nobility), and the fineness of his appearance, greatly set off by a milk-white head of hair.

*Wed., 31.*—I took a view of the stupendous bridge, about ten miles from Dunbar, which is thrown over the deep glen that runs between the two mountains, commonly called The Peas. I doubt whether Louis XIV. ever raised such a bridge as this. In the evening I preached at Berwick-upon-Tweed.[1]

## TWENTY-FIRST VISIT, 1788.

*Tues., 13 [May 1788].*—To-day we went on through lovely roads to Dumfries. Indeed all the roads are wonderfully mended since I last travelled this way. Dumfries is beautifully situated ; but as to wood and water, and gently rising hills, &c., is, I think, the neatest, as well as the most civilised, town that I have seen in the kingdom. Robert Dall soon found me out. He has behaved exceeding well, and done much good here. But he is a bold man. He has begun building a preaching-house, larger than any in Scotland, except those in Glasgow and Edinburgh ! In the evening I preached abroad in a convenient street, on one side of the town. Rich and poor attended from every quarter, of whatever denomination ; and every one seemed to hear for life. Surely the Scots are the best hearers in Europe !

---

[1] Journal, vol. iv. pp. 323, 324.

*Wed., 14.*—At five I was importuned to preach in
the preaching-house. But such a one I never saw
before. It had no windows at all : so that although
the sun shone bright, we could see nothing without
candles. But I believe our Lord shone on many hearts
while I was applying those words, "I will ; be thou
clean." I breakfasted with poor Mr Ashton, many
years ago a member of our society in London, but far
happier now in his little cottage, than ever he was in
his prosperity.

When I was in Scotland first, even at a nobleman's
table, we had only flesh-meat of one kind, but no
vegetables of any kind ; but now they are as plentiful
here as in England. Near Dumfries there are five
very large public gardens, which furnish the town
with greens and fruits in abundance.

The congregation in the evening was nearly double
to that we had the last, and, if it was possible, more
attentive. Indeed one or two gentlemen, so called,
laughed at first ; but they quickly disappeared, and
all were still while I explained the worship of God
in spirit and in truth. Two of the Clergy followed me
to my lodging, and gave me a pressing invitation to
their houses. Several others intended, it seems, to do
the same. But having a long journey before me, I
left Dumfries earlier in the morning than they expected. We set out on Thursday, the 15th, at four,
and reached Glasgow, Friday, 16th, before noon. Much
of the country, as we came, is now well improved, and
the wilderness become a fruitful field.

Our new preaching-house will, I believe, contain
about as many as the chapel at Bath. But O the
difference ! It has the pulpit on one side, and has
exactly the look of a Presbyterian meeting-house. It
is the very sister of our house at Brentford ; perhaps
an omen of what will be when I am gone ! I preached
at seven, to a tolerably large congregation, and to many
of them at five in the morning. At six in the evening
they were increased fourfold. But still I could not
find the way to their hearts.

*Sun., 18.*—I preached at eleven on the parable of the

Sower; at half-past two on Psalm l. 23; and in the
evening on "Now abideth these three, faith, hope,
love." I subjoined a short account of Methodism, particularly insisting on the circumstance,—There is no
other religious society under heaven which requires
nothing of men in order to their admission into it, but
a desire to save their souls. Look all round you, you
cannot be admitted into the Church or society of the
Presbyterians, Anabaptists, Quakers, or any others,
unless you hold the same opinions with them, and
adhere to the same mode of worship. The Methodists
alone do not insist on your holding this or that opinion,
but they think and let think. Neither do they impose
any particular mode of worship, but you may continue
to worship in your former manner, be it what it may.
Now I do not know any other religious society, either
ancient or modern, wherein such liberty of conscience
is now allowed, or has been allowed, since the age of
the Apostles. Here is our glorying; and a glorying
peculiar to us. What society shares it with us?

*Mon.,* 19.—I went to Edinburgh, and preached to a
much larger congregation than I used to see here on a
week-day. I still find a frankness and openness in the
people of Edinburgh, which I find in few other parts
of the kingdom. I spent two days among them with
much satisfaction; and I was not at all disappointed in
finding no such increase, either in the congregation or
the society, as many expected from their leaving the
Kirk.

*Thur.,* 22.—The house at Dalkeith being far too
small, even at eight in the morning, to contain the
congregation, I preached in a garden, on, "Seek ye
the Lord while he may be found"; and from the
eager attention of the people, I could not but hope,
that some of them would receive the truth in love.
In the evening I preached in the house at Dunbar,
tolerably well filled, on Job xxii. 2, 3. I believe
with

" The spirit of convincing speech."

But much more at five in the morning, Friday, 23.

And will God manifest His power among these dry bones also? Immediately after preaching we set out. How is the face of this country changed in a few years! It was twenty years ago dreary enough, but is now a pleasant garden. But what is most remarkable is, the bridge which connects the two mountains, the Peas, together; one of the noblest works in Great Britain, unless you would except the bridge at Edinburgh, which lies directly across the Cowgate: so that one street (a thing not heard of before) runs under another!

About noon we came to Berwick-upon-Tweed; but the town being all in a hurry, on occasion of the fair, so that I could not conveniently preach in the market-house, I was glad that Mr Atcheson, the Presbyterian Minister, offered me the use of his chapel. It was a large commodious place. Several of his hearers attended, to whom I spoke exceeding plain in the evening, on 1 Cor. xii. 3, and in the morning, on Isaiah lix. 1-3.

*Sun.*, *25*.—This was the day on which all the Nonjuring congregations in Scotland began, by common agreement, to pray in all their public worship for King George and his family.[1]

TWENTY-SECOND VISIT, 1790.

*[Part of the manuscript having been lost, causes a chasm here.]*

*Mon.*, *May 24* *[1790]*. — We set out at four, and reached Forglen about noon. The face of the country is much changed for the better since I was here before. Agriculture increases on every side; so do manufactories, industry, and cleanliness.

But I found poor Lady B. (one of the most amiable

[1] Journal, vol. iv. pp. 407-409.

women in the kingdom) exceedingly ill ; and I doubt whether she will be much better till she removes to her own country. I spent a very agreeable afternoon with the lovely family, and preached to a serious congregation in the evening.

*Tuesday, 25.*—We returned to Aberdeen ; and I took a solemn farewell of a crowded audience. If I should be permitted to see them again, well ; if not, I have delivered my own soul.

*Wed., 26.*—Taking the midland road, we spent an hour at Laurencekirk ; which, from an inconsiderable village, is, by the care and power of Lord Gordon, soon sprung up into a pleasant, neat, and flourishing town. His lordship has also erected a little library here, adjoining to a handsome and well-furnished inn. The country from hence to Brechin is as pleasant as a garden. Happy would Scotland be, if it had many such gentlemen and noblemen. In the evening I began preaching at Brechin, in the Freeman's Lodge ; but I was so faint and ill, that I was obliged to shorten my discourse.

*Thurs., 27.*—We went on through Forfar (now a handsome and almost a new town) and Cupar to Auchterarder. Here we expected poor accommodations, but were agreeably disappointed. Food, beds, and everything else were as neat and clean as at Aberdeen or Edinburgh.

*Friday, 28.* — We travelled through a delightful country, by Stirling and Kilsythe, to Glasgow. The congregation was miserably small ; verifying what I have often heard before, that the Scots dearly love the word of the Lord—on the Lord's day. If I live to come again, I will take care to spend only the Lord's day at Glasgow.

*Mon., 31.*—We set out at two, and came to Moffat soon after three in the afternoon. Taking fresh horses, we reached Dumfries between six and seven, and found the congregation waiting ; so after a few minutes, I preached on Mark iii. 35 : "Whosoever shall do the will of God, the same is my brother, and sister, and mother."

*Tues., June 1.*—Mr Mather had a good congregation at five. In the day I conversed with many of the people ; unlike most that I have found in Scotland. In the evening the house was filled ; and truly God preached to their hearts. Surely God will have a considerable people here.

*Wed., 2.*—We set out early, and reached Carlisle. . . .

# INDEX.

THE END.

PRINTED BY WILLIAM BLACKWOOD AND SONS.